State and Local Government

2016–2017 Edition

State and Local Government

2016–2017 Edition

Kevin B. Smith

University of Nebraska–Lincoln

Editor

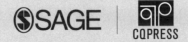

FOR INFORMATION:

CQ Press
An Imprint of SAGE Publications, Inc.
2455 Teller Road
Thousand Oaks, California 91320
E-mail: order@sagepub.com

SAGE Publications Ltd.
1 Oliver's Yard
55 City Road
London, EC1Y 1SP
United Kingdom

SAGE Publications India Pvt. Ltd.
B 1/I 1 Mohan Cooperative Industrial Area
Mathura Road, New Delhi 110 044
India

SAGE Publications Asia-Pacific Pte. Ltd.
3 Church Street
#10-04 Samsung Hub
Singapore 049483

Printed in the United States of America

Library of Congress Control Number: 2016950498

ISBN 978-1-5063-5820-8

This book is printed on acid-free paper.

MIX
Paper from
responsible sources
FSC® C014174

Acquisitions Editor: Michael Kerns
Development Editor: Nancy Matuszak
Editorial Assistant: Zachary Hoskins
Production Editor: Kelly DeRosa
Typesetter: C&M Digitals (P) Ltd.
Proofreader: Lawrence W. Baker
Cover Designer: Candice Harman
Marketing Manager: Amy Whitaker

16 17 18 19 20 10 9 8 7 6 5 4 3 2 1

Contents

PREFACE   ix
ABOUT THE EDITOR   xi

I. FEDERALISM   1

1. **Are States Still "Labs of Democracy"?**   3

    *The need for federal waivers is making it
    a lot harder for states to run social and
    economic policy experiments.*
        Donald F. Kettl, *Governing*

2. **Is Federalism Breaking Down?**   5

    *The federal and state governments used
    to have an unspoken deal—broad
    policy direction would be hashed out in
    Congress, then modified and implemented
    by states. Not anymore. The partisan
    polarization that has long marked
    Congress is now threatening to upset how
    federalism works.*
        Donald F. Kettl, *Governing*

3. **Beyond North Carolina's LGBT Battle:
    States' War on Cities**   7

    *Cities are increasingly run by liberals
    and Democrats. State governments by
    conservatives and Republicans. That's a
    recipe for conflict.*
        Alan Greenblatt, *Governing*

4. **Constitutions: Amend with Care**   11

    *Lots of people think amending the U.S.
    Constitution is a good idea. State constitutions
    get amended frequently and it turns out that
    might not be such a good deal after all.*
        Jennie Drage Bowser, *State Legislatures
        Magazine*

II. ELECTIONS AND POLITICAL ENVIRONMENT   17

5. **Voter Identification in the Courts**   19

    *Voter ID laws may be bad for some voters,
    but judging from the resulting litigation
    they have been good for lawyers.*
        Justin Levitt, The Council of State
        Governments

6. **Voter ID History**   24

    *Voter ID laws are nothing new; the first one
    was enacted way back in 1950. It was not
    until after 2000, however, that they became
    really popular.*
        National Conference of State Legislatures

7. **Aging Voting Machines Are a Threat to
    Democracy**   28

    *A lot of voting machines are nearing the end
    of their useful life. If they are not replaced,
    it may create big problems on election day.*

Lawrence Norden and Christopher
Famighetti, Brennan Center for Justice

8. **Vote-by-Mail Rates More than Double
   since 2000**   30

   *Voters are increasingly mailing it in. That's
   a good thing.*
   Sean Greene and Kyle Ueyama, *Stateline*

III. POLITICAL PARTIES AND INTEREST GROUPS   33

9. **Stronger Parties, Stronger Democracy:
   Rethinking Reform**   35

   *Political parties are changing. Can anything
   be done to make sure this change benefits the
   democratic system as a whole rather than
   narrower special interests?*
   Daniel I. Weiner and Ian Vandewalker,
   Brennan Center for Justice

10. **Rex Sinquefield: The Tyrannosaurus Rex
    of State Politics**   38

    *In Missouri, one man with a lot of money is
    having a big impact on state politics.*
    Alan Greenblatt, *Governing*

11. **Why Democratic Governors and Republican
    Mayors Have Become Rare**   42

    *Demography, geography, and electoral
    timing are having an increasingly big
    impact on which party wins elections.*
    Louis Jacobson, *Governing*

IV. LEGISLATURES   47

12. **Who We Elect: The Demographics of State
    Legislatures**   49

    *Despite notable demographic shifts, state
    legislatures still do not reflect the demographic
    diversity of the citizens they serve.*
    Karl Kurtz, *State Legislatures Magazine*

13. **Stalled Progress for Women in
    State Legislatures**   53

    *From the 1970s to the 1990s, the number
    of women in state legislatures steadily
    increased. In the two decades since, that
    growth has ground to a halt. Why?*
    Rebecca Beitsch, *Stateline*

14. **Birds of a Feather**   57

    *Legislative caucuses are groups of lawmakers
    organized to advocate and promote a
    common cause or interest. Those causes
    and interests extend far beyond the party
    caucuses that most voters are familiar with.*
    Suzanne Weiss, *State Legislatures Magazine*

V. GOVERNORS   61

15. **Experience Preferred**   63

    *Having served a stint in the state legislature
    does not guarantee success when you move
    to the governor's mansion, but it sure doesn't
    hurt.*
    Louis Jacobson, *State Legislatures
    Magazine*

16. **Rocky Roads Ahead for Governors
    with Failed Presidential Bids**   67

    *A sitting governor who fails in a run for
    the presidency may lose twice. They lose the
    White House and return to a state where
    they may have lost a lot of good will.*
    Louis Jacobson, *Governing*

17. **Scott Pruitt Will See You in Court**   70

    *Oklahoma attorney general Scott Pruitt is
    fighting for states' rights by repeatedly suing
    the federal government.*
    J. B. Wogan, *Governing*

18. **After Spending Millions Suing Obama
    39 Times, Has Texas Seen a Return on
    Investment?**   74

    *Texas attorney generals have spent years
    and millions in taxpayers' money suing
    the federal government. Has it all been
    worthwhile?*
    Lauren McGaughy, *Governing/
    Tribune News Service*

VI. COURTS   77

19. **Cases with Consequences**   79

    *Which is the most powerful and influential
    state court in the nation? Trick question.
    The most powerful state court is actually
    a federal court. The U.S. Supreme Court*

rulings have big-time consequence for states and localities.
    Lisa Soronen, *State Legislatures Magazine*

20. **States at a Crossroads on Criminal Justice Reform**   83

    Tough on crime policies have given states some of the highest incarceration rates in the world. Maybe it's time to rethink how tough on crime we should be.
      Rebecca Beitsch, *Stateline*

21. **The Unintended Consequences of California's New Criminal Justice**   87

    Proposition 47 was designed to keep non-violent offenders out of prison. It has done that. It has also made some of those offenders more likely to keep committing crimes.
      Cindy Chang, Marisa Gerber, and Ben Poston, *Governing/* Tribune *News Service*

22. **Legislators Attempt to Strip Courts of Power**   90

    Legislatures who disagree with court rulings are seeking to take away the power of the courts to disagree with them.
      Maggie Clark, *Stateline*

VII. BUREAUCRACY   93

23. **Can Government Hiring Get Out of the Stone Age?**   95

    High unemployment rates used to make filling public sector jobs easy. Not anymore. Low unemployment rates are making it harder to get qualified people to take jobs in public agencies.
      Katherine Barrett and Richard Greene, *Governing*

24. **States Employ Temporary Workers, but Often Know Little about Them**   100

    Public agencies are embracing the "gig" economy and relying more heavily on part-timers to get the job done. Temporary workers are cheaper, but are they being taken advantage of?
      Sophie Quinton, *Stateline*

25. **What Does It Take to End a Teacher Shortage?**   103

    Schools districts are finding it harder to hire and retain teachers. Low pay and high turnover contribute to a chronic teacher shortage challenging an increasing number of states.
      Sophie Quinton, *Stateline*

26. **Wisconsin Tenure Fight Likely to Spread to Other States**   106

    Wisconsin has weakened the strong tenure protections traditionally enjoyed by faculty in the University of Wisconsin System. Other states may be looking to do the same.
      Karen Herzog, Tribune News Service/ *Governing*

VIII. LOCAL GOVERNMENT   109

27. **The Illusion of Cities' Recovery from the Recession**   111

    Colorado Springs, Colorado, decided against raising taxes during the Great Recession. That kept money in taxpayers' pockets and left commuters navigating a proliferating pothole problem.
      Zach Patton, *Governing*

28. **A Checklist for Alternatives in City-County Consolidation Decisions: From Separation to Unification**   115

    Consolidating local governments has always struck many as a good way to increase efficiency in public programs and services. The assumptions underlying expectations of that happy outcome, and what they imply for successful consolidation, get examined in-depth.
      Amy B. Uden, *State and Local Government Review*

29. **What Is a Smart City?**   127

    Smart sounds good, but what does it really mean? Apparently, different things to different people.
      Sophie Quinton, *Stateline*

IX. BUDGETS AND TAXES 131

30. **Summary: Fall 2015 Fiscal Survey of States** 133

State finances continue to recover from the recession doldrums. State coffers are far from overflowing, but certainly not as empty as they were a few years ago.
National Association of State Budget Officers

31. **For First Time, Tax Revenue Has Recovered in Majority of States** 140

A post-recession milestone was reached in the final quarter of 2015. Adjusted for inflation, for the first time a slim majority of states reported that their tax revenues had recovered to their pre-recession levels.
The Pew Charitable Trusts

32. **The Curious Case of Disappearing Corporate Taxes** 144

States are relying less and less on corporate taxes. That's good for businesses, but is it good for state government finances?
Liz Farmer, *Governing*

33. **State Spending and the Search for Hidden Efficiencies** 147

A budget crisis prompted Kansas to take a hard look at its budget. Other states should not wait for a budget crisis to do the same thing.
Charles Chieppo, *Governing*

X. POLICY CHALLENGES 149

34. **Has School Choice Been All It Set Out to Be?** 151

A more market-based approach was supposed to address many of the issues of public education. Advocates say it has done that; detractors are not so sure.
Alan Greenblatt, *Governing*

35. **States to Colleges: Prove You're Worth It** 155

States are starting to grade colleges. If the colleges do not perform, it is not their GPA that takes a hit, but their revenues.
Sophie Quinton, *Stateline*

36. **Southern Louisiana Picks a Fight with Big Oil to Save the Wetlands** 158

Louisiana's wetlands are disappearing at an alarming rate and the government is planning on doing something about it: suing one of the mainstays of the state economy.
Chris Kardish, *Governing*

37. **Why Colorado's Obamacare Co-op Is Falling, and Connecticut's Isn't** 162

Obamacare depends on cooperatives to help make sure citizens have access to health insurance at reasonable prices. That's working for some states, but not for others.
John Daley and Jeff Cohen, *Governing/ Kaiser Health News*

TEXT CREDITS 164

Preface

Change is an ever-present characteristic of state and local politics, but the nature of that change—what is changing, by how much, and how fast—itself varies from year to year. What characterizes the readings in this edition of *State and Local Government* is an uptick in partisan and ideological conflict that has rippled through the federal system in the past few years.

Take for example budgets. For years, financial worries dominated the concerns of state and local government lawmakers as the Great Recession of 2008–2009 devastated government revenues and affected budgetary bottom lines long after the economy recovered. Even today, some states and localities are still struggling to regain their pre-recession financial footing. In purely economic terms, though, the financial situation has largely stabilized. The fights about taxes and spending generated by the Great Recession have morphed into more philosophical conflicts about the appropriate role of government. These more ideologically driven shocks to state and local budgeting have turned out to be just as nasty and hard to deal with as the shocks from economic declines.

It is not just budgets that partisans and ideological opponents are fighting over. Who is allowed to vote, the freedom local governments should get to act without state interferences, the freedom state governments should get to act without federal interference, the independence of the courts, the role of unions in the public and private sectors—these are just some of the issues dividing partisans in state and local government. As the readings in this book demonstrate, competing interests at the state and local levels have found a lot to fight about.

As in previous editions, this volume does not seek to cover every issue of importance to state and local government—that would require several rather large books—but to sample some of the best writing and analysis on key concerns for state and local government. This writing comes from a wide variety of published sources. Long-term readers will recognize familiar sources like *Governing* and *State Legislatures*, as well as *Stateline*, an online news platform backed by the Pew Center. The readings also draw from magazines, government associations, as well as academic studies. As always, the readings are all new to the current edition and organized by key institutions, processes, and policy areas. All of the introductions have been updated to reflect the content of the new selections and also to account for the political and policy changes that define the dynamic world of state and local politics.

Putting together this volume requires the efforts of many people, and special thanks are owed to the excellent editorial team at CQ Press: Michael Kerns, Nancy Matuszak, and Zachary Hoskins. Thanks also go to the reviewers who provided feedback for this edition: Curtis R. Berry (Shippensburg University), Bobbi Gentry (Bridgewater College), Charles Greenawalt (Millersville University), Michael E. Greenberg (Shippensburg University), Dina Krois (Lansing Community College), Adam McGlynn (East Stroudsburg University), Sandra Pavelka (Florida Gulf Coast University), Ambrus Price (California University of Pennsylvania), and Joseph Romance (Fort Hays State University). All of us hope you find what follows an engaging look into the many dimensions of state and local government.

About the Editor

Kevin B. Smith is professor and chair of the political science department at the University of Nebraska–Lincoln and has been studying and teaching state politics and policy for more than twenty years. He has authored or coauthored nine books and dozens of scholarly articles, and he is a former associate editor of *State Politics & Policy Quarterly*. Prior to becoming an academic, he covered state and local politics as a newspaper reporter.

Federalism

In a federal system, national and regional governments share the responsibility for governing. That does not mean they have to get along, though, or even like each other. The current state of intergovernmental relations is, to put it mildly, fractious. Local, state, and federal governments continue to collaborate and cooperate on a wide range of issues, programs, and policies. They have to. Their budgets, policy priorities and administrative responsibilities are intertwined in areas as varied as education, transportation, health care, public safety, and immigration. That does not necessarily mean that these governments agree on everything—or, indeed, anything—within those policy jurisdictions. States resent the federal government trying to impose its preferences on them, local governments resent state governments trying to impose their preferences on them, and these days the federal government has a hard time agreeing with itself let alone with sub-national governments feeling ill-treated by officials in the nation's capital.

The readings in this chapter reflect both sides of intergovernmental relations. The first two essays are by Donald Kettl, one of the most perceptive observers of intergovernmental relations. In the first essay, Kettl investigates whether states are still the "laboratories of democracy." As any state politics text will remind you, U.S Supreme Court justice Louis Brandeis coined this familiar saying to describe how part of the role of the states in a federal system is to try new and novel social and economic experiments. Experiments that work can be adopted by other states and the federal government, while the downside of any that fail are confined to the states that pursued them. As Kettl points out, though, it is not as hard to run an experiment as it used to be. States often need to get federal waivers to engage in the sorts of experiments Brandeis had in mind, sometimes dozens of them. That sort of bureaucratic hurdle can make it a lot harder to run a laboratory.

Kettl's second essay takes a look at how fractious relationships between federal and state governments are exporting Congress's gridlock to intergovernmental relations. Traditionally, a broad consensus on how to deal with a policy problem was hashed out in Congress, and the programs to address those problems were modified and implemented by states. No longer. These days Congress is often at ideological war with itself. States are getting in on the act, rejecting on partisan or ideological grounds not just policy directions from the federal government but sometimes billions in critically needed dollars.

The third essay, by Alan Greenblatt, shows that intergovernmental friction is not confined to federal and state governments. Cities are increasingly unhappy with their state governments, which have become more aggressive about limiting local government. Again,

at least part of the cause is partisan and ideological differences. Democrats and liberals disproportionately concentrate in urban areas so, unsurprisingly, mayors of major cities often lean to the left and pursue left-leaning policy agendas. This often does not go down well at the state level, especially if the state is dominated by conservative Republicans who are tempted to limit the movement of local governments moving leftward.

The final essay, by Jennie Drage Bowser, provides a reminder that however hard a time state and federal governments have getting along, they still have a lot to teach each other. There is a good deal of talk in contemporary national politics of amending the U.S. Constitution. For example, an amendment mandating a balanced budget has a good deal of support, as does an amendment altering the Electoral College system for electing a president. Bowser's essay basically says be careful what you ask for. Unlike the U.S. Constitution, state constitutions are frequently amended. The lesson from the states to the national government on this issue is that constitutional amendments can create as well as solve problems.

Are States Still "Labs of Democracy"?

1

The growing role of federal waivers suggest the answer isn't simple.

By Donald F. Kettl

Writing recently in *The New York Times*, Duke University business professor Aaron Chatterji painted a discouraging picture of the states' current status as "laboratories of democracy." He argued that "just when we need their innovative energies, the states are looking less and less likely" to be generating new ideas for federal policy. Has the flame of state creativity somehow gone out?

That would be a tough case to make to Michigan Gov. Rick Snyder, who is proposing a massive remake of federally funded job training, social welfare and health programs. Snyder has set out a "river of opportunity" plan that he hopes will make Michigan first in the nation in training for skilled trades, lift all third-graders to proficiency in reading and launch what he calls "Medicaid expansion done right." To accomplish his aim, Snyder has created a new department designed to weave together an assortment of federal grant programs and to combine state programs dealing with health, welfare and families.

Key to the plan are federal waivers. Snyder estimates that his program could require 145 different waivers of federal rules—"the mother of all waivers," as he told the editorial board of *The Detroit News*. If he can pull it off, Snyder's "river of opportunity" plan will unquestionably be the next big thing in intergovernmental policy.

Michigan is certainly not alone in challenging federal programs with requests for waivers. Indiana Gov. Mike Pence rolled out his Healthy Indiana Plan 2.0, which expands Medicaid to cover 350,000 Hoosiers without health insurance—but which requires them to pay for some of their health-care costs. Depending on

From *Governing*, April 2015

income, participants in the plan would be required to contribute between $1 and $27 per month.

The efforts of these two Republican governors, along with a handful of others around the country, pose tough challenges for team Obama.

Regardless of the Supreme Court's decision on Obamacare, the administration needs to get the states on board if the program is going to work. Some GOP governors have simply refused to join, but through the end of January, four Republican-led states, including Indiana and Michigan, had successfully negotiated waivers as the price for cooperation.

Some supporters of the Obama health plan worry that the administration has been too flexible on waivers. Timothy Jost, a Washington and Lee University law professor and health policy expert, has said that waivers are "pretty much pushing the limits of how far they should go, if it's not beyond it." Meanwhile, many conservative leaders have fought against signing up for any part of the plan.

In the middle are pragmatists such as Pence and Snyder, who have sought the sweet spot, counting on the administration's need to enlist the states while advancing a conservative take on social policy.

These governors are reenacting some of the arguments that surrounded President Clinton's 1996 welfare reform, and the efforts of conservative Republican governors of that era, such as Wisconsin's Tommy Thompson, to use waivers to implement their own brand of welfare policy. Thompson sought to redefine welfare by requiring recipients to seek jobs and by restructuring government programs to help them do it. That necessitated waivers from existing federal programs, and Thompson struggled for years with the Clinton administration to get them. The result was a fundamental remaking of federal welfare policy that emanated from the policy lab in Wisconsin.

Since Justice Louis Brandeis coined the "laboratories" metaphor in a 1932 U.S. Supreme Court case, there's been an ongoing battle between those on the left, who have seen the states as workshops where bold policy ideas can be tested and brought to Washington, and those on the right, who have looked on the states as places where overreaching federal policy can be constrained.

Behind all of the rhetorical posturing, however, is a very interesting experiment. Most federal grant programs include mandates that state and local governments must follow in exchange for the cash. For several decades, however, the federal government has allowed states the flexibility to launch experimental or demonstration projects in pursuit of the goals of the programs. It turns out that some of the most fascinating experiments have come when Republican governors have challenged Democratic presidents.

Presidents Clinton and Obama have needed to get Republican governors on board in order for their initiatives to have traction. Republican governors like Pence, Snyder and Thompson have taken advantage of this by pushing pathbreaking proposals to merge policy ambitions from the left with market tactics from the right.

Obama can't move far on his social agenda without the governors, since state capitols have become the front lines in implementing so many social programs. But cash-strapped governors can't get far without federal cash in advancing their agendas, even if the dollars come with strings attached.

The two sides need each other. The battles over waivers have certainly broken some test tubes, but they've increasingly become the way the laboratories of democracy work.

2

Is Federalism Breaking Down?

By Donald F. Kettl

What's the most important issue that the 2016 presidential candidates won't be talking about? A very good bet is the train wreck facing federal-state-local finances. There are lots of mega-issues on the table—international crises, immigration and health reform battles, and economic growth—but whoever wins won't be able to duck the big intergovernmental issues lurking down the tracks.

The good news is that state and local governments have recovered remarkably well from the gruesome economic collapse in 2008. Tax revenues in most states have recovered to pre-recession levels.

The bad news is that the collapse shredded the national consensus on how our federalism balancing act ought to work. As Paul Posner and Timothy Conlan from George Mason University point out in an important and far-reaching study on federalism and intergovernmental relations, we've emerged from the downturn with a "polarized federalism." Politics in the states is splitting along partisan lines, with one-party control of the legislature and governorship on the rise and sharp fractures developing between Washington and state capitols. Some states, like Kansas, came out of the recession determined to cut taxes and spending. Other states, like California, have increased taxes and broadened government's scope.

For a generation, there was an implicit deal on intergovernmental financial questions. The policy battleground would be in Congress and, once the deals were struck, most states would more or less move down the same tracks. That implicit deal is over. By Posner and Conlan's count, 21 states refused to expand Medicaid

From *Governing*, February 2015

coverage as part of the Affordable Care Act, while 27 states and the District of Columbia opted in.

The Great Recession and the rise of partisan polarization have broken the foundation on which fiscal federalism has operated since World War II. And this isn't just high-level policy polarization in state capitols. A September 2014 Reuters survey found that 1 in 4 Americans want their own state to secede from the union, an upswell fueled by contempt for politicians and concern about the sluggish recovery.

Why does this polarization matter? After all, a case could be made that the great genius of American federalism is allowing the states to chart their own course. Three big issues explain why.

One is the crumbling of the quiet consensus on the federal government's traditional role in stabilizing big economic swings and equalizing differences in fiscal capacity among the states. That could make it much harder for the feds to step in if another economic downturn cripples state finances. In the meantime, it could also make it harder to sustain the redistribution from richer states to poorer ones that lies behind much federal aid. Some of the states opting out are net winners in this game. But if they opt out of these programs, inequality across the country could increase.

The second is looming state and local infrastructure problems. Last year's spectacular water main break on Sunset Boulevard in West Hollywood was just a sample of problems brewing underneath roads around the country. The Interstate 35 bridge collapse in 2007, which crippled traffic in Minneapolis and killed 13 people, is a warning about the 1 in 9 American bridges that are structurally deficient. These problems will demand attention, either through a planned program of renovation in advance or a hurried response to the inevitable disasters to come. A go-it-alone approach could prove risky for many states and cities.

And the third is the huge tangle of issues lurking in Medicaid. Tired of escalating costs, some governors have pushed to roll the federal program aimed at funding medical care for the poor into a block grant, to give them more flexibility. Many of these governors aren't expanding the program, leaving some citizens with a "coverage gap." The Kaiser Family Foundation found significant numbers of families with incomes too high to be eligible for Medicaid and too low to receive the program's tax credit. The states will have to figure out what to do to plug the gap—or to deal with even more financial and social problems flowing from the uninsured.

An even bigger challenge is the stress that aging baby boomers will put on the Medicaid system. From 2010 to 2020, the population over the age of 65 will increase from 40 million to 55 million Americans, and 7 million Americans will join the "oldest old" of those over the age of 85. They will inevitably place more strain on Medicaid, which covers the cost of medical and nursing home care for citizens who can't afford it. Nearly one-third of the program's budget goes to long-term care for the disabled and elderly, and the program pays 40 percent of long-term care costs in the country. Many about-to-be-retirees lost a good chunk of their nest egg in the economic collapse, and others will outlive their savings. That will necessarily squeeze state budgets.

This "fend for yourself" federalism, as Posner and Conlan put it, will make it easier for presidential candidates to opt out of discussing these issues in the 2016 campaign. But they won't go away. These issues are sure to collide further down the tracks before the 2020 campaign begins.

Beyond North Carolina's LGBT Battle: States' War on Cities

3

By Alan Greenblatt

St. Louis can't get a break from its own state. Last year, Missouri enacted a law preventing St. Louis and other cities from setting their own minimum-wage rates and from banning plastic grocery bags. This year, state lawmakers have spent a considerable amount of time debating whether to prohibit the city from taxing the income of its residents and workers. The state, which took control of the St. Louis police force during the Civil War, didn't give it back until 2013, when it was forced to by a voter-approved ballot measure.

If St. Louis feels ill-treated by state officials, it's got lots of company around the country. North Carolina's legislature drew national headlines when it met in special session March 23 to block cities from passing anti-discrimination protections for lesbian, gay, bisexual and transgender people. The legislature acted in response to Charlotte's adoption of LGBT protections earlier in the year. What was sometimes lost in the media coverage was the fact that the new North Carolina law also blocks cities from setting their own minimum wage rates. Similarly, Birmingham, Ala., passed a minimum-wage increase last year, only to see the state block it and other cities from setting their own rates this year.

There's a fundamental mismatch right now between the desires of many cities and the policy preferences of states. Out of power in Congress and in two-thirds of the nation's legislative chambers, progressives from President Obama on down are increasingly turning to cities to carry out their agenda. Democrats are in charge of the lion's share of big cities. Right now, just three of the nation's 25 largest—Fort Worth, Texas; Jacksonville, Fla.; and San Diego—have

From *Governing*, March 2016

Republican mayors. Many of the current Democratic mayors are to the political left of those who governed in their cities a generation ago.

But, as in physics, every movement in politics prompts an opposite if not always equal reaction. As cities attempt to fulfill liberal wishes, they are increasingly stymied by the Republicans who dominate state offices. The GOP currently controls all branches of government in more than three times as many states as Democrats. There's rarely much doubt about who will win an argument between a Democratic city and a Republican state—the state nearly always has the upper hand. "I'm not afraid of the 'don't tread on me' complaints from the municipalities," says Missouri state Rep. Dan Shaul, who sponsored last year's preemption of local minimum-wage and garbage bag laws. "We've worked with the cities of St. Louis and Kansas City and continue to try to help them anyway we can," he says, "but our response is to do what's best for the state."

Legislators such as Shaul remain quick to praise urban areas as the states' primary economic engines. Still, they insist that businesses shouldn't have to put up with a patchwork of regulations that vary from city to city, and that citizens shouldn't have any level of government butting unduly into their lives. "What they're doing is trying to keep cities out of social policies," says Larry Shaheen, a GOP consultant based in Charlotte. "They're trying to get city governments out of the lives of their citizens."

This isn't exactly new. Cities may have been even more outmatched by states during the first half of the 20th century, before the Supreme Court abolished the practice of apportioning legislative districts by county, rather than by population. But the political dynamic between cities and the rest of their states has shifted more recently in ways that have put urban centers at a new disadvantage. Land mass no longer determines legislative power, but there's lots of room left outside the main cities for Republicans to dominate. In Missouri, there's barely a Democratic legislator who hails from outside St. Louis or Kansas City. The 113 other counties are almost all overwhelmingly Republican, giving the GOP supermajority control of both legislative chambers.

Many states follow a similar pattern. Far fewer Democrats are elected to state legislative seats outside major metropolitan areas than was the case 15 or 20 years ago.

Conversely, there aren't a lot of Republicans elected from districts representing big cities or even many inner-suburban areas. The result is that traditional regional rivalries almost perfectly align with partisan divisions.

Cities have long chafed at restrictions placed by states on their ability to raise revenue. And outstate residents and legislators have perennially cried that the leading city—whether it's Indianapolis or Louisville or Milwaukee—uses more than its fair share of resources. In Wisconsin, "the common saying goes, Madison sucks up all our tax dollars and spends it on Milwaukee or itself," says Katherine Cramer, author of the new book *The Politics of Resentment*, which looks at rural anger in her state toward big cities. "There's a perception that decisions are made in Madison and there's no respect for small towns or our way of life."

But now, in states where Democrats are in the minority, cities have few allies within majority caucuses at the state level. And Republicans are left with little incentive to help them. "If you looked at the Texas Democratic delegation, everybody in it is from an urban area, except the [heavily Hispanic] Rio Grande Valley," says Mark P. Jones, a political scientist at Rice University in Houston. "Any legislation that benefits the urban core is going to be perceived much less favorably by the Republican majority."

State lawmakers have not been satisfied with just squelching cities on contentious social issues such as LGBT rights and gun control, or labor policies like minimum-wage increases and paid sick leave requirements. States are stepping on urban toes at practically every turn, from limiting hotel taxes to banning requirements that builders install sprinkler systems. "From our legislators, I've heard some comments that 'we have those cities moving in retreat,'" says Ned Hill, a public policy professor at Ohio State University. "What they really mean are the policies of big-city mayors."

States like to complain that they are shortchanged by federal programs—receiving back less money than they send to Washington—but they feel little compunction about dealing a similar blow to their local governments. When it comes to funds for roads, schools and universities, states are becoming less likely to invest in their own major cities. A recent survey of 89 mayors in 31 states by the U.S. Conference of Mayors showed they believe relations with their states are now actually worse than relations with the federal government. One Midwestern mayor, whose party controls the legislature, said simply, "Our state is nuts."

"In many ways, the mismatch between state political power and city market power has never been more dramatic," says Bruce Katz, a Brookings Institution scholar who consults with metropolitan regions. "A lot of the focus is on the skirmishes around progressive policies, but the bigger issue is states impeding the ability of cities to realize their full economic potential."

In response to the pressures of living under a rural-dominated legislature, state Sen. Mike Colona, a Democrat who represents St. Louis, has taken what seems like a logical—if fanciful—step. He filed a pair of bills last month aimed at allowing St. Louis to secede from Missouri and become the 51st state.

Cities are now dominated almost completely by Democrats—not just in mayoral elections, but straight on up the ticket. In 2012, Obama carried the lowest percentage of U.S. counties of any winning presidential candidate in history—just 22 percent. But his vote in cities was so overwhelming as to guarantee his re-election. Obama took 69 percent of the vote in cities with more than 500,000 people, according to exit polls. A similar story can be told about the disparities in congressional voting—and, importantly, state legislative contests. It's no mystery why. The Obama coalition—racial and ethnic minorities, young people, gays and lesbians, unmarried women, and highly educated young professionals—disproportionately chooses to live in cities.

Having gained and retained political power thanks almost solely to the urban vote, Obama has turned to mayors to promote ideas that can't get through Congress. Many mayors have worked closely with the Obama administration on early childhood education, development of green energy, community policing and the president's My Brother's Keeper initiative, meant to give a boost to young African-American and Hispanic men. "In Congress, programs like that are suffocated to death," says Pittsburgh Mayor Bill Peduto. "In Pittsburgh, we're like an urban lab where they can be sent to grow."

Obama's budget for the coming year calls for expanding aid sent directly to cities in everything from poverty programs to manufacturing innovation. His most recent proposals may go nowhere, but the administration has

already had success in using cities as venues for its ideas. "We've been quite proactive throughout the administration in taking these policies around the country," says Cecilia Muñoz, director of the White House Domestic Policy Council. "It's a terrific mechanism for implementing progress and creating momentum."

Given gridlock in Washington, the absence of national policy in many areas has allowed lower levels of government to go their own way. That has sometimes set cities and states on a collision course. While most Republican governors were calling on the administration to block Syrian refugees from entering the country late last year, more than five dozen mayors signed a letter calling on Congress to keep the door open. Long before the debate over gay rights, Charlotte officials clashed with GOP lawmakers in North Carolina over broader policy toward immigrants, mirroring arguments in many states.

Last fall, Texas Gov. Greg Abbott moved to cut off state grant funding for sheriffs' offices in localities that failed to prosecute undocumented immigrants because they had enacted so-called sanctuary city policies. Just before taking office last year, Abbott complained that the state was becoming "Californiaized" by local bans on fracking and plastic bags, as well as restrictions on property use. Abbott conceded that some might see a disconnect between his actions as state attorney general, when he repeatedly sued what he considered to be an intrusive federal government, and the stance he's taken as governor, intervening to block city initiatives. But Abbott insists he's still working to protect people from encroachments on their personal liberty, from whatever level of government. "The governor believes cities are economic drivers that help create jobs," says spokesman John Wittman, "but they are often overregulated, generating unnecessary burdens on businesses."

If a state official doesn't like a city's policy, there's little penalty involved in trying to block it. A tax on earnings may be an essential source of revenue for St. Louis, but voting to kill it allows a legislator from outstate to take an anti-tax stand essentially for free. It won't in any way affect revenues or programs back home.

The same pattern of state legislative indifference to urban desires holds true for spending decisions. Consider infrastructure. The percentage of urban roads that have "poor pavement quality" has increased more than 50 percent over the past decade, according to the

Congressional Budget Office. When it comes to public transit—and light rail in particular—state officials have been abandoning projects pretty decisively in recent months. Last year, Maryland Gov. Larry Hogan canceled a $2.9 billion light rail project in Baltimore, which he described as a boondoggle. (He subsequently proposed a $135 million aid package for the public transit system.) Last fall, the North Carolina General Assembly canceled all but $500,000 of the state's $138 million commitment to light rail. "If the cities want to do it, fine," said a senior GOP lawmaker, "but the state shouldn't chip in on it."

It's a time-honored tradition in politics: Areas with clout get more goodies. The distribution of funds is always a selfish vote—"What's going to help my district?" Republicans who represent less populous parts of any state may be especially reluctant to send money to larger cities right now because the rural areas are having a hard time economically. It's a spiky economy, with an outsized share of growth occurring in a relatively limited number of metropolitan areas. It's hard for some legislators to explain why they would want to send more money to parts of the state that are already performing well in terms of income levels and jobs.

In many states, the type of contempt generally felt for Wall Street is channeled toward the major urban area. Mayors are left to complain that the easiest way for rural legislators to score points at home seems to be taking a shot at their cities. It's possible that, if it were not for the city of Portland, Maine would be the poorest state in the country. That doesn't mean rural and small-town residents want to see Portland get more money. "Local economies in small places are so endangered, and there's very little sense that anything is going to bring them back," says Cramer, the author who also runs a public service center at the University of Wisconsin. "The resentment toward the city is based on what they see as forces that are ending their way of life as they know it and want it to be."

If states were smart, they would invest heavily in their successful urban areas, suggests Katz, the founding director of the Metropolitan Policy Program at Brookings. They could do more to encourage economic development in dense areas that are most likely to be fertile for growth, spending money on things like higher education and medical centers right in the heart of cities. "If states were rational actors, what they would be doing is augmenting, not subtracting," Katz says. "Instead, it's almost like states are embarrassed by the success of their cities."

Maybe it's not embarrassment so much as a fundamental and growing mismatch. Big cities now tend to vote differently from the rest of their states. They hold different values when it comes to diversity. Their economies may be robust, but that hasn't translated to improving fortunes for other areas. Governors and legislatures aren't always at odds with cities, but when they are, they have little reason to give cities a break.

North Carolina Gov. Pat McCrory may be a former Charlotte mayor, but nearly all the top legislative leaders in his state come from much less populous, more rural areas. In addition to quashing Charlotte on gay rights, immigration and light rail, last year the legislature shifted a share of sales tax revenues from cities to more sparsely populated counties. "Before, cities were getting everything they asked for, but now the deck is stacked against them from a philosophical perspective," says Shaheen, the GOP consultant. "As a Republican, that makes me so giddy, I can barely contain it."

4

Constitutions:
Amend with Care

By Jennie Drage Bowser

"We the People of the United States, in Order to form a more perfect Union, establish Justice, insure domestic Tranquility, provide for the common defence, promote the general Welfare, and secure the Blessings of Liberty to ourselves and our Posterity, do ordain and establish this Constitution for the United States of America."

—Preamble to the United States Constitution

The U.S. Constitution is nearly 230 years old, and its longevity and seeming immutability are both a cause for celebration and a source of debate. You'd be hard-pressed to find a government document more revered. John Adams referred to its creation as "the greatest single effort of national deliberation that the world has ever seen." Benjamin Franklin teared up while signing it. George Washington called it "the guide which I never will abandon."

Most Americans agree with the sentiments of our forefathers and the values spelled out in the preamble. But not everyone agrees the U.S. Constitution should be so cherished that it's untouchable. Critics argue the country would benefit from a constitutional overhaul, or at least an update, but lament the arduous path to amending it.

Indeed, the U.S. Constitution has been amended only 27 times—a testament to just how difficult the process is. Either both houses of Congress must pass an amendment by a two-thirds vote, or two-thirds of the state legislatures must call for what's known as an Article V Convention. The amendment must then be ratified by

From *State Legislatures Magazine*, September 2015
©National Conference of State Legislatures

three-fourths of the states, either by the state legislature or by a convention, and Congress can choose which.

Among those pressing for a convention today are some who would rein in the federal government, others bound to a particular cause—balancing the federal budget or overturning what they view as unpalatable Supreme Court decisions—and still others who simply see the Constitution as outdated. Would-be changemakers might want to consider the experience of the states, where amending constitutions is relatively easy and has been done, with mixed results, frequently.

ANTIQUATED OR TIMELESS?

Georgetown University law professor Louis Michael Seidman has been vocal in his criticism of Americans' strict adherence to the document, referring to their reverence as "Constitution worship." Others defend the Constitution's relevancy, arguing its longevity reflects the genius of the Founding Fathers. Its general principles have stood the test of time and continue to reflect the values for which this country stands.

When asked whether our Constitution is still relevant hundreds of years after it was written, Richard Epstein, a professor at the New York University School of Law, says yes—at least mostly.

"Sections like the Fugitive Slave Clause are emphatically not relevant, but much of the document is a coherent institutionalization of structures and protection of rights that harness the good in self-interest, while controlling for avarice and fraud."

And on the question of whether our Constitution should be easier to amend, Epstein says no.

The strict amendment process prevents the adoption of short-lived changes and ensures the approval of only those amendments that enjoy broad support, he argues. If amendments were easy to make the result would be a document cluttered with frivolous changes. "Most amendments, especially if they themselves are amended, will make matters worse," Epstein says.

Seidman and others disagree. They argue that the difficulty of adapting the document to a changing world is out of step with contemporary needs.

According to Seidman, problems arise because some of the Constitution's provisions are simply unclear.

Political actors end up interpreting what these clauses mean, resulting in "political rather than practical" debates, he says.

To illustrate this, he points to the Affordable Care Act. The debate over its constitutionality under the Commerce Clause forces discussions, he says, that are "away from practical matters, like whether the statute will increase coverage at acceptable costs or force people into coverage they don't want. Instead, we are talking about who is a true American and who is a traitor to our foundational document."

It's simply too difficult to apply a document that's hundreds of years old to our vastly different modern world, he argues. "A lot of the problem would be solved if we better understood that the Constitution was written by ordinary human beings who suffered from the prejudices, narrowness of vision and inability to foresee the future that all of us suffer from," he says.

AMEND WHAT?

Many argue the amendments adopted so far were necessary, proof that the amendment system can work. "Today's Constitution is a realistic document of freedom only because of several corrective amendments," Thurgood Marshall, the first African-American U.S. Supreme Court justice, wrote after successfully challenging the doctrine of "separate but equal" as a violation of the 14th Amendment.

Many changes suggested over the years, however, never made it into the document. The list is long, with some proposals breaking sharply along partisan lines. Recently debated ideas include a ban on burning the U.S. flag, statehood for the District of Columbia and proposals from various points of view concerning marriage and reproductive rights.

The most popular of all successful amendment topics has been elections. Ten amendments relate to elections in one way or another, and the topic continues to come up in amendment conversations today. Current election proposals would allow foreign-born citizens to run for president, reverse the controversial *Citizens United* Supreme Court decision on campaign financing at the federal level, restructure or abolish the Electoral College and limit terms for members of Congress.

For Seidman, one of the most important changes needed—besides doing away with equal state representation in the Senate, which he says is the Constitution's most egregious flaw—is to the amendment process itself. We need to correct a system that allows "a tiny percentage of the population to block an amendment," he says.

STATE DIFFERENCES

Like the U.S. Constitution, state constitutions provide a framework of government that includes three branches. And, like the U.S. Constitution, state constitutions reflect the time period in which they were written. For instance, every state constitution written during the Progressive Era (roughly 1890 to 1920) enumerates the rights of workers, and those written after 1979 include environmental protections, points out Alan Tarr, director of the Center for State Constitutional Studies and professor of political science at Rutgers University.

From a state legislator's perspective, what may be the most important difference between state constitutions and the federal one, Tarr says, "is that, while the federal Constitution grants various powers to the legislative branch, state constitutions tend to restrict legislative powers."

Article I of the U.S. Constitution grants a long list of specific powers to Congress, such as the rights to borrow and coin money, regulate commerce, establish post offices, and define and punish "piracies."

On the other hand, state constitutions restrict legislatures' ability to enact local or special laws, create new taxes, increase existing taxes, authorize gambling or regulate the business of local governments without voter approval.

Tarr believes the authors of state constitutions put more trust in people than in politicians. By limiting the power of elected officials, they reflected a "tradition of being skeptical of the people we put into political office."

AMENDMENT PATHS VARY

There are several avenues for amending state constitutions, which are, by and large, far easier to amend than the U.S. Constitution. While the U.S. Constitution contains only 27 amendments, Alabama's has nearly 900. California's has more than 500, and Texas' 484.

The average number of amendments for a state constitution is 115.

Delaware is the only state that allows the legislature to amend the constitution without a popular vote. It has done so about 100 times. Approval comes not through a simple majority vote, but only with the support of at least two-thirds of each chamber in two votes, with an election intervening.

The other states require voters' approval before a constitutional amendment can be adopted by the legislature. In 34 states, it takes a simple majority of voters to approve a change. The requirement is a bit tougher in Florida, where 60 percent of voters must approve proposed changes, and tougher still in New Hampshire, where two-thirds of voters must approve them.

State constitutions also can be amended via a constitutional convention, which most states allow the legislature to call, sometimes requiring voter approval. The convention's members typically are elected by the voters. In Arizona, Florida and Montana, citizens can bypass the legislature entirely and call a constitutional convention themselves.

Constitutions in 14 states require voters to be asked at regular intervals, usually every 10 or 20 years, whether they'd like to hold a constitutional convention. And a few state constitutions make no mention of conventions at all—among them Indiana, New Jersey and Vermont.

In reality, state constitutional conventions are rare. Massachusetts has held five, Michigan and Missouri each have held four, and the last state to hold one was Rhode Island, in 1984.

A DIRECT CHANGE

The initiative is by far the most controversial tool for amending state constitutions. Available in 17 states (and Massachusetts in a more limited way), the process allows citizens, after acquiring enough signatures of support, to place an amendment on the ballot. The heavy users are California, Colorado and Oregon; more than 150 constitutional amendments have been proposed this way in each state. In all cases, the legislature and the governor are bypassed.

Although Colorado Representative Lois Court (D) supports the idea of a citizen initiative, she's concerned the process makes it just as easy to change the state constitution as it is to change the statutes. In Colorado, the signature requirements for getting each on the ballot are identical.

"A constitution should be a foundational document," she says. "It should not be a place for making detailed policy changes, such as the amount our minimum wage should be, or the dollar amount of a tax on marijuana, or the way we regulate wildlife."

The problem with putting the details into the constitution, Court says, is that it's too hard to change later. She points to Colorado's Amendment 64, which legalized recreational use of marijuana, as an example.

When concern grew over the danger marijuana edibles posed to children, some voters wanted a ban on that form of pot, but lawmakers were limited in how they could respond because Amendment 64 specifically legalized marijuana "in all its forms." Lawmakers eventually chose to regulate the packaging and sale of edibles, as a way around their inability to alter the amendment passed by voters.

Court would like to see proponents encouraged to pose their policy changes as statutes, rather than amendments.

Use of the initiative process varies greatly, however. In Illinois, where it is limited to just one article of the constitution, voters have been faced with exactly one constitutional initiative in state history. On the ballot in 1980, it asked voters to reduce the size of the House of Representatives from 177 to 118. Voters approved, and since 1982, there have been 59 fewer seats in the House.

DO-OVER CONSTITUTIONS

Citizens and lawmakers have been far more willing to make serious changes to state constitutions than to the federal one. Every so often, in fact, a state decides to toss out its constitution entirely and write a new one.

Nine states drafted new documents during the turbulent years between 1964 and 1975. Only two states have adopted new constitutions since then: Georgia in 1983, and Rhode Island in 1986.

Alabama is often mentioned when the idea of a constitutional convention comes up. The state's current document dates to 1901 and at 376,000 words is about 80 times the length of the original U.S. Constitution, making it by far the longest and most amended of state

constitutions. Amendments make up about 90 percent of it. Many local government functions are established by the constitution, and it often takes an amendment proposed by the Legislature to make changes to policies affecting a single county, or even a single town.

According to Nancy Ekberg, vice chair of a group called Alabama Citizens for Constitutional Reform, the state's current constitution simply doesn't serve the social and economic realities of the 21st century. She blames the document for numerous injustices, including "keeping those who can't drive or can't afford a car from job training, health care, schooling, shopping and jobs" because it prevents the state from using any vehicle fees or gasoline taxes to establish a statewide public transportation system.

In 1983, the Alabama Legislature rewrote the entire 1901 constitution and proposed it as a single amendment. But before it went to the voters, the state Supreme Court stopped it on the grounds that a new constitution could be proposed only through a convention. That gathering has yet to occur, though not for lack of trying.

An effort to call a convention failed in the 1990s because there was too much uncertainty about how it would work, says Representative Randy Davis (R), who chairs the House Constitution, Campaigns and Elections Committee. The idea was to include two people from each of the 105 House districts as members, but it wasn't clear who they would be or how they'd be appointed. How long would they meet? Where? How much would it cost? (It was looking to be very costly.) Who would control it and staff it? In Alabama, the only mechanism for calling a convention is via the Legislature, and when it came down to it, lawmakers just weren't willing to relinquish control over what had the potential to become a "three-ring circus," Davis says.

Fast-forward to the present. The effort to revise the constitution continues, but the idea of calling a convention has been set aside. Instead, the Constitutional Revision Commission, which includes Davis, meets publicly and frequently, in different locations around the state. The group takes up one article of the constitution at a time, and decides how to re-craft it. A House member writes the bills necessary to make the amendments and shepherds them through the legislative process. It then goes to the voters. Three amendments made it onto the ballot in this way in 2012;

two passed. The next batch, dealing with state government, will appear on the ballot in March 2016. So far, the commission has picked what Davis calls the "low-hanging fruit," the noncontroversial issues that are fairly easy to pass. The group hopes to address a tougher topic, education, on the 2018 ballot.

By rewriting the constitution's core elements—such as the state government sections that the 2016 amendments will address—the commission hopes to bring the 1901 document into the 21st century, and perhaps reduce the need for future amendments. It's an approach that has bipartisan support and has achieved vital change, Davis says.

"There's not much glitz in modernizing the constitution—it's just a lot of housekeeping work—but it's really important to the future of Alabama. We live in a global economy, and our constitution was getting in the way of doing business."

BUILT TO LAST

Given the procedural hurdles required for amending the U.S. Constitution, not to mention the highly politicized nature of most amendment proposals floating around these days, it's unlikely we'll see a successful effort to amend our foundational document anytime soon. More likely, we'll keep arguing about issues on the fringes but continue to let this document, so widely admired around the world and throughout history, hold together our basic governmental structure and processes.

For all its faults, the U.S. Constitution has done a remarkable job of keeping a diverse and fractious society stable throughout wars, terrorist attacks, civil strife and economic crises, and is likely to do so for many years to come.

State constitutions, for their part, will continue to change at a much more rapid pace than their federal counterpart. The initiative process isn't going anywhere in the states that have it. In fact, expect the process to gain momentum in the coming years, meaning there will be more citizen-initiated constitutional amendments on ballots nationwide.

No matter where you stand on the amendment process or the amendment proposals themselves, constitution-watching is part of our American heritage, not to mention good fun for political junkies everywhere.

THE ARTICLE V ALTERNATIVE

An Article V Convention is the "other" way to amend the U.S. Constitution. James Madison pushed to include it as a way to empower states and protect their rights. It says that if 34 states call for an amendment, then it's up to Congress to convene a convention of the states.

The method has never been used, says David Long (R), the Indiana Senate president pro tempore, "because people are afraid of a runaway convention. They fear that if you created this, there would be no way to control it and we might rewrite the Constitution."

Long is a leading voice in a group of legislators promoting the use of a convention as a way to fix problems in the federal government that Congress is just too broken to fix itself. For Long, the issue is the "serious amount of debt that's being accumulated right now."

Before specific amendments are debated, Long's group, The Assembly of State Legislatures, is attempting to first establish a structure—the rules and regulations—on how a convention would run. According to the group's website, it is committed to ensuring the states stay in charge, that any convention that gets called be controlled and be limited to the subject proposed by the states.

Driven by the belief that it's doing exactly what the founders had in mind when they wrote Article V, the group continues to seek support from lawmakers on both sides of the aisle who believe it's time to stand up to the federal government.

THE FLORIDA MODEL

Florida's Constitutional Revision Commission was created when the state adopted its current constitution in 1968. It convenes every 20 years to evaluate the document.

Florida's commission is unique in two ways. First, it's the only commission permanently established by a state constitution to convene at regular intervals. Second, it's the only state commission empowered to place recommended constitutional amendments and revisions directly on the ballot. Legislative approval isn't required, and neither is a petition process.

During 1997 and '98, the commission placed nine proposed amendments on the ballot, and voters adopted all but one. The work of the commission in 1977 and

'78 wasn't so well-received. Voters rejected all eight of the proposed amendments.

The next commission will do its work in 2017 and '18. Its 37 members will be appointed before the 2017 Legislature convenes and will mostly reflect the partisan makeup of their appointers. The governor will choose 15 members; the Senate president and the speaker of the House each will choose nine. The attorney general is an automatic member, and the remaining three will be chosen by the chief justice of the Florida Supreme Court.

Of course, Florida voters will have the final say on what is adopted, regardless of the commission's makeup.

A LITTLE TRIVIA ON THE BILL OF RIGHTS

The U.S. Constitution didn't last long before it was amended in 1789. Just two years after the document's ratification, Congress adopted a resolution proposing a set of amendments called the Bill of Rights. Freedom of speech was not originally in the top spot. It moved up to No. 1 only after the original First and Second amendments failed to be ratified by the required 10 out of 14 states at the time.

The original First Amendment proposed a way to determine how the House of Representatives would grow to reflect increases in the U.S. population. It started at one representative for every 30,000 citizens and ended at one for every 50,000. Using the U.S. Census Bureau's Population Clock, that would amount to 6,418 members in today's U.S. House. Yikes! If having 435 members makes it tough to get work done, imagine what it would be like with nearly 15 times more.

The original Second Amendment would have prevented members of Congress from giving themselves pay raises. Although dropped from the original Bill of Rights, it was eventually adopted in 1992 and is currently the last amendment to the U.S. Constitution.

II

Elections and Political Environment

Elections are the primary mechanism that connects voters to government; they are the link that insures the actions of the state reflect the will of the people. To a large extent that link is forged, managed, and operated by state governments. States control everything from voting registration and eligibility requirements, to where and when can people vote, to exactly how they vote. Local governments also play a big role in running elections. In many places, for example, county governments decide how many polling places will be available for voters to cast a ballot. The importance of those sorts of decisions was driven home in the 2016 Arizona presidential primary when thousands of Phoenix voters had to wait for hours to vote—many did not vote at all—because there were not enough polling places to accommodate voting demand. The big reason was Maricopa County's decision to slash the number of polling places from the 200 available in the 2012 elections to just 60 in 2016. On average, that meant that each polling place had to accommodate 21,500 voters, and many simply got overwhelmed by the demand.

If voting is a hassle, fewer people are likely vote. If the election infrastructure—the accuracy of voting machines and the integrity of the counting process—is weak, then elections start to lose their legitimacy—obviously a big problem for democracy. State and local governments bear much of the responsibility for insuring that the process of voting and the outcome of the ballot count are smooth and trustworthy. Of late, state and local governments have been widely criticized for not doing that job well enough.

The readings in this chapter investigate two big issues that are chipping away at trust in the ability of state and local government to insure free elections. The first issue is voter identification. More than thirty states now have laws that require voters to show some sort of government-issued identification in order to cast a ballot, though what forms of ID are allowed can vary widely. Supporters argue that these laws are necessary to reduce the possibility of voter fraud. As there is almost no evidence of any systematic problem with voter fraud, critics of voter ID laws charge they are mostly aimed at making it harder for certain demographic groups—such as minorities and the less well-off—to vote. These critics have repeatedly hauled states into court on charges that voter ID laws are unlawfully aimed at restricting the voting rights of such groups.

The first two essays in this chapter take a look at the current state of the voter ID controversy. The first, by Justin Levitt, provides a comprehensive view of the legal arguments and litigation surrounding voter ID laws. The second is a history and timeline of voter ID laws compiled by the National Conference of State Legislatures. As this essay makes clear, the history of voter ID laws goes back more than half-a-century, though it is only in the past ten or fifteen years that states have begun aggressively adopting these regulations.

The second two essays examine how citizens go about casting ballots. The first essay, by Lawrence Norden and Christopher Famighetti, examines the increasing problem of antiquated voting machines. In many places these machines are increasingly worn down, and without replacement the wear and tear puts an increasing number out of service on election day. That can lead to long lines and the sort of disaster that befell Maricopa County in 2016.

The second essay looks at a potential solution to the problem of rickety voting machines creating bottlenecks at polling stations: Eliminate the polling station altogether. Voters are increasingly casting mail-in ballots, though as the essay discusses, voters seem to prefer to drop off their "mail in" ballots at designated drop-off sites rather than actually trust their vote to the mail system.

5

Voter Identification in the Courts

By Justin Levitt

I n a polarized environment, changes to election procedures
with a perceived partisan skew are often highly controversial.
Few recent changes have been more prominent in this respect
than those regarding voter identification regulations. And predict-
ably, as voter identification regimes have changed, litigation has
followed.

A voter identification system is really just a set of procedures
to ensure that voters are who they say they are. Most of the recent
changes in state law concern the identification of voters who show
up in person at the polls. Despite widespread recognition that
absentee voting has posed more of a problem historically, few states
have changed the process for absentee voters.

FEDERAL LAW

Federal law sets a baseline for voter identification. Under the Help
America Vote Act of 2002, any new voter who registers to vote by
mail must have her identity confirmed in one of two ways.[1] First,
election officials may be able to match driver's license numbers
or Social Security digits on the registration form to other data
systems to confirm that the individual on the form is who she says
she is. If the numbers cannot be matched, then before the citizen's
ballot can be counted, the voter must provide documentation: a
photo ID card, utility bill, bank statement, government check,
paycheck, or government document with the voter's name and
address. Perhaps because this regime allows voters to confirm their
identity in several different ways, it has never been challenged in
court.

STATE LAWS

Beyond the federal baseline, every state has some means to ensure that voters are who they say they are. Some states compare signatures from the registration form to a voter's entry in the poll book. Some ask for a document from a fairly extensive list. Some ask for a government-issued photo ID from those who have one, and require a special affidavit from those who do not. In some states, similarly, voters without a qualifying ID card will be asked to vote a provisional ballot, which is counted if the voter's signature on a sworn attestation of identity matches the signature on his or her registration form.

And a few states effectively require all voters beyond a few discrete carve-outs—for example, those with a religious objection or those who are legally indigent—to present a current government-issued photo ID. A citizen without such a card will not be able to cast a valid ballot. Even within this category, there is variety: some accept some student IDs, for example, and some do not.

These more restrictive laws are at the heart of the current controversy.[2] Though most citizens have the ID required by each state, many in the more restrictive regimes do not—and these citizens without are at the center of the legal and policy battle. Indiana and Georgia passed photo-ID-only laws in 2005; Missouri followed in 2006; Kansas, Tennessee, Texas and Wisconsin in 2011; Mississippi and Pennsylvania in 2012; and Arkansas, North Carolina and Virginia in 2013.[3]

IN THE COURTS

Court challenges have followed in each state above, other than Mississippi and Virginia. Laws have been invalidated in Arkansas, Missouri and Pennsylvania; sustained against particular attacks in Indiana and Tennessee (though others have followed); and blocked (at least temporarily, but perhaps only temporarily) in Georgia, Texas and Wisconsin. Several cases are pending.

But that simple recounting of successful, unsuccessful and partially successful challenges masks substantial diversity in the litigation. Different courts are not, by and large, evaluating the same facts under the same cause of action to arrive at different results.

Instead, the impact of voter ID laws differs from state to state; the available legal claims differ from state to state; and even the quality of lawyering and litigation strategy differs from state to state. Differing outcomes sometimes reflect disagreement among judges—but they also reflect litigation under different conditions and with different legal theories. Moreover, the success or failure of particular allegations often depends as much on the particular evidence presented to a court as on the abstract merit of the claims themselves. The U.S. Supreme Court has rejected one claim that one state's voter ID law violated one constitutional doctrine—but that is not the same as deciding that voter ID laws are constitutional.

CLAIMS BASED ON IMPLEMENTATION

One set of claims has aimed not at the ultimate validity of ID laws, but at their rollout: too fast, too sloppy, too little information. Courts in Georgia and Pennsylvania pressed pause, giving states time to ensure that education and implementation were uniform; a North Carolina federal court declined to do so. In Pennsylvania, the court ultimately determined that the state would be unable to adequately implement the law as written at any point.[4]

CLAIMS BASED ON LEGISLATIVE POWER

Other claims concern the legislature's authority to enact rules like ID requirements. Most states' constitutions expressly authorize the legislature to regulate the election process—and some specify the election-related topics that a legislature may regulate. Litigation has proceeded on the premise that these authorization clauses are exclusive: if the state constitution does not expressly authorize legislative regulation of ID, the legislature may not regulate ID. State supreme courts in Georgia, Indiana and Tennessee have dismissed such claims, though the Arkansas Supreme Court struck down the state's ID law on this basis.[5]

CLAIMS BASED ON PARTISAN MOTIVE

Still another type of claim attacks the alleged partisan motivation of the legislature in enacting the new laws. These allegations have favored existing cases, but have not yet been the centerpiece of any lawsuit.[6] The Supreme Court has strongly resisted legal challenges along these lines in other electoral arenas as long as a plausible alternative purpose exists. And related, but distinct, claims of undue partisan effect have found even less hospitable legal homes.

CLAIMS BASED ON RACIAL DISCRIMINATION

Another set of claims attacks the newer ID laws as abridging the right to vote on account of race or ethnicity. ID laws are not inherently racist; neither are literacy tests, poll taxes, registration purges or district lines. But any tool can be abused. Even without intent to disenfranchise based on race, an ID law that interacts with the legacy of racial discrimination in other arenas to create a disparate racial impact may, in certain circumstances, create liability under the federal Voting Rights Act.

The racial and ethnic impact of the more restrictive ID laws is not uniform: the communities most affected in Kansas are different from those in Tennessee. Nor is the political or historical environment the same from state to state with respect to the enactment of a new regulation of the franchise. Both the Constitution and the Voting Rights Act are profoundly sensitive to local context; liability in one area need not imply liability in a different area, even for a law that looks very similar in the statute books. In areas where new laws have a more dramatically skewed demographic impact, or where there exists a more profound history of discrimination or present evidence of misconduct, these claims are more likely to resonate.

Claims of intentional racial discrimination under the Constitution are quite difficult to prove; claims under the Voting Rights Act are subject to a standard that is still a work in progress for ID laws. Most early cases under the Voting Rights Act were based on direct, and directly discriminatory, outright denials of the vote; later cases built a jurisprudence concerning redistricting. Neither line of cases fits the current ID controversies particularly well, which means that courts are just now working through the applicable standards.

The race-based claims that have succeeded are quite recent and are now proceeding through an appellate process. A federal judge struck down Texas' ID law as the product of intentional race discrimination and as a Violation of the Voting Rights Act; that decision is now on appeal.[7] In Wisconsin, a federal judge found a violation of the Voting Rights Act due to disparate impact that was in part the legacy of discrimination in other arenas; an appeals panel rejected the claim, with a significantly narrower conception of the Voting Rights Act.[8]

CLAIMS BASED ON UNEQUAL TREATMENT

Still another set of claims is premised on the assertion that the newer ID laws treat similarly situated voters differently, in an unconstitutional fashion. Some of these challenges concern the differential treatment of absentee voters and voters at the polls; others concern the differential treatment of students.[9] To date, none has succeeded, though various claims are pending.

CLAIMS BASED ON IMPERMISSIBLE COST

A further set of claims attacks the newer ID laws as imposing an impermissible cost or other property requirement, either under state constitutions or under federal statutory and constitutional prohibitions of a poll tax. Even when government-issued ID cards are available without charge, there may be travel time and effort to procure them, or a monetary cost to procure the underlying documents necessary to apply for the cards. This sort of claim was rejected in Tennessee and is pending in North Carolina. A federal court has struck Texas' ID law on this basis, but the case is on appeal.[10]

CLAIMS BASED ON UNDUE BURDEN

A final set of claims is both the most common and the most varied. The federal Constitution and many state constitutions require that electoral regulations' burdens be justified. The greater the burden, the more justification is necessary.

Proof of burden sufficient to satisfy a court has been difficult to come by. Most challenges to more restrictive

ID laws have attempted to stop the laws before they take effect. It is tricky to find people who have already been blocked from voting by a law that is still in the future, and in Georgia, Indiana and Tennessee, these challenges have failed; in Wisconsin, a challenge that succeeded at the trial court was rejected on appeal.[11] The Indiana case—one of the first challenges to restrictive ID laws in the country—was thin on empirical support and became the claim that the Supreme Court ultimately rejected. The Wisconsin case had substantially more factual development.

Other cases have turned to proxy estimates of harm, like local statistics attempting to assess the number of citizens without valid ID, and testimony speaking to the difficulties facing those without ID as they try to get an ID. In Missouri and Pennsylvania, for example, state courts found that ID laws created a burden insufficiently justified by the ostensible interest in preventing voters from impersonating others at the polls. A federal court similarly struck down Texas' new ID law, but the case is now on appeal.[12]

CASES MODIFYING VOTER ID STATUTES

The cases above resulted in injunctions against the implementation of restrictive ID laws, rejections of claims for injunctions, or temporary injunctions that were later dissolved. But a review of voter ID in the courts would not be complete without an acknowledgment of litigation that reshaped ID requirements rather than providing a thumbs-up or thumbs-down.

South Carolina passed a new voter ID law in 2011, when it was still subject to a preclearance regime requiring federal approval before implementing any electoral change. In the course of litigation, South Carolina officials explained that voters with a government-issued photo ID would be required to show it, but any voter with a "reasonable impediment" to obtaining photo ID could cast a valid ballot after completing an affidavit; virtually any reason will suffice.[13] And in Wisconsin, litigation in state court concerning the cost of ID forced the state Department of Transportation to issue a photo ID to citizens without any underlying documentation of their identity, if procuring that documentation otherwise would require paying a fee.[14]

NOTES

1. 52 U.S.C. § 21083(b).

2. There have been fewer court challenges to identification laws permitting citizens to vote a valid ballot at the polls even if they do not possess (and cannot readily obtain) a particular government-issued photo ID card, or to aspects of ID laws that apply only to certain subpopulations seeking to vote at the polls. Challenges to a Michigan requirement that voters either show photo ID or complete an affidavit were rejected by the state Supreme Court, In re Request for Advisory Opinion Regarding Constitutionality of 2005 PA 71, 740 N.W.2d 444 (Mich. 2007); challenges to an Arizona requirement that voters either show photo ID or two non-photo pieces of identification were rejected by the 9th Circuit Court of Appeals, *Gonzalez v. Arizona*, 677 F.3d 383 (9th Cir. 2012); and challenges to a Colorado requirement that voters show identification mirroring the Help America Vote Act were rejected by a state trial court, *Colo. Common Cause v. Davidson*, No. 04CV7709, 2004 WL 2360485 (Colo. Dist. Ct. 2004). Challenges to an Ohio law requiring various forms of voter identification were resolved by consent decree. Consent Decree, *Northeast Ohio Coalition for the Homeless v. Blackwell*, No. 2:06-cv-00896 (S.D. Ohio Nov. 1, 2006); Consent Decree, *Northeast Ohio Coalition for the Homeless v. Brunner*, No. 2:06-cv-00896 (S.D. Ohio April 19, 2010). And a challenge to Oklahoma's law (requiring a government-issued photo ID card, registration card, or match of voter information) is still pending. *Gentges v. Oklahoma State Election Board*, 319 P.3d 674 (Okla. 2014).

   With respect to subpopulations, for example, a federal court in Ohio struck down a state requirement that naturalized citizens, but not others, show proof of their citizenship. *Boustani v. Blackwell*, 460 F. Supp. 2d 822 (N.D. Ohio 2006). A federal court in Minnesota similarly struck down limits on tribal ID cards not applicable to other forms of ID cards. *ACLU of Minn. v. Kiffmeyer*, No. 04-CV-4653, 2004 WL 2428690 (D. Minn. 2004).

3. Some municipalities have passed their own voter ID regulations as well, for municipal elections only. For example, Albuquerque, New Mexico, requires voters at the polls to show a photo ID card, but allows for several private ID cards (like a student ID, debit card, insurance card, union card, or professional association card) in addition to government-issued ID cards. In 2008, the law was upheld against a challenge on several grounds. *ACLU of New Mexico v. Santillanes*, 546 F.3d 1313 (10th Cir. 2008).

4. *Common Cause/Georgia v. Billups*, 406 F.Supp.2d 1326 (N.D. Ga. 2005); *Common Cause/Georgia v. Billups*, 439

F.Supp.2d 1294 (N.D. Ga. 2006); *League of Women Voters of N.C. v. North Carolina*, 769 F.3d 224 (4th Cir. 2014); *Applewhite v. Pennsylvania*, No. 330 M.D. 2012, 2012 WL 4497211 (Pa. Comm. Ct. 2012); *Applewhite v. Pennsylvania*, No. 330 M.D. 2012, 2014 WL 184988 (Pa. Comm. Ct. 2014).

5. *Democratic Party of Georgia, Inc. v. Perdue*, 707 S.E.2d 67 (Ga. 2011); *League of Women Voters of Indiana, Inc. v. Rokita*, 929 N.E.2d 758 (Ind. 2010); *City of Memphis v. Hargett*, 414 S.W.3d 88 (Tenn. 2013); *Martin v. Kohls*, 444 S.W.3d 844 (Ark. 2014).

6. Memorandum Opinion and Order, *Green Party of Tenn. v. Hargett*, No. 2:13-cv-224 (E.D. Tenn. Feb. 20, 2014).

7. Opinion, *Veasey v. Perry*, No. 13-cv-00193, 2014 WL 5090258 (S.D. Tex. Oct. 9, 2014).

8. *Frank v. Walker*, 768 F.3d 744 (7th Cir. 2014), *reversing* 17 F. Supp. 3d 837 (E.D. Wis. 2014).

9. *League of Women Voters of Indiana, Inc. v. Rokita*, 929 N.E.2d 758 (Ind. 2010); *City of Memphis v. Hargett*, 414 S.W.3d 88 (Tenn. 2013).

10. Order on Parties' Motions for Judgment on the Pleadings, *Currie v. North Carolina*, No. 13-CVS-1419 (N.C. Super. Ct. Feb. 24, 2015); *City of Memphis v. Hargett*, 414 S.W.3d 88 (Tenn. 2013); Opinion, *Veasey v. Perry*, No. 13-cv-00193, 2014 WL 5090258 (S.D. Tex. Oct. 9, 2014).

11. *Common Cause/Georgia v. Billups*, 554 F.3d 1340 (11th Cir. 2009); *Democratic Party of Georgia, Inc. v. Perdue*, 707 S.E.2d 67 (Ga. 2011); *Crawford v. Marion County Election Board*, 553 U.S. 181 (2008); *League of Women Voters of Indiana, Inc. v. Rokita*, 929 N.E.2d 758 (Ind. 2010); *City of Memphis v. Hargett*, 414 S.W.3d 88 (Tenn. 2013); *Frank v. Walker*, 768 F.3d 744 (7th Cir. 2014), *reversing* 17 F. Supp. 3d 837 (E.D. Wis. 2014).

12. *Weinschenk v. Missouri*, 203 S.W.3d 201 (Mo. 2006) (en banc); *Applewhite v. Pennsylvania*, No. 330 M.D. 2012, 2014 WL 184988 (Pa. Comm. Ct. 2014); Opinion, *Veasey v. Perry*, No. 13-cv-00193, 2014 WL 5090258 (S.D.Tex. Oct. 9, 2014).

13. *South Carolina v. United States*, 898 F. Supp. 2d 30 (D.D.C. 2012) (three-judge court).

14. *Milwaukee Branch of the NAACP v. Walker*, 851 N.W.2d 262 (Wis. 2014).

6

Voter ID History

HISTORY OF VOTER ID

While voter ID has been one of the hottest topics in elections policy for the last several years, its legacy extends back to 1950.

That was when South Carolina became the first state to request that voters show some kind of identification document at the polls. No photo was required—just a document bearing the voter's name. In 1970, Hawaii joined South Carolina with a voter ID requirement. Texas (1971), Florida (1977), and Alaska (1980) rounded out the first five. In some states the request was for an ID with a photo; in others, any document, with or without a photo, was fine. In all these states, provisions existed for voters to be able to cast a regular ballot even if they did not have the requested ID.

Over time, and with little fanfare, more states began to ask voters to present an identification document. By 2000, 14 states did so. These states had Democratic and Republican majorities.

In the 2000s, voter ID as an issue began to take center stage. The Commission on Federal Election Reform (aka the Carter-Baker Commission) in 2005 made a bipartisan recommendation for voter identification at the polls.

Soon thereafter, Georgia and Indiana pioneered a new, "strict" form of voter ID. Instead of *requesting* an ID, these states required an ID. If a voter did not have the required ID at the polling place, he or she voted on a provisional ballot, and that ballot was not to be counted unless the voter returned within the next few days to an elections office and showed the required ID. These were first implemented in 2008 (after Indiana's law was given the go-ahead by the U.S. Supreme Court, in *Crawford v. Marion County).*

In 2011, 2012 and 2013, the pace of adoption accelerated. States without ID requirements continued to adopt them, and states that had less-strict requirements adopted stricter ones. Many of the stricter laws were challenged in court, with mixed results. Following is a chart with the progression of legislative enactments on voter identification from 2000 to 2016, and a detailed timeline of enacted legislation.

VOTER ID ENACTMENTS 2000–2015

2002

Missouri (SB 675, sec. 115.427): Created a non-strict, non-photo ID requirement

2003

Alabama (Act 381/HB 193): Created a non-strict, non-photo ID requirement

Colorado (Chap.164/SB 102): Created a non-strict, non-photo ID requirement

Montana (Chap. 475/HB 190): Created a non-strict, non-photo ID requirement

North Dakota (Chap. 172/SB 2394): Created a non-strict, non-photo ID requirement

South Dakota (Chap. 83/HB 1176): Created a non-strict, photo ID requirement

2004

Arizona (Proposition 200, sec. 5, approved by the voters in November 2004): Created a strict non-photo ID requirement

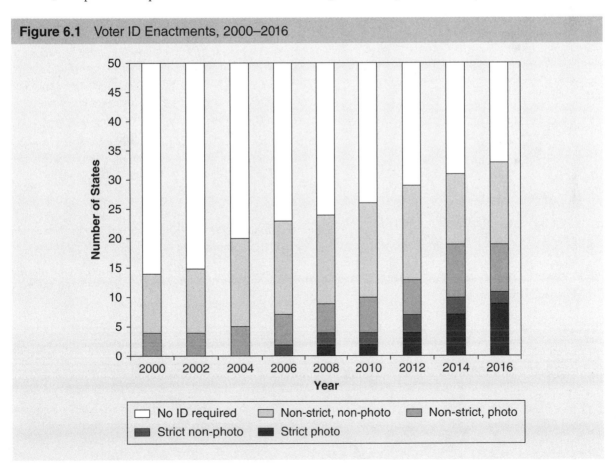

Figure 6.1 Voter ID Enactments, 2000–2016

2005

Georgia (Act 53/HB 244, sec. 59): Amended original law passed in 1997; moved to strict photo ID (not implemented until 2008 due to court challenges)

Indiana (P.L. 109/SB 483): Created a strict photo ID requirement; implemented in 2008 after being cleared by U.S. Supreme Court)

Washington (Chap. 243/SB 5499, sec. 7): Created a non-strict, non-photo ID requirement

2006

Missouri (SB 1014): Amended 2002 law; would have moved to a strict photo ID requirement but was struck down under the state constitution and never implemented

Ohio (HB 3, Sec. 3505.18(A)(1)): Created a strict non-photo ID requirement

2009

Oklahoma (SB 692): Referred a non-strict, non-photo ID requirement to the ballot by the legislature; it received voter approval in November 2010

Utah (Chap. 45/HB 126): Created a non-strict, non-photo ID requirement

2010

Idaho (Chap. 246/HB 496): Created a non-strict photo ID requirement

Oklahoma (Question 746, referred to the ballot by 2009 SB 692): Non-strict, non-photo ID requirements approved by voters

2011

Alabama (Act 2011-673, HB 19): Amendment to original law passed in 2003; created a non-strict photo ID requirement; implemented in 2014

Kansas (Act 2011-56, HB 2067): Created a strict photo ID requirement

Mississippi (citizen initiative #27): Would create a strict photo ID requirement; approved by voters but required implementing legislation in 2012

Rhode Island (Act 2011-201/2011-199, SB 400/HB 5680): Created a non-strict, non-photo ID requirement for 2012 and non-strict photo ID requirement for 2014

South Carolina (Act 27, HB 3003): Amendment to 1988 law; the law was initially declared unenforceable by the U.S. Department of Justice; after administrative changes regarding the "reasonable impediment" clause were made, it was cleared by a federal court; while the law became stricter than the original 1988 law, it is still in the non-strict, non-photo ID category

Tennessee (Act 323, SB 16/HB 7): Amended 1990 law; moved law to strict photo ID

Texas (Act 123, SB 14): Amended a 1997 law to create a strict photo ID requirement; went into effect in 2013, and has faced court challenges; in August 2015 a federal appeals court ruled it could not be enforced while the case goes back to a lower court; a final ruling is yet to come

Wisconsin (Act 23, AB 7): Created a strict photo ID requirement; after several court cases, it went into effect in 2015

2012

Minnesota (HF 2738): Put voter ID on the November 2012 ballot; it failed

Mississippi (Act 526, HB 921): Implemented strict photo ID requirement approved by voters in 2011 citizens' initiative; went into effect in 2014

New Hampshire (Act 2012-284, SB 289): Created a non-strict, non-photo ID requirement

Pennsylvania (Act 18, HB 934): Would have created a strict photo ID; struck down by courts in 2014

Virginia (Chap. 838, HB 9): Amended 1996 law; created strict non-photo ID requirement

2013

Arkansas (Act 595, <u>SB 2</u>): Strengthened existing law; moved to strict photo ID; the law was struck down by the Arkansas Supreme Court in 2014

North Carolina (Act. 2013-381, <u>HB 589</u>, Part 2): Created a strict photo ID requirement; implementation is set in the law for 2016; it was amended in 2015 to make it a non-strict photo ID requirement, still to be implemented in 2016

North Dakota (Act 167, <u>HB 1332</u>): Amended 2003 law; moved to strict non-photo ID requirement

Oklahoma (Act. 34, <u>SB 282</u> and Act 38, <u>SB 752</u>): Amended 2010 law; the law is still in the non-strict, non-photo category

Tennessee (Act 178, <u>HB 229SB 125</u>): Amended 2011 law; made law stricter by prohibiting use of county or municipal IDs for voting purposes, and allowing only state or U.S.-issued IDs

Virginia (Act 703, <u>HB 1337</u>): Amended 2012 law; moved to strict photo ID requirement

2014

None

2015

North Carolina (<u>HB 836</u>); Amended 2013 law; moved law for 2016 from strict to non-strict requirement

North Dakota (<u>HB 1333</u>): Amended 2013 law; moved to strict photo ID requirement (Note: A long-term care identification certificate from a North Dakota facility is accepted, though this is the only exception to the photo ID requirement)

Wisconsin's strict photo ID law, enacted in 2011, went into effect.

West Virginia (<u>HB 4013</u>): Created a non-strict, non-photo ID requirement, which takes effect in 2018

7

Aging Voting Machines Are a Threat to Democracy

By Lawrence Norden and Christopher Famighetti

There are some political problems that defy easy solutions—the rise of extreme partisanship, or our broken campaign finance system, for instance. But it should not be difficult to rally our elected leaders to remedy an eminently fixable problem threatening our democracy: the looming crisis resulting from our nation's outdated voting machines.

In the vast majority of states, aging voting machines are approaching the end of their useful lives. To continue to use this equipment past its projected lifespan could be disastrous. After years of wear-and-tear, machine parts like motherboards, memory cards, and touch screens begin to fail. When this happens on Election Day, machines must be taken out of service. Voters can be forced to wait in line—sometimes for hours—while repairs are made or machines substituted.

This can only shake confidence in the electoral process, and in worst case scenarios can impact election results. In the 2012 election, according to a study by political scientists from Harvard and MIT, between 500,000 and 700,000 votes were lost nationally because of long lines. Absent action to replace or upgrade machines, this problem will only grow worse.

A little history is in order. After the 2000 presidential election debacle, involving "hanging chads" on paper ballots in Florida, Congress passed a law allocating more than $2 billion to the states to replace obsolete voting equipment. By 2006, the vast majority of election jurisdictions had deployed new machines.

Voting system experts agree that most machines purchased since 2000 have a projected lifespan of between 10 and 15 years. Today, 43 states are using systems that will be at least 10 years old in 2016;

14 are using machines that will be at least 15 years old. No one expects a laptop computer to last for 10 years. It is wrong to expect these electronic voting machines, many of which use laptop technology from the 1990s, to last much longer.

For a high-profile example of what can go wrong with antiquated machines consider Virginia's 2014 election. Following reports of machines crashing or registering votes incorrectly, the state Board of Elections commissioned an expert review to look at 27 malfunctioning touch screen machines. In 26 of them, they found the glue holding the touch screens in place had degraded, knocking them out of alignment so votes were not recorded properly. That problem may not be limited to Virginia. The same model of this antiquated machine is still used in 20 states.

Security is another problem with older machines. In a related investigation, looking at a different machine, Virginia investigators found wireless cards that could allow "an external party to access the [machine] and modify the data without notice from a nearby location."

In the years since those machines were purchased, much has been learned about how to design voting systems that are more user friendly and accessible to all. We have developed techniques that can audit the count of paper ballots, to ensure that the software on new machines is correctly tallying votes.

As it is, maintaining the outdated machines used today is often a struggle. As voting systems age, the parts necessary to support them go out of production. Some election officials have to resort to finding parts on eBay.

It is too late for most jurisdictions to acquire new voting machines in time for the 2016 election. But that does not mean there is time to waste. To ensure new machines are in place before 2018 or even 2020, planning and budgeting must begin immediately.

Even in the absence of new machines, there are important steps that states and counties can take in the next several months to reduce failures or minimize their impact on voting next November. Officials should test every voting machine before Election Day to catch problems ahead of time. Training poll workers on how to deal with machine problems is also critical. Poll workers who know what to do in case of machine problems can make the difference between a major Election Day fiasco and a brief delay.

Of course, the fragile state of voting machines is no secret to those election officials who need to replace them. What too many lack is the money to do so.

Congress has a role to play. As it did 13 years ago, Washington should provide an infusion of money to help purchase new machines. But today, few in Congress of either party are talking about this problem. Realistically, given how soon action needs to be taken, states are going to have to provide the majority of funds. At a moment of intense budget pressures, replacing all of the aging machines will not be cheap—the total cost could easily reach $1 billion nationwide. But even in tough budget times, this is an essential investment. The mechanics of democracy are too important to rely on outdated systems that are increasingly prone to failure.

8

Vote-by-Mail Rates More than Double since 2000

By Sean Greene and Kyle Ueyama

The way Americans vote is changing, with more and more of them receiving and casting their ballots by mail.

The U.S. Census Bureau estimates that 10 percent of all ballots cast in the 2000 presidential election were cast by mail. By 2012, the practice had nearly doubled, to 19 percent of voters. In last year's midterms, data from the Survey of the Performance of American Elections (SPAE) found that around a quarter of all voters voted by mail.

But not all voters who receive their ballots in the mail return them that way. The SPAE estimates that in 2014 around 1 out of every 5 mail ballots nationwide were returned by hand to an official location, like an election office, drop box, or polling place on Election Day, and not mailed back to the election official.

In Colorado, Oregon, and Washington, ballots are sent by mail to all active registered voters. In Colorado, in counties with 25,000 or more registered voters, 67 percent of those who used mail ballots dropped them off. For example, in Denver County, Colorado, slightly more than 70 percent of mail ballots in the last midterm election were returned by hand to an official drop-off location, many at one of the nearly two dozen 24-hour drop boxes that were available.

But in Colorado counties with between 10,000 and 25,000 registered voters, the drop-off rate was 56 percent. And in counties with fewer than 10,000 registered voters, it was 48 percent.

THE IMPORTANCE OF DROP BOXES

A report for the Colorado Voter Access and Modernized Elections Commission found that one of the reasons for the variation between

From *Stateline*, a project of the Pew Charitable Trusts, April 2015.

Figure 8.1   Reasons for In-Person Ballot Return

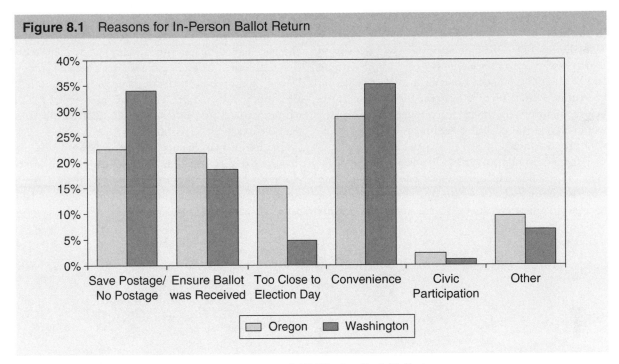

Source: 2014 Survey of the Performance of American Elections. © 2015 The Pew Charitable Trusts

counties is the state currently requires the 24-hour drop boxes be under camera surveillance. This can be cost prohibitive for some of the counties, and especially for the small and medium-sized jurisdictions.

Data from the SPAE shows a parallel trend in the two other states that hold all-mail elections, where 56 percent of voters in Oregon and 39 percent of participants in Washington decided to return their ballot in person.

In Pierce County, Washington, the second most populous county in the state, nearly 54 percent of the approximately 220,000 ballots cast were returned at a drop box. The county uses a Geographic Information System (GIS) to determine the best locations that will serve the most voters, allowing for a maximum drive time of 10 minutes. These locations are often in common public spaces, including city halls, libraries, and fire stations. The county uses large boxes that weigh 600 pounds and can hold 1,500 ballots.

A majority of voters in Arizona and California also used mail ballots in the 2014 midterm election. These states allow eligible voters to register as a permanent

absentee voter and have their ballot automatically sent to them in every election. More voters in these states mailed their ballots back, likely in part because drop boxes are not widely used in either state.

In California approximately one-fifth of these ballots were still returned by hand, while in Arizona, just 7 percent were returned by hand.

CONVENIENCE AND STAMPS

So why don't voters just drop their ballots in the mail?

In Oregon and Washington, the SPAE asked voters why they chose to hand deliver their ballots and several reasons were cited.

Convenience was the most common reason. Drop-off sites were prevalent in both states, especially in urban areas—King County, home to Seattle, had 22 locations while Multnomah County, which contains the bulk of the city of Portland, had 28. Washington mandates that each county have at least two locations where voters may return their ballot; Oregon requires that a county provide one drop off location for every

30,000 registered voters, with a minimum of two sites in a county.

A desire to save the cost of postage was the second most popular reason respondents gave in both Oregon and Washington. It appears that such concerns have not gone unnoticed. Earlier this year, the Washington Senate held a committee hearing that considered a bill which would have required ballot return envelopes to come with prepaid postage.

Fifteen percent of voters in Oregon who hand delivered their ballot said they did so because it was too close to the day of the election to return their ballot by mail, compared to only 5 percent of respondents in Washington. In Oregon, ballots must be received, either in person or by mail, by 8 p.m. on Election Day. The Secretary of State's office recommends that voters who return their ballots less than a week before Election Day use a drop box to ensure their votes are counted. Washington only requires that a ballot returned by mail be postmarked, and not necessarily received, no later than the day of the election.

The use of mail ballots is growing steadily, and the trend is likely to continue in the 2016 election cycle. However, as seen in states that rely on vote by mail, "mail voting" more aptly describes how voters receive their ballots, not how they return them.

Political Parties and Interest Groups

Figuring out where a special interest group ends and a political party begins is not always easy. Both advocate their policy preferences, push agendas, support candidates, and try to make the merits of their cause clear on every media platform from Facebook feeds to bumper stickers. Technically speaking, though, political parties and special interest groups are different creatures that, despite their often unsavory reputations, provide important services to democratic politics.

According to political scientists this is the big difference that separates the two: Political parties run candidates for office under their own label, while special interest groups do not. That difference has huge implications. It means while special interest groups might influence government, only political parties will actually organize and run government. With one exception (non-partisan Nebraska), state legislatures are organized and run by political parties, and the power and influence of a given legislator within a chamber depend not on his or her standing with a special interest group, but on which party controls the chamber, and his or her standing in the party caucus. To be sure, political parties and special interest groups do a lot of similar things: mobilize voters, support candidates, and advocate particular points of view. The bottom line, though, is that only political parties actually run government.

The readings in this chapter, though, suggest that the traditional distinction between special interest groups and political parties is not as sharp as it used to be. The first reading, by Daniel Weiner and Ian Vandewalker, is the introduction to a much larger

33

report on the state of the modern political party (you can download the full report at: http://www.brennancenter.org/sites/default/files/publications/Stronger_Parties_Stronger_Democracy.pdf). The central premise of this essay is that the traditional notion of what a political party is and what it does is changing. This includes questioning what really separates a political party from a special interest group, and maybe rethinking what a political party is. Parties increasingly seem to be diffuse networks that include political action committees and nonprofit groups, some of which have pretty narrow interests. In short, at least parts of the groups integrated into these party networks look awfully like special interest groups. Indeed, in some ways, political party organizations are "swallowing" special interest groups. As parties change, Weiner and Vandewalker question what political parties are actually evolving into, and what reforms might support and strengthen the benefits these organizations have traditionally provided democracy.

The second essay, by Alan Greenblatt, takes a look at one of the biggest contemporary concerns about special interest groups. More accurately, the concern is about the interests of a small group of deep-pocketed individuals who, thanks to recent court rulings, are free to deploy their wealth to wield extensive influence on government and politics. This essay focuses on Rex Sinquefield, who has become a big power broker in Missouri, using his considerable resources to advocate his political positions, up to and including recruiting and backing candidates for office who back his agenda.

The final essay, by Louis Jacobson, takes a look at how demography, geography, and electoral timing is shaping partisan success—or lack thereof—from City Hall to the Electoral College. In brief, these factors give Democrats an advantage in pursuing the presidency and mayoral races. The same factors give Republican candidates an advantage in winning gubernatorial races, congressional majorities, and generally doing better in off-year elections.

9

Stronger Parties, Stronger Democracy: Rethinking Reform

By Daniel I. Weiner and Ian Vandewalker

Political parties are a core ingredient of representative democracy. A robust debate has recently developed, however, concerning whether organized parties can still provide the sorts of democratic benefits they traditionally supplied to our political system and, if not, what to do about it. This paper examines these questions from the perspective of campaign finance law. We ask whether there are changes that can be made to the rules governing party fundraising and spending that will enhance parties' democratic strengths without expanding the risks associated with unfettered money in politics.

Over the last century, parties have been changed, and some would say undermined, by significant legal and societal forces. These include the expansion of party nominating primaries, institutional shifts in Congress and state legislatures, and the emergence of television advertising as the key medium for political persuasion. Today, elections are far more focused on individual candidates than on the parties. And in recent years, even the parties' important supporting role has been increasingly eclipsed, as financial resources have flowed outside formal party institutions to new, purportedly independent entities like super PACs.

Campaign finance law, many argue, has played an important role in these changes. In particular, the balance of power is said to have shifted more quickly away from parties in the last decade thanks to both the heightened fundraising restrictions in the Bipartisan Campaign Reform Act of 2002 (BCRA), also known as the McCain-Feingold law, and the Supreme Court's elimination of restrictions on purportedly independent non-party groups, most notably in *Citizens United v. FEC*. The resulting accelerated waning of organized parties is blamed for a host of problems, ranging from greater polarization and gridlock, to instability caused by the weakness of party leaders, to vanishing transparency in political spending, to declining participation by ordinary voters. One often-proposed solution is to allow parties to accept bigger checks: to deregulate party fundraising by repealing or significantly altering not only much of BCRA, but also the older framework of federal contribution limits and restrictions in place since passage of the original Federal Election Campaign Act (FECA) in 1974.

Others dispute that the parties have been significantly weakened. They note that party committee fundraising has been relatively steady since BCRA, and contend that party leaders in Congress exert a historically high amount of control over their caucuses. This camp sees polarization and gridlock as the products of broader political forces, such as Americans' residential sorting by political views, to say nothing of strategic choices by party leaders. They question whether changes to campaign finance regulation can fix these problems, and are especially skeptical of many calls for deregulation.

This is an important debate, but it tends to obscure two threshold questions: *First*, what is a party? When practitioners in the field speak of parties, they are usually referring to the institutions run by the traditional party establishments—e.g., the Democratic and Republican National Committees and the two major parties' respective congressional committees, as well as the many state and local party committees. But a growing number of scholars argue for a broader conception of the parties as diffuse networks connected to a common brand, encompassing both established party organizations and a variety of other individuals and entities affiliated with them, including ostensibly independent but party-aligned super PACs and 501(c) nonprofit groups. Clarity on this point is important, because the broader one's conception of the parties, the less it makes sense to think of them as competing with other political actors so much as themselves encompassing an array of competing interests. Since the various factions within parties differ in their democratic character—some include party activists and organizers while others are controlled by elite donors—the result of this intraparty competition has potentially significant effects on the parties' contribution to the health of the republic.

Second, what is the ultimate goal of efforts to "strengthen" parties? For example, many argue that strengthening traditional party leaders will promote the stability and compromise necessary for divided government to function. Others advance different goals, like empowering the so-called party faithful (i.e. the party's rank-and-file activists and volunteers) to make wider party networks more accountable to ordinary voters. While there is significant tension between such objectives, a common thread running through the arguments of many party-boosters is the need for parties to raise more money. Yet, as a consequence of the Supreme Court's *McCutcheon v. FEC* ruling and the recent roll-back of national party contribution limits by Congress, party committees can already accept vastly larger contributions than they could just a few years ago. Such changes may have strengthened the parties in some sense, but they have not necessarily enhanced the attributes that make organized parties attractive as political actors.

Hanging over all such discussions, moreover, are familiar concerns about corruption and political misalignment. It has long been understood that large contributions to parties, like those to candidates, pose an inherent risk of *quid pro quo* corruption and its appearance. There are many examples in American history of corruption scandals in which the *quid* took the form of contributions to a political party. The more money a small class of wealthy donors can give to the parties, the greater danger that the parties, dependent on those contributions, will sell policy outcomes in exchange. In addition, there is a growing body of evidence to suggest that the views of the donor class (which has always been small and unrepresentative of the public at large) have an outsized impact on policy decisions, creating misalignment between public opinion and policy outcomes. Too often, middle and working class voters already find themselves shut out of the policymaking process. Sweeping deregulation of party fundraising risks exacerbating such problems.

All of these concerns—especially the perennial threat of corruption—have driven decades of campaign finance regulation directed at the parties. One need not advocate wholesale abandonment of this traditional regulatory paradigm, however, to realize that the current system is not enough, especially in an era dominated by an activist

Supreme Court majority hostile to many of its central components.

Ultimately, legitimate concerns about corruption and misalignment resulting from party fundraising must be balanced against the reality that party institutions *do* play a salutary role in our democracy, one that risks being eclipsed in the new era of unlimited fundraising by both party-affiliated and truly independent outside groups. Not only do the parties offer a number of avenues for political engagement by their core supporters, they also continue to drive voter registration and turn-out efforts on a scale that few other political actors can replicate. As presently constituted, moreover, organized parties plainly are more transparent than the shadow parties and other outside groups competing with them for resources.

Whether the wholesale lifting of party contribution limits would enhance these positive attributes is an open question but, in any event, there are other ways to strengthen traditional party organizations that do not raise comparable corruption and misalignment concerns. We advocate for targeted reforms to *build up the institutional parties as meaningfully transparent organizations that function as engines of broad participation in politics.* This approach eschews complete deregulation of party fundraising, instead embracing other, more targeted measures to strengthen organized parties, including:

- Making public financing available to parties;
- Raising or eliminating coordinated spending limits and other limits on party contributions to candidates;
- Lessening federal regulation of state and local parties;
- Relaxing certain disclosure requirements whose burdens outweigh their benefits while strengthening others; and
- Relaxing certain restrictions on contributions to parties.

A thoughtful policy agenda combining one or more of these measures stands the best chance of producing a more inclusive, fair and transparent democracy. This is not intended as a single package of reforms, but rather as a set of discrete suggestions, and some combinations may not be desirable.

10

Rex Sinquefield: the Tyrannosaurus Rex of State Politics

By Alan Greenblatt

Republicans are in firm control of the Missouri House of Representatives, and they run a good whip operation. If they can't get a bill passed with a solid GOP majority, they don't bring it to the floor. They'd rather not advertise dissension within party ranks. A couple of years ago, however, the leadership made a big exception to that rule. They knew they lacked the Republican support to override Democratic Gov. Jay Nixon's veto of an $800 million state income tax cut, but they still called the package up for a vote, forcing all legislators to go on record, including 15 Republicans who ended up bucking the party majority and opposing the cut.

Rank-and-file members are convinced this all took place to please one man. A decade after returning to the state with a fortune he earned managing money in California, 70-year-old Rex Sinquefield has become a powerful presence in Missouri politics. Unlike most people who disagree with the positions politicians take, Sinquefield has the resources to make them pay. Last year, he and campaign committees he funded helped recruit candidates to run in primary contests against several of the Republicans who had broken party ranks on the tax cut vote. Each of the challengers was offered six-figure support. "He came after me with a lot of money and a very, very negative campaign," says Nate Walker, one of the targeted House members. "I had to go and mortgage my house so I could at least fight back a little bit."

The issues that concern "Rex," as he is universally referred to in political circles, have become central to the state's agenda in recent years. In addition to his campaign contributions, Sinquefield

From *Governing*, June 2015

has spent millions on lobbying efforts and on the Show-Me Institute, a free-market think tank he established in St. Louis. Last year, he estimated his lobbying operation employed about 1,000 people "the last time I looked at my checkbook." It's hard to tell to what extent he was kidding, but he didn't seem to be joking when at the same event he twice referred to Nixon as an "idiot." (Sinquefield declined requests to be interviewed for this story.)

Democrats from the governor on down have accused Sinquefield of trying to buy state government. U.S. Sen. Claire McCaskill uses him as the centerpiece of her campaign to bring contribution limits back to the state, arguing that legislators too often ask themselves "What does Rex think?" instead of sticking with the wishes of their constituents. Big majorities in both chambers of the legislature have indeed accepted campaign contributions from Sinquefield. "His influence is enormous," says Sean Soendker Nicholson, executive director of Progress Missouri, an advocacy group on the left. "Legislators and leaders are very attuned to what he wants and what all of his lobbyists want to see happen."

What Sinquefield wants to see happen doesn't always transpire, though. Each of the legislators who was challenged for their votes, including Walker, survived the 2014 election. So did a county judge who had ruled against Sinquefield on a ballot question and subsequently found herself subject to a $300,000 campaign onslaught. To a certain extent, the St. Louis billionaire is like a would-be Michael Corleone of *The Godfather* who targets his enemies but frequently fails to take them out. "Truly, it would have changed the face of politics in Missouri had he unseated us," says Lyle Rowland, another GOP representative targeted for his 2013 tax vote. "Then it wouldn't have mattered who we were or what we stood for—whoever had the most money could win the election."

Sinquefield has devoted many millions to the idea of eliminating income taxes and replacing them with sales taxes, but the effort has not progressed either at the ballot box or in the legislature. A ballot measure he bankrolled last fall to change teacher evaluation methods and weaken tenure proved so unpopular that the campaign backing it went dormant weeks before the election. It ended up getting only about a quarter of the vote. "I think he has bad instincts overall," says Ken Warren, a

pollster and political scientist at Saint Louis University. "He's backed a lot of causes that simply lose."

But while Sinquefield's batting average isn't as high as he'd like, he has had some game-changing victories. After the failure on the tax veto override, Sinquefield and his squad tried again last year. That time, legislators succeeded in overriding a Nixon veto, offering Missourians their first income tax cut in nearly a century. Nixon complained publicly about spotting Sinquefield's fingerprints on parts of the package. Ron Richard, the Republican leader in the state Senate, says Sinquefield deserves some, though not all, of the credit for pushing the tax cut through. "He has the ability and wherewithal to move ideas that need to be debated," Richard says. Sinquefield devoted $10 million to Missouri candidates and campaign committees in 2014 alone, helping to support more than 160 campaigns.

Win or lose, the ongoing Sinquefield saga in Missouri sheds light on the central role money plays in contemporary American politics, as well as its limits. While many megadonors, such as billionaires Charles and David Koch, continue to be cash machines for federal candidates, others are finding they can get more for their money by focusing on a single state. Not every state has a Sinquefield, but quite a few do. And some of these state moneybrokers, such as Republicans Art Pope in North Carolina and Bruce Rastetter in Iowa, and Democrats Tim Gill and Pat Stryker in Colorado, threaten to amass the kind of clout in individual legislatures that was held more than a century ago by railroads and mining companies, and triggered Progressive Era campaign finance limits in the first place. "It costs less currying favor with state lawmakers," says Kenneth Vogel, author of *Big Money*, a book detailing donations in the current super PAC era, "and bills are actually moving. They don't have the same level of gridlock as Washington."

There's no question such donors are playing an outsized role. Their influence is sometimes felt in ways that aren't easy to detect, such as bottling up bills that may never come to a vote. Nevertheless, they can't always get what they want. "They're spending in such a ham-handed way that they become a public villain, in some cases," Vogel says. "They often seem to prompt a backlash."

That has happened with Sinquefield. Few Missouri politicians turn down his money, but some are starting to make calculations about whether it's ultimately more of a handicap than an advantage. Most rural Republicans, for example, have no use for his school reform ideas, and Tom Schweich, the state auditor who committed suicide in February, intended to make Sinquefield's dollars a central theme of his campaign for governor in 2016. At his campaign announcement, Schweich accused Sinquefield of engaging in "corrosive tactics" through "an army of mercenaries. If they run our state, we won't have a debate over whether it's Missour-ah or Missour-ee. It will be Missour-Rex."

Schweich's death and the subsequent suicide of one of his campaign aides have cast a pall over Missouri politics and opened wide rifts within GOP circles. Former U.S. Sen. John Danforth, a Schweich ally, received national attention for a eulogy in which he decried negative campaign tactics. There isn't any indication that Sinquefield had anything to do with a whisper campaign about Schweich's religious affiliation or an attack ad that called Schweich a "weak candidate." It is clear that Sinquefield's favored candidate for governor, former state House Speaker Catherine Hanaway, however, has been thrown off course by the whole affair. She suspended her campaign for a month out of respect for Schweich.

Sinquefield has given $1 million to Hanaway's campaign. In fact, he's already contributed heavily to an entire slate of candidates seeking statewide office in 2016, including $1 million to Bev Randles, who is running for lieutenant governor. Whether his preferred candidates end up winning or losing will say a lot about the extent of his reach. "So far, he hasn't been successful, by and large," says former Democratic Gov. Bob Holden. "By the same token, if he continues to put money in cycle after cycle after cycle, he could have tremendous impact."

Sinquefield learned to hate taxes at his mother's knee. His father died when he was 7, and money was scarce. In straitened circumstances, his mother resented having to pay the 1 percent tax imposed on earnings of people who work or live in St. Louis. "I can't afford this damned tax," he recalls her saying.

She was able to keep her older daughters at home, but she placed Rex and his brother in an orphanage for several years. After that, Sinquefield considered entering the priesthood, but he was precociously interested in the stock market and ended up studying business. After earning an MBA from the University of Chicago, he helped pioneer index funds, which track markets broadly rather than picking out individual stocks. Eventually, he cofounded a California-based investment firm, Dimensional Fund Advisors, that was managing $398 billion worth of assets as of March 31. Sinquefield won't divulge his net worth; *Forbes* estimates the fortune of his Dimensional cofounder, David Booth, at $1.6 billion.

Retiring back home to St. Louis a decade ago, Sinquefield became a major charitable benefactor. He put the city on the map as a chess capital, underwriting the move of the World Chess Hall of Fame from Miami to his St. Louis neighborhood, where he provides six-figure purses annually for the U.S. chess championships and the Sinquefield Cup. He's a big backer of chess programs in area schools as well, and a huge donor to scholarship funds. Sinquefield has also given generously to the St. Vincent Home for Children, where he spent part of his childhood. "It's just home to him," says Mike Garavalia, development director at St. Vincent. "He has returned and given back to us manyfold, not just monetarily but with his time and commitment."

Sinquefield has done a lot of things in St. Louis that Mayor Francis Slay and other prominent Democrats applaud. After the city failed for years in the legislature in its attempt to win control of its own police force, which the state had taken over during the Civil War and never given back, Sinquefield sponsored a successful statewide ballot measure to make that change in 2012. He's also been a big backer of efforts to get the city and St. Louis County, which are entirely separate entities, to cooperate more on a regional basis.

If all his money went to boosting St. Louis and helping the city cope with its problems, "lots of statues" would be erected in Sinquefield's honor, says Rowland, the GOP representative. But his charitable giving is vastly exceeded in statewide public attention by the money Sinquefield puts into politics. His single largest political expenditures have come in his efforts to abolish the earnings tax. In 2010, he spent $11 million successfully backing a statewide ballot targeting the tax. Thanks to its passage, citizens in St. Louis and Kansas City now have to vote affirmatively every five years to keep the earnings tax on the books. They've done so once already, but city officials and bond rating agencies wonder how the lost revenues could ever be recouped if the tax is voted down.

Altogether, Sinquefield has devoted nearly $40 million to candidates and political committees in Missouri, which is the only state with no limits on campaign contributions or lobbyist gifts. No legislator anywhere wants to be accused of letting money sway his vote, but in Missouri, politicians employ what might be called a police-lineup defense, saying they've never spoken to Sinquefield or barely seen him around. "I've only met Rex one time," says Will Kraus, whose campaign for secretary of state received a $100,000 Sinquefield donation last fall. "I think I met him once," says GOP state Sen. Rob Schaaf, who took in more than $50,000 in Sinquefield funds last year. "He hasn't influenced me."

Missouri legislators such as Kraus and Schaaf have semiplausible deniability because money often flows not directly from Sinquefield but through PACs he bankrolls, such as Grow Missouri and the Missouri Club for Growth. Even before limits on individual donors were abolished in 2008, Sinquefield gave as freely as he wished through more than 100 different PACs. That's why even if Democrats succeed in restoring contribution limits through a ballot measure—and they've been talking about launching such an effort for years, to little noticeable effect—money from Sinquefield and other large donors will still find its way into the system.

Sinquefield is certainly not shy about his political giving. Donations over $5,000 have to be disclosed within 48 hours to the Missouri Ethics Commission, and for years Sinquefield made a habit of writing checks for $5,001. Politicians tend not to like that. Once they are known to have tapped into the Sinquefield vein, it can be a struggle to convince anyone else that more money might still be required.

Although the bulk of his money has been spent on Missouri politics, Sinquefield and his team have spread the gospel of tax cuts to governors and lawmakers in other states, including Louisiana, Nebraska and Oklahoma. Sinquefield called the big program of tax cuts enacted in Kansas under Republican Gov. Sam Brownback "a stroke of genius." During an appearance on St. Louis Public Radio in January, Sinquefield said that the growing budget shortfall in Kansas "has very little to do with taxes per se," blaming it on poor revenue projection instead.

Despite a shortage of evidence from the Kansas experiment thus far, Sinquefield is a believer in the domino theory of state tax rates. If a state lowers its taxes, he argues, its neighbors are sure to follow. Sinquefield wants Missouri to eliminate personal and corporate income taxes altogether, partially replacing the lost revenue with a broader sales tax that would be capped at 7 percent. "He was one of the guys early on who really started to see the connection between low-tax policies and growth," says Stephen Moore, chief economist at the conservative Heritage Foundation and, along with Sinquefield, co-author of a book last year arguing that lower taxes and anti-union policies drive economic and population growth. "A huge number of states are looking at cutting rates," Moore says, "and state taxes are a lot lower than they were 10 years ago."

No one outside Sinquefield's orbit seems to believe that Missouri is about to eliminate its income tax. But Sinquefield has good reason to believe further tax cuts are coming down the road. Even if Hanaway fails to win the nomination for governor, the eventual GOP nominee will likely favor tax reduction. That's also the position of the probable Democratic nominee, state Attorney General Chris Koster, who has received large donations from Sinquefield in the past. "We're playing offense and the other side is constantly and chronically playing defense," Sinquefield said a few years back.

Even the biggest donor in a state is not going to win every political battle. Still, although Sinquefield has not enjoyed nearly the level of return on his political investments that he found in the financial markets, he clearly has plenty of money left for both charity and political campaigns. "Candidly, they've wasted a lot of their money through bad decisions," says Holden, the former governor, "but they've got the money to waste."

While many legislators have balked at parts of Sinquefield's agenda, Sinquefield can take some satisfaction in the fact that many of his critics won't be around all that long. House and Senate members in Missouri are limited to eight years in office; if the current cohort is hard to persuade, the next generation of legislators may feel it's not worth the aggravation of standing up to him and enduring thousands of dollars in attack ads as their reward. And Sinquefield doesn't intend to stop writing checks until he can succeed in reshaping Missouri more to his liking. He once grandiosely declared that he refused to die until his favored tax and education policies had been adopted. "There's more coming down the pike," says Travis Brown, Sinquefield's lobbyist. "He's got a very ambitious agenda."

11

Why Democratic Governors and Republican Mayors Have Become Rare

By Louis Jacobson

U sually, this column takes a granular approach to politics. Most often, we're handicapping gubernatorial and legislative races. But for this one time, we're taking a look at the big picture in American politics today—the *really* big picture.

While there's no single theory that can explain all political behavior in America, there's still reason to believe that distinct patterns are emerging at four different levels of government, and that those patterns are almost perfectly balanced by party.

Let's start at the presidential level, where demographic patterns are making it increasingly challenging for the Republican Party to win the White House. By the same token, structural factors are making it increasingly difficult for the Democrats to take control of either chamber of Congress.

Meanwhile, state elections timed for the midterm cycle will continue to make it hard for Democrats to win governorships, and local demographic and political shifts will make it increasingly harder for Republicans to win mayoral elections.

Put it all together and each party should have an edge in two political arenas—the Democrats with the White House and mayoral offices, and the Republicans in congressional and gubernatorial elections. Depending on your perspective, this is either a recipe for long-term gridlock or an opportunity for each party to enact its agenda at a different level of government.

Let's take a closer look, level by level.

THE PRESIDENCY

Simply put, Democrats have an edge in the Electoral College, though it's not an insurmountable one.

From *Governing*, July 2015

Here's how: Any credible Democratic candidate would start with an almost certain base of 170 electoral votes (California, Connecticut, Delaware, the District of Columbia, Hawaii, Illinois, Maryland, Massachusetts, New Jersey, New York, Oregon, Rhode Island and Vermont). It's probably safe to add another 27 electoral votes (Minnesota, New Mexico and Washington state). Together, that adds up to 197 votes. If you add in three swing states that haven't voted Republican for president since 1988 (Maine, Michigan, Pennsylvania and Wisconsin) that gets a Democratic nominee up to 247, or just 23 swing-state electoral votes short of the 270 needed to win the presidency.

By contrast, the Republicans start out with 143 solid electoral votes (Alabama, Alaska, Arkansas, Idaho, Kansas, Kentucky, Louisiana, Mississippi, Montana, Nebraska, North Dakota, Oklahoma, South Carolina, South Dakota, Tennessee, Texas, Utah, West Virginia and Wyoming). It's also reasonable to add four Republican leaning states with a collective 48 electoral votes (Arizona, Georgia, Indiana and Missouri). Together, that's 191 electoral votes, or 206 if you include North Carolina, which voted Republican in five of the last six elections. This lineup requires the GOP to win 64 swing-state votes—almost three times as many as the Democrats would need.

Under this scenario, the swingiest of the swing states, which we've categorized as belonging to neither party's lineup, control the 85 pivotal electoral votes—Colorado, Florida, Iowa, Nevada, New Hampshire, Ohio and Virginia.

In reality, it's not at all clear that the GOP will inevitably lose Maine, Michigan, Pennsylvania and Wisconsin for the foreseeable future, meaning that Democrats don't actually have a lock on the presidency. Still, for Democrats, it's a nice edge to start with, and more important, it's fortified by demographic changes helpful to their party.

As political analysts Charlie Cook and David Wasserman recently noted, the racial and ethnic diversification of the electorate continues. Cook and Wasserman foresee the likelihood that the white share of the electorate, which forms the core of the Republican Party, will shrink from 72 percent in 2012 to 70 percent in 2016. Those two lost percentage points would be redistributed to Hispanics and Asian-Americans, two groups more favorable to Democratic candidates. "If the 2012 election had been held with that breakdown (keeping all other variables stable), President Obama would have won by 5.4 percentage points rather than by his actual 3.85-point margin," Cook and Wasserman write.

They add that "the group with which the GOP does best—whites without college degrees—is the only one poised to shrink in 2016. . . . In other words, the GOP doesn't just have a growing problem with nonwhites; it has a shrinkage problem as well, as conservative white seniors are supplanted by college-educated millennials with different cultural attitudes."

While this doesn't equate to a recipe for certain victory, it's not a bad position to be in if you're a Democrat.

CONGRESS

Where the Democrats have an edge in the presidency, Republicans have the advantage in Congress.

This is clearest in the House. The clustering of Democratic voters in densely populated urban areas means that any reasonably compact district will likely include many "wasted" Democratic votes—that is, Democratic support levels far above 51 percent in a given district, which could otherwise be used to dilute Republican strength in neighboring districts. This clustering was exacerbated by a strong Republican election cycle in 2010, when voters, even in otherwise Democratic-leaning states, elected GOP legislators and governors who proceeded to draw district lines favorable to the GOP. This is a key reason why a purple-to-blue state like Pennsylvania has a 13–5 Republican lead in its House delegation and why a swing state like Florida has a 17–10 GOP edge.

The combination of clustering and redistricting has produced a House electoral landscape in which few seats are genuinely competitive. To become a majority in the 435-member chamber, a party must assemble at least 218 votes. Currently, the House GOP has a 246–188 edge, not counting one vacant seat. As of now, the *Cook Political Report* has rated just 29 seats as competitive, either as tossups or as leaning toward one party or the other. That's not even enough competitive seats to sway the balance of power.

This statistic shows how hard it will be for Democrats to take back the House anytime soon—but it gets even worse for the party. Of those 29 competitive seats, only 22 are Republican-held. So, the Democrats would not only have to hold onto their own seven endangered seats, but would have to sweep every single one of the competitive Republican-held seats and then flip eight more GOP-held House seats that aren't currently considered competitive—all in order to achieve a bare, one-seat majority.

Securing a Democratic majority more solid than that would require even more seats, which is tough when so few seats in either party are even remotely competitive. Just four House GOP winners in 2014 failed to get to 50 percent; another nine won with 50 or 51 percent; and another 10 won with between 52 and 55 percent of the vote. All told, that's less than 10 percent of the GOP caucus that had even vaguely close races in 2014.

Superficially, the Senate offers more hope for Democrats. The map of seats being contested in 2016 is favorable to the Democrats, with the GOP having to defend more incumbents and open seats, and many of those elections taking place on reasonably favorable territory for the Democrats. Because of this, Senate Democrats have a real chance of seizing the chamber in 2016, just two years after losing it.

If you take a longer, more structural view, though, the situation is less rosy for the Democrats in the Senate. That's because the Senate gives equal weight to states, not to population. To explain, let's give each party two Senate seats for its "strong" states, and split the two Senate seats between the parties for the 12 swing states. How does this shake out? Using these presidential preferences as a guide, Republicans would have 46 seats in the strong states and another 12 in swing states. That's 58 seats, or just two short of a filibuster-proof majority. The Democrats, by contrast, would have 30 seats in strong states and 12 in swing states, for just 42 seats total, dooming them to long-term minority status.

While incumbency can certainly keep a state's weaker party in a Senate seat, retirements and deaths in office eventually give the state's dominant party a good shot at taking that seat back. And given the geographical structure of the Senate, this favors the GOP.

GOVERNORS

The biggest surprise on this list may be the outlook for gubernatorial elections. Here, Republicans have reason for optimism.

Historically, gubernatorial elections have tended to be up for grabs between the parties. Statewide electorates are sufficiently eclectic to encourage candidates in both parties to run toward the center, expanding their bases. But the pattern of results is changing, and for an unexpected reason.

For obscure reasons, 36 states hold their gubernatorial contests during midterm cycles. This hasn't seemed to matter much in the past. But in recent elections, the types of voters who cast ballots in midterm elections has diverged significantly from those that do in presidential cycles. Midterm electorates tend to be smaller, whiter, older and more Republican; presidential electorates tend to be larger, more demographically diverse, and more Democratic.

This pattern helped Republican gubernatorial candidates in 2010. That year, the GOP won governorships in such bluish states as Maine, Michigan, New Mexico and Wisconsin. But it proved to be an even bigger help in 2014, another GOP wave year. On the eve of the 2014 election, *Governing*'s final handicapping of the gubernatorial seats included an unusually large field of 12 tossup races. In a neutral environment, one would expect these races to go roughly half to one party and half to the other. Instead, Republican candidates won eight of those 12 races, plus another contest in Maryland that had been rated lean Democratic. Highly vulnerable Republican incumbents, such as Sam Brownback in Kansas, Scott Walker in Wisconsin, Rick Scott in Florida and Paul LePage in Maine, also won new terms, buoyed by the GOP-friendly electorate.

Currently, the breakdown of the gubernatorial ranks is 31 Republicans, 18 Democrats and one independent. Historically, the number of Republican governors has only been that high on rare occasions, so it's likely that the GOP number will fall somewhat in the coming years, especially after the 2018 election, when a number of two-term Republican governors will be term-limited out, creating competitive open seats. Still, on balance, it's going to be a tough challenge for Democrats to take back governorships when so many of them are contested during midterm election cycles.

MAYORS

As we've noted before, the GOP is having an increasingly difficult time winning mayoral races in big cities. Of the nation's most populous cities, only a few have

Republican mayors. They include three city-county hybrids where suburban voters can play an outsized role (Indianapolis, Jacksonville, Fla.; and Miami), and a few Sun Belt cities (Albuquerque, N.M.; Fort Worth, Texas; Oklahoma City and San Diego). Gone, apparently, are the days when a Republican like Rudy Giuliani could be the mayor of New York or Richard Riordan could be the mayor of Los Angeles.

Here, as with the U.S. House, geography is destiny. Cities have been magnets for younger, more diverse populations that tend to be socially liberal. This makes the Republican Party, with its national image of social conservatism, a tough sell. Indeed, such mayors as Bill DeBlasio of New York, Ed Murray of Seattle and Bill Peduto of Pittsburgh have been pursuing agendas that are unapologetically progressive.

The clearest example is the spread of minimum-wage hikes. Already, Los Angeles, San Francisco and Seattle have set themselves on a course to raise the minimum wage to $15. Chicago's is set to rise to $13. By contrast, President Obama got nowhere in Congress with his longstanding efforts to institute a more modest raise to $10.10.

The minimum-wage debate highlights a key consequence of the parties' varying holds on the levers of power: When stymied at one level, you can try another. Just as Democratic mayors are sidestepping GOP opposition to minimum-wage hikes in Congress, Republican governors are trying to block what they don't like from Obama's Democratic administration, such as elements of the Affordable Care Act or action on climate change.

Whether such combat is a boon for federalism—or a recipe for conflict between the branches—is in the eye of the beholder. Either way, the multipolar skirmishing between the two parties may well be with us for many years to come.

IV

LEGISLATURES

Alan Rosenthal, one of the great scholars of state politics and governance, called state legislatures the "engines of democracy."[1] And with good reason. Though Congress might get most of the attention, Rosenthal argued that it is down at the state level where legislators routinely make decisions that have big impacts on the day-to-day lives of citizens. Given that impact, who is actually doing the legislating and whose interests are actually being represented in state houses is a big deal.

That is the main point driven home by the readings in this chapter. The common theme here is that who we elect matters. The first essay, by Karl Kurtz, is an in-depth study of the demographics of state legislatures. What this essay makes clear is that state legislators, at least demographically, are not really reflective of the citizens they represent. The typical state lawmaker is still a middle-aged, college-educated, white male. Virtually every other demographic group is underrepresented in state legislatures, and this certainly includes women, minorities, and the young. There is also a clear lack of diversity in religious beliefs and education levels among state lawmakers.

The second essay, by Rebecca Beitsch, focuses specifically on one of those underrepresented categories: women. Between the early 1970s and mid-1990s, the numbers of women in state legislatures increased at a steady clip, increasing roughly five-fold from less than 5 percent of the number of lawmakers in 1971 to nearly 25 percent. That growth stalled towards the end of the 20th century—since the late 1990s the percent of state legislators who are female has remained flat. Why? Why is the gender that makes up slightly more than half the population still only a quarter of the lawmakers who represent that population? Beitsch suggests several potential answers and also explores the considerable variation in female representation in state legislatures. Those state-to-state differences may also hold clues as to why women are less likely to run for office than men.

The final essay, by Suzanne Weiss, is focused less on describing what groups are or are not proportionally represented in state legislatures and more on why it matters. A legislative caucus is defined as a group of lawmakers who organize and seek to systematically advocate and promote a set of shared goals or policy preferences. The best known legislative caucuses are party caucuses, where Democrats and Republicans seek to advance the interests of their respective partisan groups.

As Weiss makes clear, however, political parties are not the only groups that form effective and influential legislative causes. Caucuses can form around a wide variety of common goals or characteristics, some of which may cross party lines. Legislators representing similar geographic regions may band together to advance common interests regardless of party affiliations. These affiliations can also be based on some of the same demographic characteristics investigated in the first two essays. The Texas legislature, for example, has a black caucus, a Mexican American caucus and women's caucus. California Legislative Black Caucus, for example, has been going strong for nearly half-a-century. One of its newest caucuses is the Young Texans Legislative Caucus, formed in 2013, and whose members were all under 40. These sorts of caucuses help insure that even though particular groups may not be proportionally represented in state legislatures, they are not without influence.

NOTE

1. Rosenthal, Alan. (2008.) "Engines of Democracy: Politics and Policymaking in State Legislatures." Washington, DC: CQ Press.

12

Who We Elect: The Demographics of State Legislatures

By Karl Kurtz

Who is the "average" lawmaker in America today? A white, male, Protestant baby boomer, with a graduate degree and a business background—a stereotype of the American "establishment." But the truth is, there's nothing average about the nation's 7,383 legislators; in fact, only 50 actually have all six of those characteristics.

State lawmakers are less diverse than the country in general, but they reflect the wide variety of people they serve more closely than ever before, according to a new joint study by NCSL and the Pew Charitable Trusts.

WOMEN, MINORITIES UNDERREPRESENTED

There are six times as many women serving in state legislatures today than in 1971. By 2009, their portion had grown from a meager 4 percent to nearly 25 percent, where it is today. But women comprise 51 percent of the country's population. They have a long way to go to reach parity. If they would run at the same level as men, they might get there. When they're on the ballot, they win as often as men.

Likewise, African-Americans, between 1971 and 2009, jumped from 2 percent to 9 percent of all state lawmakers. They currently make up 13 percent of the U.S. population. But since 2009, the advances of women and blacks in legislatures have stalled.

Gains for Hispanic legislators have come primarily in the past six years, but at 5 percent, they are well short of their 17 percent slice of the total population pie. Low voter registration and turnout

From *State Legislatures Magazine*, December 2015
©National Conference of State Legislatures

among Hispanic immigrants and their wider dispersal (compared with blacks) throughout the general population explain why there are fewer Latino-majority legislative districts.

There are slightly more women in house chambers (25 percent) than in senates (22 percent), but the difference is not statistically significant. Between political parties, however, the difference is larger. Women comprise 34 percent of the Democratic lawmakers and 17 percent of the Republicans. In Colorado, Idaho, Montana and Utah, women make up the majority of the Democratic legislators. In Hawaii, women hold half the eight Republican seats in the Hawaii Legislature.

Minorities also are better represented among Democrats (33 percent) than Republicans (5 percent). Minorities (combined) now fill the majority of Democratic seats in the Arizona, California and Nevada legislatures. In nine Southern states, a majority of Democrats are black, while in New Mexico, the majority are Hispanic. In Hawaii, minority lawmakers (mostly of Asian and Pacific Islander descent) constitute majorities among the Democrats and Republicans alike. In all of these states, except California, Hawaii and New Mexico, Republicans are in the majority.

One of the arguments made for term limits during the 1990s was that they would allow the number of women and minorities serving in state legislatures to increase. But 25 years later, in the 15 states still with limits, that hasn't occurred. Minority legislators average 19 percent of the membership in term-limited states and 17 percent in the other states, a statistically insignificant difference. The proportion of female members, as well, is virtually the same in the two types of legislatures. In fact, of all these demographic categories, the only one that has been affected by term limits is age.

Educated to a Degree

The majority of legislators and members of Congress have a college degree, and the numbers are about the same for Democrats and Republicans. But the fact that two-thirds of members of Congress and 40 percent of state legislators have graduate or professional degrees, compared with 11 percent of the U.S. population, is remarkable. The proportions of doctoral and master's degrees are about the same in Congress as in

state legislatures. But in the area of law, 39 percent of the members of Congress have law degrees compared to only 17 percent of state lawmakers.

The state legislative education data, however, are incomplete for nearly a quarter of the members. It is tempting to speculate why lawmakers would not share their educational background, but we'll leave any guessing up to the reader.

On Top

Portion of Legislators With Advanced Degrees

60%	New Jersey
58%	New York
56%	Virginia
54%	Maryland
52%	Nevada/Oregon

LAWMAKERS ARE OLDER AND . . .

The average age of all state legislators is 56, compared with 47 for the adult U.S. population. But the average term-limited legislator is three years younger than his or her peers. That's no surprise since, by definition, term-limited legislatures have fewer long-serving—and therefore older—members.

Across the country, the average female legislator is two years older than her male counterpart. Likewise, senators tend to be about two years older than house members, probably reflecting a tendency for legislators to serve first in the house or assembly, then move on to the senate. Probably for the same reason, the average age of members of Congress is 59, as most people serve at the state level before running for national office.

There are no differences in ages between members of the two political parties or among various regions of the country.

Legislators from the baby-boomer generation have a disproportionate influence in America's legislatures, with nearly twice as many members as their overall share of the U.S. population would warrant. The millennial generation (1981–1997) is seriously underrepresented in both state legislatures and Congress. A positive sign for the younger generation, though, is that their share of the state legislative population has grown from 1 percent in 2009 to 5 percent in 2015.

Among those who reported their birth year in this study, Representative Saira Blair (R) of West Virginia was the youngest at age 19, and Representative John Yates (R) of Georgia—one of four nonagenarian lawmakers—was the oldest at 94.

Average Ages	
56	Legislators
47	U.S. Adults
59	Congress

THE YOUNG, THE OLD AND THE STATISTICALLY SIGNIFICANT

- Senators, on average, are two years older than House members.
- Lawmakers in term-limited legislatures are three years younger than those in the other states.
- Female lawmakers, on average, are two years older than their male counterparts.

Religion Reflects Society

The religions of state legislators appear to reflect those of the U.S. population as a whole: Protestants and Catholics predominate, with a large number of "unaffiliated."

While only nine of the 535 members of Congress list no religious affiliation, 22 percent of Americans report having no religious affiliation, according to the U.S. Census Bureau. Interestingly, among state legislators, 42 percent choose not to report their religious preference. It's hard to say why, but the reasons for choosing not to state a religious preference may differ from why one chooses to be unaffiliated, so the two categories should not be compared directly.

At just less than 2 percent, Jews make up the largest number of non-Christian legislators nationally, although more than 5 percent of the legislatures in New York, Florida, Maryland and Illinois are Jewish. Only six legislators in the country report being Buddhist, Hindu or Muslim. The only state legislator who identifies himself as an atheist is the long-serving, iconoclastic Nebraska Senator Ernie Chambers (NP).

The Oldest	
(Average Age of Members)	Legislatures
66	New Hampshire
63	Idaho
62	New Mexico
61	Vermont
The Youngest	
50	Puerto Rico
50	Michigan
51	Florida
52	Wisconsin
52	Ohio

The Work of Legislators

NCSL has been collecting data on the occupations of state legislators for nearly 40 years. Their jobs and professions provide a broad-brush view of members' backgrounds. People engaged in business, many of them small-business owners, make up the single largest category.

Faith	
Many lawmakers choose not to identify their religious preference.	
Protestant	38%
Catholic	16%
Other Christian	2%
Non-Christian	2%
Unspecified/Not Available	42%

There are substantially fewer lawyers serving in state legislatures than there were 40 years ago, and farmers and ranchers have declined by half, from 10 percent to 5 percent. New Jersey, Louisiana, Virginia and South Carolina top the list of states with at least one-quarter of their members practicing law. Not surprisingly, Nebraska, South Dakota, Wyoming, North Dakota and Montana all have more than 15 percent of their members working in the agricultural sector.

The number of people who report their occupation as "full-time legislator" has declined recently, perhaps because of the current widespread, public distrust of full-time politicians. Nevertheless, nearly half the members of the Pennsylvania General Assembly list their occupation as "legislator," followed by at least a third of the lawmakers in Illinois, Massachusetts, New York and Wisconsin. Yet, in California, arguably the most "full-time" state legislature, only 8 percent of the members report their occupation as legislator, about the same as in Missouri, Colorado and Kentucky.

This points out the flaws of relying on self-reporting in general. Many legislatures collect and publish information on their members, but the definitions, categories and coding can vary widely. In the end, we can only accept the information for what it is—a broad overview of the types of people who make up our lawmaking bodies, with a pinch of healthy skepticism about conclusions drawn from the details.

Descriptive Representation

These demographic characteristics of legislators make up what political scientists call "descriptive representation"— a way to measure the extent to which legislators mirror the population as a whole. While reflecting the demographics of one's constituents may be a nobel goal to strive for, in practice, with single-member legislative districts, it's almost impossible to achieve.

There's a lot more to representation than simply sharing the characteristics of your district.

Good representatives, according to the late political scientist Alan Rosenthal, "are continuously sensitive to the opinions, interests and demands of their constituents"— what Hannah F. Pitkin called "a constant condition of responsiveness, of potential readiness to respond," in her classic book, "The Concept of Representation." After all, representation is in the doing, not the belonging.

The Study

This joint study by NCSL and the Pew Charitable Trusts was conducted by compiling data gathered between May and September 2015 from the following sources:

- KnowWho, a directory publisher that gathers information from legislative websites, accessed in May 2015
- Project VoteSmart
- The Pew Research Center's 2014 U.S. Religious Landscape Study
- The Census Bureau's American Community Survey, accessed September 2015
- Legislators' personal websites
- Membership lists from the National Black Caucus of State Legislators, the National Hispanic Caucus of State Legislators and the Asian Pacific Islander Legislative Caucus.
- Key state legislative staff offices.

Complete data were obtained for members of Congress in all categories and for state legislators on gender, race and ethnicity. Other categories have incomplete data: Researchers found the occupation of 95 percent of lawmakers, the educational level attained for 77 percent, the ages of 75 percent, and the religion (or none) for only 58 percent. Analysis of the categories with incomplete data must be done with caution.

Stanford University intern Michael Gioia, NCSL's Brian Weberg, University of Rochester Professor Lynda Powell and the Pew Charitable Trusts' Rica Santos assisted in collecting and analyzing the data. This project was funded by NCSL and the Pew Charitable Trusts.

Their Other Jobs

Occupation	Total
Business	30%
(Owner—13%)	
(Other—11%)	
(Real Estate—3%)	
(Insurance—2%)	
Attorney	14%
Legislator	12%
Retired	8%
Consultant	8%
Nonprofit Professional	
Educator	6%
Agriculture	5%

13

Stalled Progress for Women in State Legislatures

By Rebecca Beitsch

In 2015, female candidates for state legislative seats are just as likely to win as their male competitors. The challenge is getting them to run.

A quarter of the nation's state legislators are women, according to a new survey of the composition of the nation's 50 state legislatures by *Stateline* and the National Conference of State Legislatures. That's up dramatically from the 5 percent figure of the early 1970s. But the percentage hasn't budged much in more than a decade, prompting many to question what can be done to encourage more women to seek state elective office.

Party leaders are less likely to recruit female candidates—and women are less likely than men to run without being asked. Many younger women worry about balancing a political career with family obligations. And because Republicans have been less successful in recruiting female candidates, their recent dominance at the state level has contributed to the stalled progress.

It may not take a woman to speak up on issues that are important to women, but state legislators and researchers who have studied the issue say regardless of party, women often bring a different working style and more varied life perspectives to the legislative arena, in addition to a stronger focus on women, children and family issues.

"Women bring different perspectives and considerations," said Kira Sanbonmatsu, a Rutgers University professor who studies women in politics.

Many political observers have credited women with helping to end the 2013 federal government shutdown, generally describing women as better at setting aside egos to get work done.

From *Stateline*, a project of the Pew Charitable Trusts, December 2015.

But even with the good qualities they may bring to politics, women tend to be more hesitant to seek office.

RECRUITED TO RUN

"Women just don't wake up one day and look at themselves in the mirror the way men quite frankly do and say, 'I should run for office,'" said Liz Berry, who recruits many candidates through her role as state president of the National Women's Political Caucus of Washington.

Jennifer Lawless, director of the Women and Politics Institute at American University, agreed. "Women don't assess themselves the same way when deciding if they're qualified for office," she said. "They perceive themselves as being less qualified."

Many women agree to run after being recruited, but that requires parties and state legislators to reach out to them. Most party leaders and legislators are white men, and when they look for recruits, they turn first to people like them.

"Women are less likely to run unless they're recruited, and they're less likely to be recruited," said Debbie Walsh, director of the Center for American Women and Politics at Rutgers University.

Another challenge is that it takes more time to convince female recruits to take the plunge, which means recruiters have to be determined—and patient.

"When women first think about running up until the time that they actually run is about three years. For men, it's about three weeks!" said Washington state Sen. Christine Rolfes, who helps recruit Democratic candidates in her state.

Many recruited women delay candidacies because they worry about how their families will be affected, especially if their children are young. Even as men take on a greater share of family responsibilities, research shows that in most households, women still bear the heavier load. Convincing them that they can balance their legislative, professional and family duties—not to mention addressing their concerns about unpleasant political realities like negative campaigning and constant fundraising—takes time.

Some state legislatures are full-time while others are part-time, but the structure of the legislature doesn't have much impact on the percentage of female members. Either way, it's a time commitment that many women are reluctant to make.

When she was first approached to run for office, Rolfes' children were toddlers, and she said the thought of leaving them "made me sick to my stomach. But when they were a little older I was ready."

Rolfes, whose children are now in high school, is one of the few female Washington state legislators with children at home. For women who want to rise through the political ranks, delaying a run until their children are older can be costly, because they don't have as much time to earn the seniority that delivers real power—and often the chance to run for a higher office.

STATE VARIATION

The percentage of female state legislators varies widely from state to state—but in no state do women make up close to 50 percent.

Walsh said women tend to do better in states where recruiting is focused more at the local, rather than the state, level, but there are geographic and cultural differences as well.

The Northeast and the West have had more success in getting women to serve as lawmakers. The Northeast has more citizen legislatures, where legislators represent fewer people, and the role isn't viewed as a profession, so people cycle in and out more, Walsh said. In the West, the relatively high percentage of female lawmakers may have its origins in a settlers' culture in which women and men worked side by side. Western states also were among the first to grant voting rights to women.

States legislatures in the conservative South, where traditional gender roles hold greater sway, have the lowest percentages of women.

Until recently, Republican Sen. Katrina Shealy was the only woman in the South Carolina Senate. Shealy said most of her colleagues have been respectful—but not all of them. Shealy's said her neighbor on the Senate floor, Republican Sen. Tom Corbin, often made comments to her, once joking about her wearing shoes, saying women should be barefoot and pregnant. During a dinner where reporters were present, he referred to women as a "lesser cut of meat."

"I always told him to stop, and I didn't treat it like a joke, but I didn't say anything else because I didn't want to come off like I was whining because I was the only girl in the room, and I can't take care of myself," she said. But once his comments became public, "I had to respond because you have to say something for all the women that will come behind you."

Shealy later addressed the Senate, saying, "These type remarks are never acceptable in public or in private. . . .[W]hether the person speaking them thinks they are in jest or not, these words are hurtful and disrespectful. We are all created equal and, as such, deserve respect."

A second female senator, Democrat Margie Bright Matthews, recently joined Shealy. Matthews was elected to replace state Sen. Clementa Pinckney, who was killed in last June's mass shooting at a Charleston church. Shealy said she has reached out to Matthews to work on some of the children's issues Shealy is most passionate about, hopeful that partnering on legislation will help it get passed.

Cary Brown, director of Vermont's Commission on Women, credits the small size of the state's districts for its relatively high percentage of female legislators. In tiny Vermont, women can campaign among their neighbors and don't have to travel far to get to the Capitol. Nevertheless, few women there have been elected to a statewide or federal office.

"We have over 40 percent women in the state Legislature, but we've never sent a woman to Washington, so we've still got work to do," Brown said.

In Washington, the percentage of female legislators has dropped, from 40 percent in 2001 to 33 percent now. "We stopped putting so much effort into recruiting, and it was a big mistake," said Berry, of the women's political caucus.

KEPT ON THE SIDELINES

In legislatures with few women, those who are elected say they are more likely to be kept on the sidelines.

While they may be present at committee meetings, women may not always be part of the socializing that takes place outside of the statehouse, where many informal decisions are made.

Just 13 percent of Wyoming's legislative seats are held by women, and Democratic state Rep. Cathy

Connolly is the only woman on the House Appropriations Committee. Her male colleagues have discussed getting together to play basketball before the meetings.

"Do I either go stomping around complaining about boys, or do I do something different? So I say, 'Sure I'll play, but only if I can be quarterback,'" Connolly joked. Though she's not particularly interested in playing basketball, Connolly said she makes a point of accepting invitations for fear of missing out on important networking. "There are an awful lot of informal discussions and an awful lot of planning that happens in that environment."

Her colleague, Democratic state Sen. Bernadine Craft, agreed.

"There are a lot of networking and social situations where you get a lot of information and you can get a lot of support to get your bills passed," said Craft, the only woman in the Wyoming Senate.

Craft said a female colleague in the House complained to her about returning to a committee meeting after a quick break, only to find her male colleagues had made some informal decisions on legislation.

"She joked, 'Have you guys moved these meetings to the men's room because if so maybe I should come too,'" she said.

Donna Boley, the only female state senator in West Virginia and a member of Republican leadership, said she feels respected by her male colleagues, though she passed up an invitation to discuss legislation at a bar one night. They promised not to have late night meetings at a bar again.

PARTY GAP

Sixty percent of female state legislators are Democrats, while 40 percent are Republicans. More than a third of Democratic state legislators are women, compared to less than a fifth of Republicans. Given those disparities, Republican gains at the state level over the past decade may be one reason the overall percentage of women in state legislatures has been stuck at 25 percent.

More women are registered as Democrats, but the GOP also has been less active in recruiting female candidates and has lagged behind the Democratic Party in providing trainings, PACs and support targeted to women, Walsh said.

Emerge America, created by Democrats to recruit like-minded women into office, has established campaign schools in 14 states. Emerge Maryland Director Diane Fink said she has seen women with all kinds of family situations go through the program and make sacrifices to serve—including one woman who interviewed for the program only to give birth later that night.

"If it means sitting there half in labor to get the training you want, that's what you do," Fink said.

American University, in Washington, D.C., runs a similar program, WeLead, for young women of both parties, but Lawless said promoting the campaign spirit early is no guarantee they'll run.

"Some want to work on other campaigns, or be a lobbyist or be a campaign consultant," she said of the participants. "Even in a politically active group of women, the desire to run is not universal."

14 Birds of a Feather

By Suzanne Weiss

Following a tradition thought to be as old as state legislatures themselves, a handful of Texas House freshmen in 2013 created a mechanism to work together, across party lines, to advance a shared agenda.

The members of the Young Texans Legislative Caucus, all of whom were under age 40, were focused on issues important to their generation and the next, from college affordability to entrepreneurship to natural resources management.

Today, with just two sessions under its belt, the 32-member caucus has put together a string of modest but notable successes. Among them are bills expanding the use of crowdfunding for small businesses, creating incentives to use alternative fuels and encouraging financial institutions to establish branches in Texas' "banking deserts." The caucus also pushed successfully for a bill mandating that public universities strengthen policies on campus sexual assaults, and another requiring hospitals to give parents of newborns safety information that includes a warning against leaving children in hot cars.

"Nearly six in 10 Texans are 40 years of age or younger, and that demographic definitely deserves to have a stronger voice in our legislative deliberations," says Representative Eric Johnson (D), who co-founded the caucus. "When I looked at the makeup of the House, I realized we had a solid core of younger members on both sides of the aisle that we could organize around to get some things done."

ALWAYS ON THE SCENE

Affiliations of like-minded lawmakers are nothing new, says Peverill Squire, a University of Missouri political science professor and an

From *State Legislatures Magazine*, October 2015
©National Conference of State Legislatures

expert on American legislatures. "Caucuses have probably always been part of the legislative scene," he says, and they have endured for a simple reason: "Their members see value in them."

Squire cited a couple of ways in which caucuses benefit individual legislators and invigorate the policymaking process.

First, they provide a mechanism to "circulate information and collectively develop ideas, including ideas that, for one reason or another, committees won't take up," Squire says. "They provide a chance for things to gain traction." In this way, caucuses "serve as alternative routes, as a challenge to existing structures and as a competing source of power to established leadership."

Membership in a caucus also helps legislators "send a signal to their constituents that an issue is important to them," he says. And because they are generally bipartisan, caucuses can serve as a countervailing force to the polarization that increasingly afflicts legislative deliberations.

James Henson, director of the Texas Politics Project at the University of Texas at Austin, agrees. "Caucuses allow legislators to sidestep partisan conflicts and coalesce around issue areas," he says.

Consider, for example, the experience of two members of the Louisiana Legislature's Acadiana Caucus—Senator Dan "Blade" Morrish (R) and Representative Jack Montoucet (D), who consider themselves party stalwarts and at opposite ends of the political spectrum.

For nearly a decade, the two have worked closely on a wide range of issues, from coastal restoration, bridge projects, flood insurance and workforce training to increased state support for the French-immersion language programs that serve more than 4,000 students, from kindergarten through the 12th grade, in the 22 parishes that make up the state's Acadiana region.

"As caucus members, Jack and I work together to do what's best for the people we represent," Morrish says. "Democrat and Republican? That never enters into the picture."

LINKED BY PARTY, PRIORITIES, PASSIONS

By far the most established and powerful legislative caucuses are partisan—one for the minority party and one for the majority, in each chamber. They are given staff, office space and other resources to carry out their business—setting rules, electing leaders, formulating policy and strategy—much of which is done behind closed doors.

By contrast, nonparty caucuses like the Young Texans are both more informal and more open, and typically receive no funding. Most are co-chaired by a Republican and a Democrat. Often, they come and go in the space of several years, giving way to new interests, priorities and affiliations.

In 2005 and again in 2013, NCSL surveyed legislative clerks and secretaries to get a clearer picture of the number and kind of special caucuses operating within the chambers in each state. Many of those caucuses no longer exist, according to a recent survey that included a 50-state search of legislative websites.

The survey showed that about one-third of states have no caucuses other than party caucuses. The other two-thirds have nonparty caucuses numbering from one or two—typically a women's and a black or Latino caucus—to between 15 and 20.

But the survey also showed that new caucuses are popping up all the time: in Virginia, a 20-member New Americans Caucus, which pledges to address issues involving undocumented residents and other immigrants; in Connecticut, a 27-member Intellectual and Developmental Disabilities Caucus; and in Utah, a 21-member Clean Air Caucus.

The most numerous and longest lasting nonparty caucuses are those based on demographics. They emerged in the mid-1970s as the number of blacks, women and Hispanics elected to legislatures began to increase. Today, 35 states have black caucuses, 23 have women's caucuses and 16 have Hispanic/Latino caucuses. Nineteen states have Native American caucuses tied to a national network.

Other ethnic and cultural affiliations around which caucuses have coalesced are Asian (California and New York), Filipino (Hawaii), Irish (Pennsylvania) and Italian-American (Connecticut). Among the newest are California's three-member Armenian Caucus and a nine-member Jewish Caucus, both formed in the past year.

The majority of demographic caucuses, according to their websites, are open to all legislators, regardless of party, race/ethnicity or religion. But in fact, Democrats have long dominated the larger racial/ethnic caucuses—in some cases, to the point of excluding the other party.

When California Assemblyman Rocky Chavez (R) asked to join the 24-member Latino Caucus last year, for example, he was turned away and told that he ought to form his own caucus, where Republicans would be more welcome. Chavez complained publicly, accusing the caucus of discrimination.

MOSTLY BIPARTISAN, BICAMERAL

By and large, however, most caucuses are both bipartisan and bicameral.

About half of the nation's legislatures have caucuses focused on regional needs and interests: the Everglades in Florida, for example, or the coastal counties of Maine, Massachusetts, Oregon and Washington, or rural and agricultural areas, such as Alaska's Mat-Su Valley and California's Inland Empire.

Some caucuses are organized around the interests of certain industries or sectors, from arts, culture, aviation and aerospace to coal, fisheries, manufacturing, steel and vineyards.

Michigan, for example, has a caucus promoting the growth of the state's biosciences industry and another, the Dutch Caucus, nurturing long-term business, civic and cultural relationships between the Netherlands and the western region of the state.

In Texas, 16 legislators banded together in 2012 to create the Farm-to-Table Caucus, which supports the production and wider availability of home-grown foods, craft beers and regional wines. Lawmakers in Hawaii and North Carolina last year established similar groups.

The year-old TechHub Caucus in Massachusetts aims to further the state's national and global leadership in the Big Data sector, which includes a range of advanced high-speed computing industries and data-analysis companies. And in Washington, a Competitive Caucus was established earlier this year with the goal of safeguarding the state's competitiveness in international trade by, among other things, streamlining regulatory processes.

Another major caucus category includes those leading the charge on behalf of a special issue. Some work

broadly on big topics such as education, the environment, mental health or transportation, whereas others are tightly focused on autism, hunger, outdoor recreation, diabetes, community colleges or veterans' benefits.

In many cases, issue caucuses are part of a network, tied to national organizations—the National Caucus of Environmental Legislators, for example, or the National Assembly of Sportsmen's Caucuses, which has more than 2,000 members in 47 states.

Over the last several years, ideological groups—Mississippi's Conservative Caucus, Utah's Patrick Henry States' Rights Caucus, Article V caucuses focused on federalism and limited government—have sprung up in about 20 states.

Finally, there are a handful of caucuses formed specifically for spiritual fellowship or social activities; they range from Bible study and prayer groups to Illinois' White Sox Caucus and Pennsylvania's Karaoke Caucus.

BRIDGING POLITICAL DIVIDE

A new wrinkle is the formation of bipartisan legislative groups modeled along the lines of the Young Texans Caucus, and part of a network called State Future Caucuses, whose stated goal is to "break through partisan gridlock and create a more constructive governing environment for the next generation."

In Maine, where there are now 13 legislators under age 30, the newly established Youth Caucus works to broaden education, training and employment opportunities for the state's young people.

Similarly, the PA Future Caucus, established last year by and for Pennsylvania's under-35 legislators, has set its sights squarely on working across the political divide to get things done.

The tendency of millennials to vote and otherwise engage in politics at a lower rate than older citizens, says Representative Nick Miccarelli (R), the new caucus' co-chairman, is not so much political apathy as "an expression of frustration at the lack of progress and results." He listed measures to address the related problems of soaring college tuition costs and high levels of student loan debt as the top items on the caucus' agenda.

Although many legislative caucuses meet infrequently and focus their efforts on a handful of issues, others put together ambitious agendas, issue news releases, maintain websites and make use of Facebook, Twitter and other social media.

The Utah Legislative Clean Air Caucus, for example, recently held a news conference at which it unveiled a package of 17 proposed bills and six appropriation requests totaling more than $5.4 million. The proposals ranged from a higher sales tax on tires and new incineration regulations to a measure allowing the state to adopt pollution standards stricter than those set by the U.S. Environmental Protection Agency.

CHANGING THE CONVERSATION

Of course, not every bill backed by a caucus becomes law. But having a caucus to champion a particular measure provides a collective history that can strengthen members' commitment to introducing it year after year.

The Hawaii Legislature, for example, last year passed a bill ensuring that women who are victims of sexual assault are provided with "accurate, unbiased information" about—and access to—emergency contraception when receiving care at hospitals. It had taken nearly two decades for the measure to gain acceptance, says Senator Rosalyn Baker (D), a 21-year legislative veteran, adding, "We just kept at it."

In Nevada, the 10-member Hispanic Legislative Caucus recently scored victories on two measures that had died in committee for several years running. One is a $50 million program underwriting, for the first time, English-language-learning programs in the state's school districts. The other is a law allowing immigrants in the country illegally to obtain a driver's privilege card, if they carry auto insurance.

"I wasn't sure these things would happen in my legislative career," says Senator Mo Denis (D), who was the only Hispanic in the Nevada Legislature when he was elected in 2004. "The Hispanic community is starting to come of age."

The recent successes resulted from better strategies on the part of the caucus, coupled with movement into leadership positions by Denis and several other caucus members, says Andres Ramirez, who runs a political consulting firm in Las Vegas.

In years past, the Hispanic caucus largely touted its ability to stymie what it viewed as anti-immigrant legislation, Ramirez says. More recently, the caucus has moved from defense to offense, and managed to change the legislative conversation, he says.

"The tone of the past two sessions has been not about how to harm or exclude Latinos, but how do we help them and incorporate them in this state," Ramirez says. "That's a dramatic and tectonic shift."

Not all caucuses will effect change on such a scale, of course. But in joining forces, often across party lines, legislators are finding ways to make progress on goals that otherwise might be impeded by partisanship or inertia. Their flexibility to coalesce and dissolve as needed can infuse caucuses with a sense of purpose, the urgency of a mission, not to mention the strength of numbers.

Considering the success these coalitions have enjoyed since the early days of the republic, and the appeal they have for a new generation of lawmakers, they're likely to remain a fixture on the legislative scene for quite some time.

GOVERNORS

Governors hold one of the most important and influential elective offices in the United States. Being governor is certainly the most powerful elected executive office someone can hold outside of being president. Governors, however, are not the only powerful elected executives in state government. Unlike the federal government, many states elect a range of executive offices, from state treasurer to insurance commissioner. Some of these jobs are relatively low profile. Others work in political spotlight bright enough to sometimes outshine the governor. Arguably the second most important and influential executive in state government is the attorney general, who has a broad ranging policy brief to protect the rights and interests of state citizens in the legal area. Being an attorney general is a great way to build a platform capable of launching someone into higher office.

The broad theme of the readings in this chapter is what it takes to be a successful state executive. The focus is on governors and attorney generals as two of the most high profile executive branch jobs in state government. The first essay, by Louis Jacobson, takes a look at how legislative experience can help a governor. Service in the legislature is no guarantee of success in the governor's mansion, but as Jacobson makes clear, it sure doesn't hurt. The ability of most governors to achieve their policy aims is critically dependent upon their ability to persuade the legislature to support their agenda. That is often easier if you are familiar not just with the legislators, but with the legislatures rules, processes, and culture.

The second essay, also by Louis Jacobson, takes a look at what happens to governors who fail on the biggest stage in national politics. More than one governor has looked for a promotion from state chief executive to national chief executive. In the last presidential primary cycle a number of sitting governors ran for the GOP presidential nomination, including the governors of Wisconsin (Scott Walker), Lousiana (Bobby Jindal), New Jersey (Chris Christie), and Ohio (John Kasich). As a general rule, these presidential bids did not do much for their reputation as governors. Pursuing the White House requires a lot of time, attention, and energy, pulling presidential hopefuls away from their day jobs as governors. Failing in that bid often means returning to lowered popularity, legislatures resentful that the home state was put on the back burner, and diminished influence.

The final two essays in this chapter shift the focus from governors to attorney generals. One of the notable phenomena of President Barack Obama's presidency was the aggressive agenda waged by Republican attorney generals in red states to curtail or even eliminate federal policy priorities in programs. J.B. Wogan's essay focuses on Scott Pruitt, who became Oklahoma's attorney general in 2010. In the following years Pruitt regularly sued federal agencies in an attempt to turn back

Obama administration initiatives in areas ranging from air pollution to health care. The basis for Pruitt's legal activism is not simply a partisan, prominent conservative Republican's attempt to limit the actions of a more liberal leaning Democratic administration. Pruitt argues he is fighting for states rights generally, a point of principle he argues extends beyond contemporary partisan disagreements.

If any attorney general could rival Pruitt in being a legal thorn in the Obama administration's side it is Texas attorney general Ken Paxton and his predecessor Greg Abbott (Abbott left the attorney general's office to successfully campaign for governor). Between them, Paxton and Abbott spent millions on dozens of lawsuits suing the federal government on everything from Obamacare to pollution regulations. Like Pruitt, the broader argument behind Texas's legal crusade against the federal government is states' rights advocacy. Abbott and Paxton have clearly politically benefited from repeatedly dragging the federal government into court, but the state is losing at least as many of those lawsuits as it wins and some are starting to question whether the millions expended are worth it.

15

Experience Preferred

By Louis Jacobson

Stamping a little pig on line-item vetoes for appropriations he felt were wasteful didn't exactly endear Minnesota's then-Governor Jesse Ventura to the Legislature. The former professional wrestler was elected in 1998 with zero legislative experience, and it showed. His lack of understanding of and appreciation for the legislative process handicapped his entire governorship, says Carleton College political scientist Steve Schier.

"He viewed legislators as cowards and . . . the Legislature returned the favor by ignoring much of his agenda as his single term wore on," says Schier.

Ventura may be an anomaly, but as legislative sessions start up in most states this month, governors will be there, working with lawmakers to promote their policy goals. Will their legislative experience (or lack of it) matter? Based on interviews with a wide range of political observers, lawmakers and governors, the answer is a qualified "yes." Legislative experience can help, but it is hardly a guarantee of success, nor is a lack of experience necessarily a barrier to gubernatorial achievement.

For Jim Douglas, a former Republican Vermont governor and House majority leader, "Legislative experience was a plus . . . lawmakers knew I had some of the same experiences they were having. I was familiar with the protocols and the committee process. I could relate to their problems, and they knew they couldn't snow me, either."

About 50 percent of recent governors from both parties and among all states have previously served in state legislatures. Currently, 21 governors have had experience in the legislature, and

From *State Legislatures Magazine*, January 2016
©National Conference of State Legislatures

many others have previous experience in other statewide elected positions, such as attorney general or secretary of state.

THE SKILLS ADVANTAGE

Examples abound of how skills honed in the legislature can make a difference in a governor's ability to lead effectively.

Former Arkansas Governor Mike Beebe, a Democrat, is a good example. He served two terms until his retirement in 2014. Hal Bass, an Ouachita Baptist University political scientist, points to Beebe's record on budget negotiations and his ability to work with Republican lawmakers to enact the "private option"—a free-market approach to expanding Medicaid under the Affordable Care Act—as examples of how "state legislative experience was clearly a factor" in Beebe's success.

The governor's legislative skills became particularly important in negotiations with junior lawmakers, who made up much of the Republicans' newly installed legislative majority. Beebe had served 20 years in the Senate before becoming governor, and he believes "it was an invaluable asset for my time in the governor's office."

Legislative experience also aided Michigan's John Engler, says Bill Ballenger, the founder of Inside Michigan Politics. A three-term Republican governor, Engler had served two decades in the Legislature before making the switch. Some saw him as having an "LBJ-style genius for cracking whips" to get the Legislature to comply with what he wanted—something that wouldn't have been possible without the time he spent in the Legislature building relationships and gaining respect.

There are plenty of other examples—from Republicans Rick Perry of Texas, Norm Bangerter of Utah and Victor G. Atiyeh of Oregon, to Democrats Lawton Chiles of Florida and David Ige of Hawaii—of how governors benefited from their ability to relate to state legislators, particularly those of the opposite party or in times of economic stress.

Governors who have served in legislatures know the importance of building personal relationships with lawmakers and meeting regularly with leaders from parties. They also know how to do the "little things like offering praise at public events, which not only translate into better relationships but also can help ease the passage of portions of the governor's agenda," says Christopher W. Larimer, a University of Northern Iowa political scientist who is writing a book on Iowa governors.

NO GUARANTEES

There are limits on the importance of experience, however. For starters, a governor's personal style can play a larger role than legislative work history. In South Carolina, for instance, Mark Sanford "had difficulty getting along with legislators," says College of Charleston political scientist Jack Bass. His lack of legislative experience was secondary to his well-known prickly style of interacting with lawmakers.

Having legislative experience means having a voting record that's open to attack by opponents. And, not all experience is equal. Leadership experience is typically much more useful than experience as a rank-and-file legislator. Experience can also grow stale with time, particularly in states with term limits.

How much Ohio's Republican Governor John Kasich's legislative service aided his successful run as governor is difficult to determine since so much time passed in between. After leaving the state legislature in the early 1980s, he had a long career in the U.S. House, followed by a stint in the private sector before winning the governorship. Very few of his legislative colleagues hung around that long.

Likewise, in California, former governors Pete Wilson (R) and Gray Davis (D) both had experience in the Legislature, but the lawmakers they had worked with had mostly been term-limited out by the time they held the governorship.

"Legislative experience may confer an advantage if members a governor served with are still serving, but I see little evidence that it provides a leg up if the governor was a legislator long before he became governor," says Garry South, a Democratic strategist in the state. "The issues and internal dynamic of the chambers will have significantly changed."

LACK OF RELATIONSHIPS

Governors who come to the office through some other route—private business or show business, for example—have had mixed success. For some, lack of experience and knowledge of legislative processes have resulted in fumbled legislation and contentious relationships with lawmakers.

Nevada Governor Kenny Guinn (R), for example, failed to pass a large tax increase in 2003, partly, says longtime political journalist Jon Ralston, because he had no relationship with lawmakers. He challenged lawmakers, "lectured them, berated them, even called them 'irrelevant,'" which served only to "help coalesce the opposition," Ralston says.

In today's highly partisan environment, in which the art of corralling bipartisan support is more challenging than it used to be, "having a legislature of the same party has become considerably more significant for a governor than legislative experience," says Oregon political columnist David Sarasohn.

But not always.

In North Carolina, for instance, Republican Governor Pat McCrory has had "a rocky relationship with the General Assembly," says Mark Binker, who covers the state Capitol for WRAL-TV in Raleigh. "He recently sued them over how they structured certain boards and commissions, and despite being a Republican dealing with a Republican-led legislature, has seen some of his vetoes overridden over the past three years." Binker says he suspects that McCrory "would have had a leg up had he spent some time in Raleigh before being elected governor."

Like McCrory, Florida Governor Rick Scott, a Republican, is working with a Republican Legislature, but Scott also has struggled at times, battling lawmakers over a variety of issues, notably health care budgets.

"I think that Rick Scott not having any real government experience has caused him difficulty with the Legislature," says University of Central Florida political scientist Aubrey Jewett.

"Even though he had broad partisan support in the Legislature, his relationship has been conflicted. Scott has simply not paid attention to worrying about the Legislature or addressing its concerns."

EXPERIENCE NOT MANDATORY

Still, a lack of legislative experience doesn't necessarily preclude a good working relationship with lawmakers.

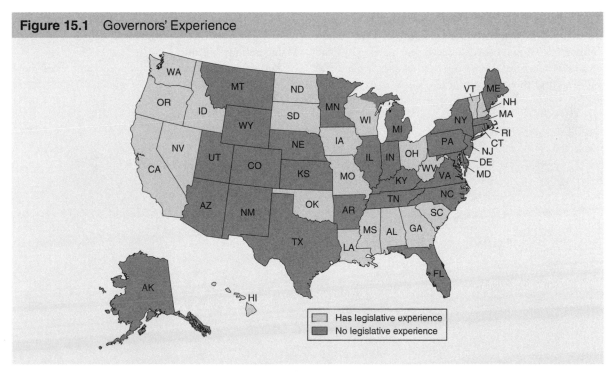

Figure 15.1   Governors' Experience

Has legislative experience
No legislative experience

Twenty-one governors have prior experience serving in legislatures.

John Lynch (D) of New Hampshire didn't have a legislative background, but he had a successful tenure due in part to the management skills he honed in the business world, says Andrew Smith, a University of New Hampshire political scientist.

In California, Arnold Schwarzenegger was a virtual political novice when he became governor, yet he was able to win over members of the Democratic legislative majority in order to make deals, at least for a portion of his term, says California-based consultant Harvey Englander. "He had a major charm offensive going that enabled him to get quite a bit of his agenda through," Englander says.

In Montana, recent governors have used a variety of tactics to get around their lack of legislative experience, says former Senator Dave Wanzenried, including using the bully pulpit to eclipse a Legislature that meets only biennially. "Qualities and experiences other than those forged through legislative service tend to influence a governor's success in dealing with the Legislature in Montana," he says.

In Indiana, Governor Mike Pence (R) has faced significant governing challenges, but working effectively with the legislature hasn't been one of them. He came from Congress with no state legislative experience and "immediately upon taking office, began meeting in small groups with lawmakers of both parties to get acquainted, get ideas and show them that he 'gets it' as to their role in the process," says Ed Feigenbaum, the publisher of *Indiana Legislative Insight*.

"He has been extremely respectful of the General Assembly, effectively tossing out broad concepts that suggest what he would like to get accomplished, letting them largely shape it and then working with them toward the end of each session to fine-tune things," Feigenbaum says. "In his first term he sought a big individual income tax rate reduction, but the legislature came back to him with a broader tax reduction package that he ultimately pronounced to be better than what he had proposed."

University of Maine political scientist Kenneth Palmer says only one of the governors he considers to be his state's three most successful—Democrats Ed Muskie and Kenneth Curtis and Independent Angus King—had experience as a legislator. That was Muskie, who served six years as a legislator.

"None of the three had a party majority in the Legislature," Palmer says. "Still, they brought about significant accomplishments in tax policy, environmental protection and education. The keys to their success included personal political skills, a willingness to compromise, a moderate style of politics with little concern for ideology and a strong emphasis on problem-solving. In short, they worked with much understanding of the Maine political culture."

And that, more than legislative experience, may have made all the difference.

16

Rocky Roads Ahead for Governors with Failed Presidential Bids

By Louis Jacobson

"Come at the king, you best not miss," Omar from the TV show "The Wire" famously advised a rival in the drug trade after he shot him. That advice, in its own way, is applicable to ambitious governors as well. Namely, if you run for president, make sure you win. If history is any guide, your future gubernatorial career after losing a presidential race will be about as healthy as one of Omar's adversaries.

In recent decades, just two sitting governors have won the presidency: Bill Clinton and George W. Bush. But the list of sitting governors who have either lost or dropped out of a race for president is much lengthier. In most cases, these candidates' gubernatorial careers suffered after they lost their bid. It's happened to Democratic and Republican governors alike.

This pattern will be particularly relevant in 2016. Already, we've seen the most sitting governors running in at least four decades. While Scott Walker of Wisconsin and Louisiana's Bobby Jindal have dropped out of the Republican contest, Republicans Chris Christie of New Jersey and John Kasich of Ohio remain in the race, although neither is polling in the top tier.

In fact, three of those four sitting governors are at or near their lows in popularity back home.

A University of New Orleans survey in November found Jindal had an overall 20 percent approval rating, with even a majority of Republicans disapproving of him. In an electoral rarity in the Deep South these days, Jindal will be succeeded by a Democrat, John Bel Edwards, in January.

Similarly, in Wisconsin, Walker isn't doing much better. Walker received 37 percent approval from voters in a Marquette University

From *Governing*, January 2016

Law School poll shortly after he left the presidential race. Six of 10 voters in the state say they wished he hadn't run for president.

And in New Jersey, Christie has hit new lows with just a 33 percent approval rating despite winning his 2013 re-election in a walk, according to the Rutgers Eagleton poll. If Christie loses his presidential bid, "he will return to a New Jersey with his power substantially weakened," said David Redlawsk, director of the Eagleton poll. "The Democratic majority in the legislature has no interest or incentive to work with him anymore."

The one exception, in 2016 and potentially ever, is Kasich. His continued popularity—62 percent approval in an October Quinnipiac poll—appears to stem from the fact that he is running as the clearest pragmatist in a primary notable for its ranks of staunch ideologues.

"In Ohio, we've seen pretty much across the board pride in John Kasich's efforts," said Douglas J. Preisse, a principal with Van Meter, Ashbrook & Associates, Inc. and a longtime Republican strategist in Ohio.

Unless things turn around for Kasich's companions in the presidential race, they'll soon be joining the following governors who limped back to the governor's mansion in defeat.

FORMER TEXAS GOV. RICK PERRY (R)

Initially, Perry seemed like a promising candidate, having served for more than a decade as governor of one of the nation's largest states. But he stumbled badly in the wide-open presidential contest, including the infamous debate performance in which Perry couldn't remember one of the federal departments he wanted to close.

"The collapse of Perry's 2012 presidential bid damaged his image in Texas as an invincible political juggernaut who had never lost a campaign in his political career," said Rice University political scientist Mark P. Jones. "While I believe Perry was already leaning towards not running for re-election in 2014, his failed 2012 presidential bid certainly emboldened potential challengers and likely influenced his decision to not stand for re-election."

FORMER NEW MEXICO GOV. BILL RICHARDSON (D)

By the time he was elected governor, Richardson had already put together a long career in the U.S. House of Representatives and in the presidential cabinet. Therefore, it was hardly a secret to New Mexico voters that Richardson had higher political ambitions.

But after dropping out of the 2008 presidential race—following a distant fourth-place finish in the New Hampshire primary—things turned sour for Richardson. His "need for big-donor dollars to compete on the national stage seems to have caused him to squeeze so hard and in so many places that it all came crashing back down on him," said one political observer in the state.

This played out in two legal cases that cast a shadow over Richardson's final two years in office—a grand jury investigation of a kickback scandal involving highway funds and a wider scandal involving state investments. Richardson was never charged with wrongdoing, but it kept him from taking a position as commerce secretary for Obama. Aspects of the cases continue to play out years later.

The investigations, combined with the budgetary fallout from the Great Recession, "resulted in the once popular governor becoming one of the most reviled politicians in the state," said Steve Terrell, a political journalist with *The Santa Fe New Mexican*. "He seemed almost paralyzed for his last two years in office. He remains unpopular, and Republicans still use him as a boogeyman."

Indeed, New Mexicans elected a Republican, Gov. Susana Martinez, to succeed him in 2010.

FORMER CALIFORNIA GOV. PETE WILSON (R)

Wilson, a moderate Republican, won the governorship in 1990 in a landslide. He then easily won a second term in 1994. But then, just two years later, he ran for president. "Californians were not amused that he went off to run for president right after being re-elected, and the fact that he also ran badly didn't help," recalled Garry South, who was at the time chief of staff to Lt. Gov. Gray Davis, a Democrat. "Wilson's poll numbers never really recovered, and Gray was able to run and win in 1998 against someone who had become a very unpopular and discredited GOP governor."

A California law puts the lieutenant governor in charge when the governor leaves the state, and Wilson was often gone while campaigning for president. He sought to change the law to take the lieutenant governor out of the line of succession. But Davis' stature had grown during Wilson's frequent absences, and the move ultimately backfired with voters.

What's more, Wilson contested his party's presidential nomination by running to the right, seemingly in a bid to rebut the notion that he was too moderate to win the nomination. Most notably, he championed Proposition 187, which barred the use of most state services for undocumented immigrants. The measure passed, but, for the state GOP, it proved to be a pyrrhic victory: The state's fast-growing Latino population shifted decisively toward the Democrats and turned California into a solidly blue state, a pattern that still holds more than two decades later.

FORMER VIRGINIA GOV. DOUG WILDER (D)

In 1989, Wilder became the first African-American since Reconstruction to win a state governorship. He decided just two years later to run for president.

Although he dropped out early on, the presidential bid "made Wilder very unpopular and limited what he could do for half of his one four-year term," said University of Virginia political scientist Larry Sabato. "It probably also kept his poll numbers low when he ran for Senate in 1994, after leaving office."

In addition, voters elected Republican George Allen to succeed him in 1993.

In *Son of Virginia*, Wilder wrote, "In retrospect, I can see that my run for president hurt my standing with Virginia voters. The polls were evidence of their displeasure, and I accept that." Indeed, Wilder wrote that when he announced to the General Assembly that he would quit the presidential race and return to the governorship, he received "the largest, heartiest cheer I'd ever heard from that body."

FORMER MASSACHUSETTS GOV. MICHAEL DUKAKIS (D)

Unlike the others on this list, Dukakis actually won his party's nomination before losing the 1988 presidential race. But that didn't ease his return to the governorship, where he had two years remaining in his term.

"Dukakis came back to a state that was about to face some of the worst economic conditions in memory," said Maurice T. Cunningham, a political scientist at the University of Massachusetts-Boston. "The 'Massachusetts Miracle' he had run on had passed and soon the state budget was a mess, necessitating unpopular cuts and new taxes."

It didn't help that during the budget fight, Dukakis—nearing the end of his third nonconsecutive term—came to be seen as a lame duck. "Dukakis became a political target even among some Democrats, such as John Silber, who took the nomination," Cunningham said. In the end, voters elected a Republican, William Weld, to the governorship in 1990.

CALIFORNIA GOV. JERRY BROWN (D)

Several of the other governors on this list, such as Dukakis and Wilder, have gone on to productive "elder statesmen" roles in politics following their governorship. But none had quite as strong a comeback as Brown, who was elected governor in 2010 and again in 2014.

One reason for Brown's current gubernatorial success, however, is that he's no longer focused on the presidency. "His running for president a second time in 1980 as a sitting governor paved the way for his own defeat in the Senate race in '82," said South, a veteran Democratic consultant in the state. "It infuriated many Democrats that he took on a sitting Democratic president who was already having troubles and who later was beaten in the 1980 general election. He also ran badly, with his bizarre, haphazard campaign, which became the butt of many jokes.

His image developed into one of a scatter-brained dilettante who was less interested in being governor than being a gadfly on the national stage."

Ultimately, Brown was succeeded by a Republican, George Deukmejian.

17

Scott Pruitt Will See You in Court

By J. B. Wogan

When the Environmental Protection Agency proposed rules regulating carbon dioxide emissions from coal-fired power plants, Scott Pruitt sued. When the Justice Department offered legal status to young undocumented immigrants, Scott Pruitt sued. And when the Obama administration sought to give tax credits to states that hadn't set up their own health insurance exchanges, Scott Pruitt sued.

Since becoming Oklahoma attorney general in 2010, Pruitt has filed or joined lawsuits against federal agencies at least a dozen times. Even when Oklahoma isn't an actual party in litigation, the state often submits a legal brief against the federal government. Besides air pollution, immigration and health care, Pruitt has fought federal laws and regulations on banking, contraception and endangered species. These days, whenever states go to court against the Obama administration, the chances are that Pruitt is somehow involved.

Not that Pruitt is alone. During Obama's presidency, the entire cadre of Republican attorneys general (27 at present) has coordinated cases against federal agencies at an unprecedented pace. But Pruitt is at the center of the action. He has set up a first-in-the-nation "federalism unit," which seeks to combat instances of federal overreach by every possible means: letters, comments during the rulemaking process, congressional testimony, legal briefs and, most conspicuously, lawsuits. When Pruitt became chairman of the Republican Attorneys General Association (RAGA) in 2012, he took the strategy national by launching the group's "Rule of Law" campaign to help RAGA members research cases related to state autonomy, the Constitution and federalism.

From *Governing*, September 2015

"He's completed the shift for attorneys general nationally who realize now how important it is for states to push back against the federal government," says former Nebraska Attorney General Jon Bruning, a Republican ally of Pruitt who left office in January.

The legal justification for Pruitt's court challenges is almost always related to states' rights. It's easy, though, for his critics to presume an alternative explanation. He is, after all, a conservative politician filing lawsuits to undermine the liberal policies of a Democrat in the White House. But Pruitt insists that today's hyperpartisan world misinterprets him. He claims he is merely trying to reassert limits over executive power and would do the same regardless of the president's political affiliation. In Pruitt's view, Congress should make laws and the executive branch should administer them. Everything else should be left to the states. Instead, Pruitt says, "you see federal agencies taking license. That's simply not how our checks and balances work."

This isn't just some academic point for Pruitt. He believes the American system of government is under attack by a president unwilling to respect the constitutional limits of his office. Amid partisan gridlock in Washington, Obama has promised to use "a pen and a phone" to accomplish as much as he can through administrative action. That has won praise from liberals, but it has horrified Pruitt, who sees attorneys general as a critical firewall against federal officials infringing on state sovereignty and making national policy without Congress.

While Pruitt admits that he disagrees with Obama's positions on immigration, health care and the environment, he insists that those concerns are secondary to a more "transcendental" issue: maintaining the system of government as the framers intended it, with no single branch wielding unilateral control. That mission should matter to Democrats, he argues, because they may one day face a Republican president intent on bypassing a Democratic majority in Congress in the same way. In Pruitt's view, today's court battles will affect American governance long after Obama leaves office. "We live in a consequential time," he says. "Precedent is being set."

Pruitt, who is 47 years old, projects a political identity that took root more than a decade ago, when he was a state senator from Broken Arrow, a suburb of Tulsa. He framed his early campaigns around shrinking the size of government. He supported a cut to the state income tax and wanted to adopt a formula that would limit future spending growth. At the time, Oklahoma was one of the few states to offer in-state tuition to undocumented immigrants, and Pruitt was among the chorus of Republicans who wanted to restrict that benefit to citizens. (The state reversed its policy after he left the legislature.)

After three years in the state Senate, Pruitt mounted an unsuccessful campaign for Congress. In 2006, rather than seek re-election, he ran for lieutenant governor and nearly upset the Republican House speaker, losing in the primary by less than 1 percent of the vote.

In his second attempt at statewide office, in 2010, timing helped. Obama wasn't on the ballot that year, but he might as well have been. Pruitt continually portrayed the president as a big-government Democrat working to increase regulations on health insurance and fossil fuel production. To some degree, Pruitt was tapping into populism that's always been a part of his state's politics, says Keith Gaddie, a political scientist at the University of Oklahoma. "Standing up to those fancy Eastern Yankees is very much a tradition in Oklahoma." Pruitt's résumé turned out to be an ideal one in a state where voters in both parties largely shared his fears about federal encroachment.

The Republican primary for attorney general focused on the legal challenges to the Affordable Care Act. The outgoing Democratic governor and attorney general both refused to join a multistate lawsuit against the health-care law, with then-Gov. Brad Henry calling it "an exercise in legal futility." By contrast, both Pruitt and his opponent in the primary promised to join the lawsuit. But Pruitt went further. He pledged to establish the nation's first federalism unit focused entirely on fighting attempts to expand the federal footprint.

Pruitt's disclaimers aside, it's impossible not to interpret the federal-state court battles of recent years as contests of both party and ideology. Empirical research supports that view. Paul Nolette, a political scientist at Marquette University, analyzed 20 years of U.S. Supreme Court cases and found that blocs of state attorneys general were challenging the federal government on a partisan basis much more often than they had in the past.

When attorneys general sued the Clinton administration in the 1990s, the coalitions they created tended to be bipartisan. In instances where most of the challengers came from a single party, they were usually Democrats suing a Democratic president. By comparison, the major lawsuits of today feature a homogeneous slate of Republican attorneys general litigating against the Obama administration, with a similarly homogeneous slate of Democrats filing friendly legal briefs in support of Obama.

Nolette says attorneys general are taking legal positions for political purposes and that both parties are doing it. He gives the example of the two same-sex marriage cases decided by the Supreme Court in 2014. Both parties found legal rationales that fit their political ideologies. A bloc of Democratic attorneys general wanted the court to respect state sovereignty when it meant allowing states to legalize same-sex marriage, but also wanted the court to strike down a California law that banned same-sex marriage. Likewise, Republicans argued for states' rights to save California's ban on gay marriage, but invoked federal supremacy to maintain a definition of marriage that excluded gay couples.

Until relatively recently, the office of state attorney general was seen for the most part as free from both ideology and partisanship. But that began to change at the start of the 2000s, when the Republican Party set up a group dedicated to electing conservatives to the post. A few years later, Democrats countered with their own group.

Pruitt continues to reject the insinuation that his work is driven by a partisan agenda. "Opponents want to present it that way," he says. "It's not that way at all for me." Nonetheless, the fact remains that he consistently finds legal justifications for policies popular among conservative Republicans, while challenging policies that his party opposes. From the outside, the lawsuits seem to be less about state sovereignty and more about a broader Republican strategy to upend the president's domestic policy agenda.

When he isn't challenging Obama directly, Pruitt frequently can be found weighing in on other disputes that clearly divide liberals from conservatives. Much of the time, these center on religion. As attorney general, Pruitt released an official legal opinion in favor of distributing Bibles in public schools; he defended the installation of a religious monument on state Capitol grounds; and in a legal brief in support of an Oklahoma-based business, Hobby Lobby, he argued that businesses should be able to refuse to cover the cost of employees' contraception on the basis of religious liberties.

"There are broader trends that have been going on for a few years now where the attorneys general have been far more activist," Nolette says. "But it still requires some sort of entrepreneur to pick it up and press the extent of the power." Pruitt has been that kind of entrepreneur.

One example is the *King v. Burwell* case. The plaintiffs in the case mounted an argument that actually was first embraced by Pruitt. The case hinged on language in the Affordable Care Act that said tax credits were to go to individuals who purchased health insurance through an exchange set up by the state. Yet in practice, the federal government has awarded tax credits through both state-based and federal exchanges. If the tax credits were invalid in states with federal exchanges, the law would unravel. Ultimately lower courts didn't agree on whether the broader context of the law—aimed at getting people to sign up for health insurance—meant that federal agencies could ignore an oversight in the statute. The U.S. Supreme Court decided against Pruitt's position in late June.

"Dozens of think tanks and attorneys general have been analyzing ways to challenge the law," says Bruning, the former Nebraska attorney general. "It's been part of the law for years. Many of us didn't see it." While Pruitt himself didn't come up with the novel argument presented in *King v. Burwell*, he was the first to use it as the basis of a lawsuit. At the time, the architects of the argument—Jonathan Adler of Case Western Reserve University Law School and Michael Cannon of the libertarian Cato Institute—were having trouble getting Republican state officials to mount a challenge based on what seemed like a highly technical reading of the law's mechanics. Even though other plaintiffs filed lawsuits later on that advanced beyond Pruitt's case, he was the first attorney general to recognize the potency of Adler and Cannon's analysis.

So far, Pruitt's willingness to wade into controversial issues has made him a celebrated figure in conservative circles. In 2014, he ran unopposed for his second term, and he's on a short list of candidates mentioned prominently for the Oklahoma governorship. But there's one issue on which he has rankled fellow Republicans. It concerns a lawsuit filed last year by Pruitt and Bruning against Colorado's legalization and regulation of marijuana. In most of Pruitt's other high-profile disputes, he has argued against federal intrusion, but in this case, he and Bruning say federal law banning the use of marijuana should preempt state law in Colorado and other jurisdictions that have legalized it. That position strikes many as inconsistent with Pruitt's efforts to defend state prerogatives. "I think that's misplaced," replies Pruitt, who alleges that Colorado's law has increased illegal drug trafficking in nearby states, including his own. "What about the states' rights of Oklahoma?"

While both Oklahoma and Nebraska have argued for federal supremacy in the marijuana case, it's also clear that Pruitt and Bruning disagree with legalization on policy grounds. "It's about what's good for our country in the long term," Bruning says. "I see a slacker culture that makes me think of the fall of Rome. I don't want to hire employees who smoke marijuana on their lunch break."

Adler, the law professor who was Pruitt's ally in the challenge to the Affordable Care Act, summed up conservative dismay over Pruitt's challenge to Colorado in an op-ed article earlier this year. "It is as if their arguments about federalism and state autonomy were not arguments of principle," Adler wrote, "but rather an opportunistic effort to challenge federal policies they don't like on other grounds. It makes Oklahoma and Nebraska look like fair-weather federalists."

18

After Spending Millions Suing Obama 39 Times, Has Texas Seen a Return on Investment?

By Lauren McGaughy/Tribune News Service

Texas Attorney General Ken Paxton has taken up his predecessor's crusade against the federal government, spending nearly a quarter of a million dollars suing the federal government in six new legal challenges since taking office in January.

Elected in a tea party wave that swept several other social conservative Republicans into office, Paxton waited just two months before he sued the Obama administration for the first time over its policy of extending spousal benefits to married same-sex couples.

Five more lawsuits soon followed.

Since President Barack Obama was first elected in 2008, Paxton and former Attorney General Greg Abbott, now governor, have spent more than $5 million in taxpayer money suing the federal government 39 times, according to information provided by the attorney general's office.

Texas' Republican leaders long have defended the lawsuits as a means to push back against what they characterize as an overzealous federal government encroaching on states' rights.

"The lawsuits we've launched against the Obama Administration seek to protect Texans from massive and unlawful federal power grabs that would often impose costly new burdens on families and businesses. Just to put things in perspective, our Obamacare lawsuit alone concerns a $120 million annual new tax on the state," Paxton

From *Governing*, November 2015
©Tribune News Service

spokesperson Cynthia Meyer said, referring to the state's most recent challenge to the federal Affordable Care Act. "That's why the Paxton administration has launched six lawsuits against the Obama administration thus far. It's our duty to defend the rule of law against an aggressive federal government."

Paxton and Abbott's efforts to fight the federal government have been lauded by many conservative politicians and policymakers in the Republican-dominated state, including leaders at the Texas Public Policy Foundation, the capital's premier conservative think-tank. Robert Henneke, head of the foundation's Center for the American Future, last month called Paxton's most recent suit "an assertion of Tenth Amendment sovereignty against an oppressive regime aimed at harming middle class families."

'WASTE OF MONEY'

Critics, however, say the lawsuits represent little more than conservative politics run amok.

"It's a significant waste of money and resources that can easily be spent far better protecting our air and water from polluters," said Tom "Smitty" Smith, director of the consumer watchdog group Public Citizen Texas. "Certainly, it can be used for consumer protection or going after a variety of corporate criminals that have defrauded the state."

More than half of the state's legal challenges, 21 out of 39, have been aimed at the U.S. Environmental Protection Agency, a favorite political punching bag of Republicans.

In its most recent suit against the agency, the state already has spent more than $82,000 in one month fighting the federal government's plan to cut carbon emissions by 30 percent by 2030.

The challenge to the Obama administration's Clean Power Plan, and the dozen other suits that remain pending against the federal government, was the subject of a speech Paxton gave Thursday at a TPPF conference on energy and climate change.

"The fight against EPA is not just about growing the economy, protecting private property, or even saving jobs," Paxton said. "It's about standing up for the Constitution and the rule of law. It's about taking power out of the hands of un-elected bureaucrats and returning it to the people."

He later told reporters, "We think we're going to win this case."

MIXED SUCCESS

If so, it would be Texas' eighth victory against the federal government since Obama took office. The state already has eight losses, according to a *Houston Chronicle* analysis of the cases. The office of the attorney general only counts five as losses, however, and considers the other three—all challenges against a series of EPA rules promulgated in 2010—as "mixed outcomes." They count mixed outcomes when a court ruling or compromise resulted in the EPA partly acquiescing to the state's wishes, but not wholly to its demands.

While the state has gone after the EPA more than any other agency, the lawsuits with the biggest price tags have involved voting issues.

Texas has spent $1.6 million on its bid to force the federal government to accept its voter ID law, which was called discriminatory by a panel of federal appeals judges in August. The state has appealed, and asked for a rehearing before the full court.

Nearly $1 million has been spent to force the Obama administration to accept the state's 2011 redistricting maps for congressional and legislative seats. That case ultimately was withdrawn by the state in 2013 after the U.S. Supreme Court struck down a key section of the Voting Rights Act, which required certain states to get the federal government to sign off on changes to voting maps.

OTHER COSTS

The $5 million tab does not include all money the state has spent defending its laws against challenges from the federal government. Paxton and Abbott, for example, have spent more than $8 million defending voter ID and redistricting against charges from the administration that they are thinly veiled attempts to disenfranchise minority voters in a state with an increasingly diverse population.

Paxton's first challenge against the feds over gay marriage was settled in June, when the U.S. Supreme Court upheld the right for same-sex couples to wed. He dropped the state's lawsuit the next month. Outcomes in his five other cases, and eight remaining from his predecessor, remain pending.

©2015 the *Houston Chronicle*

VI

Courts

State criminal justice systems have had a tough decade. The Great Recession financially squeezed court and corrections systems, which were already creaking under the demands of astronomically high caseloads and incarceration rates. Naked partisanship is increasingly seeping into judicial elections, where deep-pocketed interest groups aggressively campaign to advance their preferences by getting a favored candidate elected. In that sort of political environment, whatever judges decide can end up being pilloried as legislating from the bench. And even in the normal course of things, courts view and rule on similar issues differently, meaning the legal view in one state can be different from its neighbors.

The readings in this chapter highlight and explore these stresses and strains. The first reading, by Lisa Soronen, examines how decisions by the U.S. Supreme Court are having a big impact on the states. It may seem somewhat unusual to kick off a chapter in a book on state and local government and politics with an essay on the top federal court. Keep in mind, though, that the U.S. Supreme Court sits at the head not just of the federal court system, but also the court systems of the states.

Under the nation's system of dual constitutionalism, the United States effectively has two parallel court systems, the federal system, which deals with issues of federal law, and the individual state systems, which deal with state law. At least in theory, these systems are separate—a state court has no jurisdiction over matters of federal law, and a federal law has no jurisdiction over issues of state law. In practice, though, state lawmakers and state judges make decisions that raise issues relevant to federal law and the U.S. Constitution. The most prominent recent example was gay marriage; some states decided under their constitutions that it was allowed, and others outlawed same-sex unions. The legality of gay marriage thus varied from state to state to state, and raised the question of whether homosexual couples had a right to marry under the U.S. Constitution. Only the U.S. Supreme Court can impose uniformity across all the states on these sorts of questions, and that's just what the court did in *Obergefell v. Hodges*, ruling that same-sex couples had a constitutional right to marry. In her essay, Soronen explores this and other cases where U.S. Supreme Court rulings have had big implications for state and local governments.

The second essay, by Rebecca Beitsch, takes a look at sentencing reform in the states. Many states are staggering under the financial burdens of historically high prison populations. During the 1980s and 1990s many states passed tough-on-crime laws that precipitated an explosion in incarceration rates for non-violent offenders. Many state correction systems are now bursting at the seams, and states are starting to rethink the tough-on-crime approach of the past few decades.

The third essay, by Cindy Chang, Marisa Gerber and Ben Poston, takes a look at some of the unintended consequences that some of these reforms may bring. In California, the passage of Proposition 47 in 2014 is having a mixed impact. The central aim of Proposition 47 was to reduce and reclassify non-violent property and drug crimes from felonies to misdemeanors. The idea was to stop putting people in prison for committing crimes such as shoplifting or personal drug use. Proposition 47 has had some success in doing exactly that. However, it also seems to have encouraged some petty criminals to become serial offenders, secure in the knowledge that their criminal activity will not land them behind bars.

The final essay, by Maggie Clark, takes a look at a new trend of legislatures seeking to strip courts of their power. Fed up with courts making decisions that they disagree with, some state legislatures are actively pursuing legislation to reduce or even eliminate state court powers of review, or the power to interpret what the state constitution does or does not allow. This has alarmed a wide range of good government advocates who see it as undermining an independent judiciary.

19 | Cases with Consequences

By Lisa Soronen

The U.S. Supreme Court's recent rulings on same-sex marriage and Obamacare drew enormous interest from court watchers and the public alike. Several other cases—on redistricting, fair housing and Medicaid, for example—got less notice, but could have far-reaching consequences for the states.

Here's a recap of what was decided and a note on what lies ahead as the court enters its 10th year with Chief Justice John Roberts in the center seat.

REDISTRICTING

By a 5-4 decision in *Arizona State Legislature v. Arizona Independent Redistricting Commission*, the court held that the Constitution's Elections Clause permits voters to vest congressional redistricting authority entirely in an independent commission. The ruling is an affirmation of direct democracy. NCSL filed an amicus brief supporting the Arizona Legislature.

Justice Ruth Bader Ginsburg's majority opinion relies on the history and purpose of the Elections Clause, and the "animating principle of our Constitution that the people themselves are the originating source of all the powers of government," in ruling that redistricting commissions may operate independently of state legislatures.

Founding-era dictionaries typically defined legislatures as the "power that makes laws." In Arizona, that includes the voters, who may pass laws through initiatives.

From *State Legislatures Magazine*, September 2015
©National Conference of State Legislatures

EPA REGULATIONS

In *Michigan v. EPA*, the justices held 5–4 that the Environmental Protection Agency acted unreasonably in failing to consider cost when deciding whether to regulate mercury emissions from power plants. Twenty-three states challenged the regulations.

The Clean Air Act requires the EPA to regulate air pollution from stationary sources based on how much pollution the source emits. But the agency may only regulate emissions from fossil-fuel-fired power plants if it finds that regulation is "appropriate and necessary."

EPA found it appropriate and necessary to regulate mercury emissions, but did not consider costs when determining whether power plants should be regulated. The majority of the court, in an opinion written by Justice Antonin Scalia, concluded that the agency's interpretation of appropriate and necessary to exclude costs wasn't reasonable.

The opinion leaves unanswered questions, including how the EPA may account for costs and whether the agency may consider ancillary benefits in the cost-benefit analysis.

FAIR HOUSING

In *Texas Department of Housing and Community Affairs v. Inclusive Communities Project*, the court held 5–4 that disparate-impact claims may be brought under the Fair Housing Act.

In a disparate-impact case, a plaintiff claims that a policy used by a government agency, private real estate firm or developer isn't intentionally discriminatory but nonetheless has a disproportionately adverse impact on a particular group.

The federal courts of appeals had ruled that such claims were possible. The Supreme Court, which had twice agreed to take up this question only to have the cases settle before the justices could rule, has finally resolved it.

While state and local governments are more likely to be sued under the FHA, they do occasionally sue others for violating it. Justice Anthony Kennedy pointed out at the end of his majority opinion that the city of San Francisco filed an amicus brief supporting disparate-impact liability under the FHA despite being a "potential defendant."

Same-Sex Marriage

Obergefell v. Hodges has been both celebrated and condemned.

In a 5–4 decision written by Justice Kennedy, the court held that same-sex couples have a constitutional right to marry. All state laws and court decisions banning same-sex marriage are now invalid.

The court relied on the 14th Amendment's Due Process and Equal Protection clauses in its opinion, rejecting the argument that sufficient debate had not occurred on this issue. It noted that "individuals need not await legislative action before asserting a fundamental right."

Kennedy wrote in his majority opinion that the "hope [of the same-sex couples in this case] is not to be condemned to live in loneliness, excluded from one of civilization's oldest institutions. They ask for equal dignity in the eyes of the law. The Constitution grants them that right."

AFFORDABLE CARE ACT

The third time was a charm for the Affordable Care Act. *King v. Burwell* is the first complete victory for the law. In a 6–3 decision, the court ruled that health insurance tax credits are available on the 34 federal exchanges. The court's opinion focused largely on the consequences of ruling to the contrary: the destruction of health insurance markets.

The ACA allows the states and the federal government to sell insurance on health care exchanges. The law states that tax credits are available when insurance is purchased through "an Exchange established by the State." So the technical question in this case was whether a federal exchange is "an Exchange established by the State" that may offer tax credits.

The court said yes, and as a result, the status quo remains unchanged. If a person otherwise eligible for a tax credit buys health insurance on a state or federal exchange, the tax credit will be available.

FREE SPEECH AND GOVERNMENTS

You know it's going to be a good day for state government when the Supreme Court begins the analysis portion of its opinion with this: "When government speaks, it is not barred by the Free Speech Clause from determining the content of what it says."

In *Walker v. Sons of Confederate Veterans*, the court held 5–4 that Texas may deny a proposed specialty license plate design featuring the Confederate flag, because specialty plate designs are government speech.

In a vigorous dissent, Justice Samuel Alito questioned much of the majority's analysis. He pointed out that only within the last 20 years has Texas allowed private groups to put messages on license plates, adding that the state allows messages on license plates to make money, not to convey ideas it supports.

Nine states—Alabama, Georgia, Louisiana, Maryland, Mississippi, North Carolina, South Carolina, Tennessee and Virginia—allow Confederate flag specialty plates, according to *The New York Times*. States may ban these plates and others as a result of this decision.

STATE BOARDS AND COMMISSIONS

In *North Carolina State Board of Dental Examiners v. FTC*, the court held 6–3 that state licensing boards whose members are market participants are not immune from antitrust laws. Immunity applies only if the state actively supervises the board.

The North Carolina's Board of Dental Examiners is a state agency mainly charged with licensing dentists. Six of its eight members must be practicing, licensed dentists. After the board issued cease-and-desist letters to teeth-whitening service providers, who were not dentists, the Federal Trade Commission charged it with violating antitrust law.

In a previous case, the court held that states are immune from antitrust law when acting in their sovereign capacity. In this case, the court said that even though the board is a state agency, it must be supervised by the state in order to enjoy immunity. The "formal designation given by the States" does not necessarily create immunity, wrote Justice Kennedy. "When a State empowers a group of active market participants to decide who can participate in its market, and on what terms, the need for supervision is manifest."

Although it's generally seen as a win for consumers, the case reduces the authority of state legislatures to compose state agencies, boards and commissions as they prefer and could require additional state resources to actively supervise boards.

MEDICAID REIMBURSEMENT

In *Armstrong v. Exceptional Child Center*, the court held 5–4 that Medicaid providers cannot rely on the Supremacy Clause to sue states to enforce a Medicaid reimbursement statute.

What's Ahead for the Court's Next Term?

- The court agreed to hear a major affirmative action case concerning a public university's use of race as a factor in student admissions. It will be the second time the court has heard *Fisher v. University of Texas at Austin*, a challenge from a Texas woman, Abigail Fisher, who is white, targeting the admissions policies at the school.
- The court will decide whether public-sector unions may require workers who are not members to help pay for collective bargaining. A ruling against them could deal a severe blow to organized labor. That case, *Friedrichs v. California Teachers Association*, was brought by California teachers who said that being compelled to pay union fees to subsidize activities they disagreed with violated their First Amendment rights.
- The court surprised observers when it decided to hear *Evenwel v. Abbott*. The issue in the case is whether state legislatures can use total voter population—rather than simply total population, which is the long-standing precedent—when apportioning state legislative districts. Over the last 25 years, the court has repeatedly refused to hear cases arguing that voter population must be equalized. The court will also decide two other redistricting cases next term.
- The court has accepted three death penalty cases and one case involving life in prison without parole.

(Continued)

(Continued)
- Although nothing was on the court's calendar as of press time, the justices also are likely to hear a case involving state restrictions on abortion.

Sources: CNN, *The New York Times*, SCOTUSblog, *The Week.*

Medicaid requires states to ensure that Medicaid providers are reimbursed at rates "consistent with efficiency, economy and quality of care" while "safeguard[ing] against unnecessary utilization of . . . care and services." Medicaid providers sued Idaho, claiming that its reimbursement rates were too low.

Congress did not create a private right of action in the Medicaid statute allowing providers to sue states to enforce the statute.

The court rejected the argument that the Supremacy Clause creates a private right of action. "It instructs courts what to do when state and federal law clash, but is silent regarding who may enforce federal laws in court, and in what circumstances they may do so."

The court's rejection of a private cause of action under the Supremacy Clause has implications well beyond this case. Had the Supreme Court ruled otherwise, the Supremacy Clause would have provided a cause of action for every federal statute that arguably conflicts with state law.

TAX ON INTERNET PURCHASES

In *Direct Marketing Association v. Brohl*, Justice Kennedy wrote a concurring opinion stating that the "legal system should find an appropriate case for this Court to reexamine *Quill.*"

In the 1992 case *Quill Corp. v. North Dakota*, the court held that states cannot require retailers with no in-state physical presence to collect a use tax.

To improve tax collection, the Colorado legislature in 2010 began requiring remote sellers to annually inform Colorado shoppers of their purchases and send the same information to the state Department of Revenue. The Direct Marketing Association sued Colorado in federal court, claiming that the notice and reporting requirements are unconstitutional under *Quill.*

The question the court decided was whether this case could be heard in federal court (as opposed to state court). Although the justices said yes unanimously, the case is significant for states because the court's most influential justice expressed skepticism about whether *Quill* should remain the law of the land.

DEATH PENALTY

In *Glossip v. Gross*, the court held 5–4 that death-row inmates are unlikely to succeed on their claim that using midazolam as a lethal injection drug amounts to cruel and unusual punishment. Death-penalty opponents have persuaded manufacturers to stop producing sodium thiopental and an alternative, pentobarbital. As a result, Oklahoma and other states began using midazolam as the first of three drugs administered during executions. But prisoners claimed the state's use of midazolam violates the prohibition against cruel and unusual punishment because it fails to render them insensate. In Justice Alito's majority opinion, the court concluded that because the use of midazolam does not likely violate the Eighth Amendment, states may continue to use it in executions.

In his dissent, Justice Stephen Breyer, joined by Ruth Bader Ginsburg, called for a "full briefing on the basic question" of whether capital punishment is unconstitutional. His statement invites a case challenging the constitutionality of capital punishment, one that could have far-reaching and significant implications for states where the death penalty is used.

20

States at a Crossroads on Criminal Justice Reform

By Rebecca Beitsch

After two decades of "tough on crime" policies, many states are taking a hard look at the way people are charged, how much time they serve, and what happens when they are released from prison.

While bills governing the use of body cameras and other police-related measures are likely to be considered this year, many states are looking at growing prison populations, obstacles to drug treatment, and high recidivism rates as reasons to re-evaluate their criminal justice systems.

The U.S. has the highest incarceration rate in the world, and many states are at a crossroads, weighing whether to build new prisons or change how they sentence people as well as how they guide them through parole and probation.

Several states, including Alaska, Maryland and Rhode Island, are considering sweeping criminal justice changes that would ease some of the punitive policies of the 1980s and '90s, especially when it comes to drug offenders. In some places, lawmakers will consider recommendations made by criminal justice task forces, often with the guidance of outside groups such as the Council of State Governments (CSG) and The Pew Charitable Trusts (Pew also funds *Stateline*).

"If there's a theme or common denominator, it is policymakers asking what the science says will work," said Michael Thompson, director of the CSG's Justice Center. "The question they're asking is, 'Can we get a better return on our investment?'"

SENTENCING REFORM

States that want to decrease the number of people going to prison often turn to reducing sentences, either by scrapping mandatory

From *Stateline*, a project of the Pew Charitable Trusts, January 2016.

minimums or reclassifying some felonies as misdemeanors. They may also divert people into treatment for drug addiction or mental illness.

Nicole Porter with the Sentencing Project, which advocates for shorter sentences, said when states do reclassify crimes, it tends to be lower level felonies, such as drug possession and property crimes like theft under a certain dollar value.

Porter said some states may be inspired by what California voters did in 2014, approving Proposition 47, which reduced some felonies, such as nonviolent property theft and drug crimes, to misdemeanors.

Not only did the state decrease the number of people going into prison, but thousands of inmates were eligible to be released early under the new law. As of September, nearly 4,500 people were released under Prop. 47. And the state's Department of Corrections estimates 3,300 fewer people will be incarcerated each year.

Holly Harris with U.S. Justice Action Network, a coalition of liberal and conservative groups pushing for criminal justice changes, said reducing felonies to misdemeanors could have a big impact on women. Though they are the fastest growing segment of prison population, many women are nonviolent offenders or are serving time for drug crimes that might be reclassified.

In Alaska, the state's Criminal Justice Commission in December called for limiting prison beds to serious and violent offenders, reclassifying many of the lowest level misdemeanors as violations punishable by a fine, and shortening jail time for more serious misdemeanors to no more than 30 days. The panel also called for changing simple possession of heroin, methamphetamine and cocaine to a misdemeanor.

But states that are adjusting sentences aren't just shortening them. Last year, Maine legislators reduced sentences for some drug possession crimes, but increased them for cocaine and fentanyl powder, one of the opioids that have concerned state leaders as they battle heroin addiction.

"The dichotomy feels like legislators have a split personality," said Alison Holcomb, director of the American Civil Liberties Union's Campaign for Smart Justice, which lobbied against the increased sentences in Maine. Holcomb said while attitudes around some drugs have relaxed, some states that are trying to crack down on the abuse of opiates have imposed harsher sentences.

But reducing sentences could have unintended consequences. In Utah, state Rep. Eric Hutchings, a Republican, said the reclassification of some crimes as misdemeanors blocked some people from drug courts and treatment programs meant only for felons—something he said the state will fix this year.

Many states may also consider ending some mandatory minimum sentences, which have helped to swell prison populations in several states. Iowa Attorney General Tom Miller, a Democrat, said he wants the Legislature to eliminate mandatory minimums for less serious crimes, which under current law can land someone behind bars for decades.

Bills in several states, including Florida, Massachusetts and Virginia, would either scrap mandatory minimums or give judges more power to depart from them when issuing sentences. Last year, Maryland, North Dakota and Oklahoma gave judges more discretion to exempt some people from mandatory minimums, according to Alison Lawrence with the National Conference of State Legislatures.

CHANGES TO PAROLE AND PROBATION

States are also looking to get people who are already in the criminal justice system out faster and to help them transition back into society while on parole.

One option is "presumptive parole," which means presuming that inmates are eligible for parole, rather than requiring them to convince the parole board they should be released, an approach Mississippi adopted in 2015. Michigan's House is currently weighing the policy, something the state's Department of Corrections estimates will free up enough beds to save the state $82 million a year.

"It puts the burden on the state to show a compelling reason why you should not be released on parole," Harris said. States may also consider scaling back the amount of time prisoners must serve before they become eligible for parole. Mississippi used to require convicted felons to complete 85 percent of their sentence before they were eligible, but changed the law in 2014. Now nonviolent offenders must serve 25 percent of their time, while violent offenders must serve 50 percent, before they can be considered for parole.

Some states are trying to make their parole process more responsive to parolees' behavior.

Several states, including Alabama and Utah, have adopted "swift, certain, fair" approaches, which aim to provide an immediate response to parolees' behavior, whether it's jail time after a failed drug test or a reduced parole term if someone has been following the rules and making a lot of progress in post-prison life.

Hutchings said Utah legislators passed such a measure last year after examining the recidivism rates of parolees. One-third were back in prison because they had committed new crimes, but two-thirds were there for parole violations.

People need a quick, clear response when they do something wrong in order to change their behavior, Hutchings said, but the state was taking too long to get people in front of a judge when they violated parole—and they were often sent back to prison for too long.

"These are not people we're afraid of. They're just people who are not doing what they said they were going to do," he said. "It's kind of like the game Chutes and Ladders. You get your stuff together but then one slip-up and you're back at the beginning. Even if you just get sent back to jail for 60 days, you don't show up for work so you lose your job. You can't make your car payments so it gets repo'ed. You go all the way back to zero."

The state adapted one of its facilities to include a special section for parolees and probationers, giving them access to drug treatment, therapy, and their parole or probation officer. Officers can also order parolees and probationers to sleep at the center for a few nights, to make sure they stay out of trouble, or to be locked up for up to five days—or even longer with a judge's approval.

Michigan state Sen. John Proos, a Republican, said he wants to expand his state's "swift and certain" program, which now operates only in some counties. He'd also like the state to open it up to probationers.

But he also wants to understand why prison doesn't better prepare inmates for parole. "Do we need more education? Do we need more resources?" he asked.

Several states already provide some resources, including substance abuse and mental health treatment, before people even go to prison.

Maryland's working group on criminal justice reform found the state spends about $26 a day to incarcerate one person, versus $4.55 per person for probation and parole. To reduce the number of people entering prison, the group proposed starting a grant program to cover the county costs of specialty courts and re-entry programs.

COLLATERAL CONSEQUENCES

Some states are likely to consider ways to remove some of the barriers that make it difficult for people to make a life for themselves once they get out of prison.

Each year, several states take up "ban the box" legislation, which blocks employers from asking on job applications whether someone has served time. The idea is that if employers have a chance to get to know applicants before finding out about a criminal past, they are more likely to give them a second chance.

While 19 states have some sort of ban the box policy, sometimes it only applies to the state or its contractors, but not private employers. Arkansas state Sen. Jeremy Hutchinson, a Republican and the chairman of the Senate Judiciary Committee, said he expects the state to consider such a policy this year, but he's not sure how far he wants to go.

"There's a lot of hesitancy, even on my part, to dictate to employers what should be on their job application, but the state can be a model," he said.

States are also likely to consider laws that allow for the expungement or sealing of records, or certificates of rehabilitation, which allow a state to vouch for the good reputation of people who have been convicted of crimes and served their time.

This month, the Kentucky House voted to let people convicted of most Class D felonies—the lowest level of felony, punishable by one to five years in prison—erase their criminal records and get a second chance at jobs, housing and other opportunities sometimes denied felons.

JUVENILE JUSTICE

Some states are also reevaluating their juvenile justice systems and trying to open them to an older population, prompted in part by new brain science which suggests cognitive abilities are not fully formed until age 25.

In New York, after failing to change the state's status as one of the few where 16- and 17-year-olds are automatically tried as adults, Democratic Gov. Andrew Cuomo issued an executive order in December requiring that young prisoners be housed separately from older inmates—an idea that has been talked about in other states as well.

21

The Unintended Consequences of California's New Criminal Justice

By Cindy Chang, Marisa Gerber, and Ben Poston/Tribune News Service

Semisi Sina has kept sheriff's deputies busy in the last year.

The 30-year-old has stolen bicycles from his Hacienda Heights neighborhood. He has skipped out on drug treatment and kept up his meth habit.

He has racked up 16 arrests, earning himself a place near the top of the Los Angeles County Sheriff's Department's list of repeat offenders picked up for theft or drug use. And he says a new law has made it easier for him to commit crimes.

"Now, you can get away with it because of Proposition 47," Sina said recently in an interview at his parents' home. One year after voters approved the landmark ballot measure, Proposition 47 has dramatically altered California's criminal justice landscape. The proposition, which downgraded drug possession and some theft crimes to misdemeanors, made good on its pledge to reduce prison and jail populations by thousands of inmates. Tens of thousands more people with older felony convictions have been able to wipe their records clean, giving them the chance to qualify for new jobs and other benefits.

But law enforcement officials and others have blamed Proposition 47 for allowing repeat offenders like Sina to continue breaking the law with little consequence.

Crime has risen in the state's largest cities, setting off debate over whether the proposition is responsible. In some areas, street cops are making fewer narcotics arrests.

From *Governing,* November 2015
©Tribune News Service

And without the threat of a felony conviction and a lengthy stint behind bars, fewer drug offenders are enrolling in court-ordered treatment.

"Proposition 47 was good and bad," said Thomas Loversky, a Manhattan Beach–based criminal defense attorney who has clients in drug court. "The good part is we have people who shouldn't be spending time in jail not spending time in jail. The bad part of Proposition 47 was there was no hammer to force people who needed treatment to get it."

Lenore Anderson, executive director of Californians for Safety and Justice and an author of the measure, said courts and law enforcement agencies need to adjust to the new landscape by innovating—for example, by funneling offenders into treatment before they even see a judge. Misdemeanors, which can carry one-year sentences, can be used in the same carrot-and-stick way as felonies, she said.

"Proposition 47 is working," Anderson said. "It's reducing the state prison population, it's giving people second chances and it's saving state money that has never been saved before."

Los Angeles County Sheriff Jim McDonnell is among the law enforcement officials who believe that Proposition 47 has led to more crime while forcing fewer addicts into treatment.

"We've removed the disincentive, but we haven't created a meaningful incentive," McDonnell said in an interview last week. "We're putting the people we're trying to help in a position where we can't help them." McDonnell said he agrees with the goals of the proposition: reducing incarceration while providing treatment for drug addicts.

A drop in the state prison population because of Proposition 47 is expected to save about $100 million annually, according to a state estimate. Under the terms of the law, that money will go toward treatment and education programs beginning in late 2016.

But McDonnell and others questioned whether that windfall will be enough to cover all those who need help.

At some point, McDonnell said, he might advocate for the proposition to be revised—for example, by increasing the penalties after repeat misdemeanor convictions.

Sheriff's deputies are sometimes passing up narcotics arrests altogether, since it can take hours to book a suspect they believe is unlikely to incur much of a penalty. Narcotics arrests by sheriff's deputies are down 30 percent from a year ago, despite McDonnell's orders to his deputies to keep making arrests.

At the same time, areas of Los Angeles County patrolled by the Sheriff's Department have seen property crime climb nearly 8 percent from last year. Auto thefts alone are up over 20 percent. Sheriff's officials say there is a link between drug and property crimes as some addicts steal to support their habits.

Statewide, property crime has increased in nine of California's 10 largest cities this year, a *Los Angeles Times* review found. Violent crime has increased in all 10.

Proponents of Proposition 47 say it is too soon to connect the ballot measure to rising crime and question why police aren't making misdemeanor arrests.

Criminologists also caution against attributing fluctuations in crime to a single cause.

Keramet Reiter, a criminology professor at the University of California, Irvine, said the ballot measure has been used by critics as a "convenient scapegoat" for the rise in crime. The reality, she said, is more complicated in a state that is undergoing broad changes to its criminal justice system, including a massive shift of inmates from state prisons to local jails.

The Los Angeles Police Department has reported a double-digit increase in property crime so far this year, but Chief Charlie Beck said it is premature to fault Proposition 47.

"The studies are not done and the results aren't in," Beck said. County jail populations were down by about 12 percent statewide in the first quarter of 2015, the most recent figures available, according to the Board of State and Community Corrections. Counties are not required to put their cost savings into programs.

In Los Angeles County, which has the largest jail system in the country, Proposition 47 has opened up beds for some offenders to serve more of their sentences rather than being released early. County-sentenced inmates are serving about 70 percent of their sentences versus 20 percent before the measure passed.

As the criminal justice system adjusts to the ballot measure, repeat offenders are sometimes being sentenced to jail time or drug treatment on misdemeanors, court records show. But getting them to follow through with the treatment can be a challenge.

Judges got tougher on Sina, the Hacienda Heights offender, as his rap sheet grew. After a May 7 arrest, he spent two months behind bars.

Shortly after he was released on July 9, he resumed his criminal activities. On July 31, he pleaded guilty to stealing a bicycle from a shopping mall employee while she was at work. A judge sentenced him to nine months behind bars.

Last month, he left jail to finish his sentence in a work program. Sina said he rejoiced when he first heard about Proposition 47. He said he didn't start stealing bicycles until the proposition raised the threshold for a felony theft to $950.

"Proposition 47, it's cool," Sina said. "Like for me, I can go do a (commercial) burglary and know that if it's not over $900, they'll just give me a ticket and let me go."

He was sentenced to rehab five times this year but did not show up for a single session.

"I know it's up to me to change. I wasn't ready. I probably still am not. I'm not going to lie—I'm still not ready to quit," he said last week on a break from shoveling dirt at a sheriff's training facility in Whittier.

©2015 *Los Angeles Times*

22 Legislators Attempt to Strip Courts of Power

By Maggie Clark

Frustrated with what they see as "activist judges" who make policy through their rulings, lawmakers in New Hampshire and Tennessee have proposed bills that would end the judicial branch's ability to rule on the constitutionality of legislation.

"The executive, legislative and judicial branches were created separate but equal, but the judiciary has overstepped their bounds," says Republican state Senator Mae Beavers, the lead sponsor of the Tennessee bill. Beavers wants to amend the state code to take away the state Supreme Court's jurisdiction to rule on the question of whether a law is or is not constitutional. "They're not just interpreting the law, but making policy."

Beavers is not the first Tennessee lawmaker to try and limit the state's courts. Last year, a bill to amend the state constitution to instruct judges that they may only "strictly construe the enacted text" of a law passed the Senate unanimously. But the legislative session ended before the House could vote on the bill.

In New Hampshire, a feud between the state judiciary and House Republicans reached a peak last October. The state Supreme Court had issued an advisory opinion that the legislature did not have the power to force the attorney general to join a multi-state lawsuit against the federal health care overhaul. The House then overwhelmingly passed a resolution repudiating the court's opinion. During the House debate, Republican Dan Itse called judges "unelected bureaucrats," who "usurp and pervert the power of the people, destroying their liberty."

This year's bill goes much farther than a repudiation. It attempts to amend the state Constitution so that "the supreme court shall

From *Stateline*, a project of the Pew Charitable Trusts, January 2016.

determine the constitutionality of judicial acts and the legislature shall determine the constitutionality of legislative acts."

The amendment's lead sponsor, Republican state Representative Gregory Sorg, says he's introduced this amendment for the last four legislative sessions, and each time the interest has grown. "(Judicial review) makes judges more powerful and helps legislators avoid making tough calls," Sorg says. "There are more who think like I do now. It was much more lonely in 2003 when I first introduced the bill."

For New Hampshire to amend its constitution through an act of the legislature, the amendment must pass both houses with a three-fifths majority. Then, it must pass a popular vote with a two-thirds majority.

These attacks on the courts, says Bill Rafferty, editor of the National Center for State Courts' Gavel to Gavel blog, are indicative of a general feeling among some legislators that the courts are just a recalcitrant state agency, not a co-equal branch of government.

"The only other time the courts have seen their jurisdictions removed is when they're transferred to other courts, like when a state creates a new court of appeals, or a tax court—but that's administrative," Rafferty says. "What's unprecedented about these bills is the extent to which they're removing the court's jurisdiction altogether, in effect, hobbling them."

Although legislators have never liked it when judges struck down their laws, Rafferty says, they have traditionally tried to work with the courts to amend the laws in question. "Now it's not a disagreement about the law," Rafferty says. "We're seeing that rather than changing the laws, they're going after the judges."

VII

Bureaucracy

Legislatures may be rapidly gaining in the unpopularity sweepstakes, but bureaucracy continues to retain the dubious honor of being the least loved part of government. It is not hard to figure out why. Ask someone what they associate with bureaucracy and the answer is likely to be something like "red tape," "incompetence," or "inefficiency." These stereotypes are deeply ingrained in peoples' perspectives of government agencies and stubbornly resistant to change. Yet despite the public's lack of love for the bureaucracy, people would have an awfully hard time getting along without it.

In reality there is no such thing as "the bureaucracy." Broadly defined, bureaucracy consists of all public agencies of the programs and services they implement and manage. That is a lot of agencies and programs, some of them doing a great job, some a not-so-good job, and most of them only vaguely connected to each other in the sense that they are primarily lumped into the executive branches of state and local government. When you look at "the bureaucracy" close up, what your find are schools, police departments, health departments, and public universities. What these agencies truly have in common is that they are all tasked with the implementation, management, and enforcement of public policy. When a legislature passes a law—be it a speed limit or a grade school testing requirement—a government agency, in other words a bureaucracy, is tasked with translating that law into action. It is mostly a thankless job. Legislators might get pats on the back for championing strong academic standards for schools. School administrators have to do the dirty work of insuring students actually meet those standards and for their trouble they are less likely to get pats on the back than get it in the ear from teachers, students, and parents upset at the focus on standardized tests. For bureaucracies, though, that's the gig—doing the dirty work of government.

The main theme of the readings in this chapter is the people who do this dirty work. The first essay, by Katherine Barrett and Richard Greene, takes a look at public sector hiring. It has been a tough decade for public sector job hunters. The Great Recession pressured state and local governments to shed jobs and reduce wages. The tough economic times also made a lot of public agencies top heavy—older workers held on to their jobs rather than retiring. This upshot was a tight labor market with a lot of qualified people chasing a relatively small number jobs. That is changing. Many agencies are facing a wave of retirements, trying to recover pre-recession staffing levels, and dealing with a low unemployment rate that gives job seekers lots of options.

The second essay, by Sophie Quinton, looks at the growing temporary employee phenomenon in public agencies. This trend is particularly noticeable in higher education, where part time adjuncts—considerably cheaper than full-time instructors—are teaching more and more classes. This trend extends far beyond higher education, however. The public sector generally is reflecting the rise of the temporary worker in a "gig" economy.

The final two essays take a look at pay and benefits in two of the largest state and local bureaucracies: K–12 public school systems and public higher education systems. The first, also by Sophie Quinton, looks at the chronic teacher shortage in some states. As states scramble to address this shortage, they are trying to figure out what is driving the lack of teachers. Low pay is certainly a factor. But there is also a lot of turnover in the teaching ranks, and schools often find it hard to retain good teachers.

The final essay, by Karen Herzog, takes a look at tenure, long viewed as an essential job protection by professors who fear that without it they could be pressured to avoid teaching controversial topics, or going down educational or research paths that might upset powerful political constituencies. Historically, those most likely to oppose strong tenure protections are conservatives, but conservative voices within the academy are speaking out in defense of tenure.

23

Can Government Hiring Get Out of the Stone Age?

By Katherine Barrett and Richard Greene

During the Great Recession years, filling jobs in the public sector was uncomplicated. With unemployment rates high, there was no shortage of applicants. "When we had the downturn, we had no troubles hiring," reports Rock Regan, the former chief information officer of Connecticut. "We got a lot of people."

The unstable economy also meant that a huge group of older workers ready for retirement did not step down. The devastating impacts of the stock market near-crash between 2007 and 2009 caused many older workers to defer plans to live on retirement income and benefits.

Today, the hiring situation has been reversed. Although the number of applicants for most public jobs is still relatively high in many states, the national unemployment rate is hovering around 5 percent. That means the number of qualified candidates is shrinking. States and localities are trying to attract new employees by dipping into the same limited personnel pool as other governments and, more notably, the private sector. "When private industry is expanding and the economy is growing, we can't compete," Missouri's then-CIO Tim Robyn told a National Association of State Chief Information Officers' (NASCIO) conference last spring.

At the same time, the groundswell of retirements is materializing. Men and women who delayed that decision are beginning to leave their government jobs—ready or not. "You can delay retirement, but you can't delay aging," says Neil Reichenberg, executive director of the International Public Management Association for

From *Governing,* February 2016

Human Resources (IPMA-HR). "So baby boomers are leaving their jobs one way or another."

Numbers underscore the openings in government ranks. In its annual survey, the Center for State and Local Government Excellence found that 73 percent of states and localities were hiring—up from 66 percent in the previous year's survey. For many governments, the report noted, "there is a sense of urgency about recruitment, retention and succession planning."

Urgency or not, many governments are locked in antiquated systems and outdated processes that stand in the way of bringing in the best and brightest. At a time when state budgets are loosening their strings and dormant programs are being refreshed, human resources departments are faced with the need to focus on improving their capacity to hire and to retain employees. Many governments are finding that if they want to hire the next generation of public employees, they'll need to shift from the old ways of doing business.

In the meantime, governments are dealing with the consequences of being unable to hire the most competent people. One effect is that employees are overworked. A number of states are already experiencing that. In Pennsylvania, average overtime costs per employee have gone up 15 percent since 2010. In Arizona, overtime rose about 25 percent between 2011 and 2015.

In some departments, when hiring doesn't keep up with necessary staffing, it can create unsafe conditions. Corrections departments are a case in point. A study in 2015 by West Virginia's Joint Committee on Governance and Finance warned that the increased inmate-to-staff ratio "can increase staff overtime and stress levels while reducing inmate and staff communication. This can affect the safety and security of the institution."

Inadequate hiring protocols can affect economic development. If states and localities are going to attract businesses and citizens, they need to provide services that are competitive with other places. "Minnesota provides great service," says Ann O'Brien, assistant commissioner of enterprise human resources in that state. "If we don't get the talent we need to provide those services, then we're failing."

Difficulties in hiring depend on a number of variables. If a facility is in an out-of-the-way place—prisons and rural health-care clinics, for instance—it's tougher to find applicants. There are also certain positions for which hiring is particularly demanding, such as with jobs with hazardous working conditions, with a clientele that can be difficult or even hostile, or with irregular hours where employees have to work weekend or overnight shifts.

Additionally, jobs that require very specialized skill sets often remain vacant for a longer period. In the Center for State and Local Government Excellence Survey, hard-to-fill positions included accountants, corrections officers, dispatchers, engineers, firefighters, information technology professionals, mental health professionals, nurses, police officers, public works employees, social workers and water treatment plant employees.

The image of the public workforce has also taken hits, and that doesn't help with hiring or retaining employees. "Some people are saying that when they go to a party," O'Brien reports, "they don't tell people they're state employees because they'll be embarrassed."

Attracting millennials remains a challenge too. By 2025, they'll make up 75 percent of the world's workforce, so the search for ways to reach the group has become hugely important. The old approaches no longer apply. "The way people traditionally did recruitment was to throw an ad in the newspaper," Connecticut's Regan says. "Now the millennials say, 'What's a newspaper?'"

The flip side of hiring is the constant challenge of making sure employees don't leave. "You can't talk about hiring without talking about retention," says Candy Sarvis, deputy commissioner at Georgia's Human Resources Administration. "We're just not seeing quality applicants, and to the extent that we find them, we're not able to retain them." Turnover rates in her state have been on the rise, from 15.6 percent in 2011 to 18.4 percent in 2015.

Turnover is being pushed, in part, by aging employees. A fast-growing portion of people in mid- and upper-level management jobs are retiring. Delayed by the 2008 recession, they are finally departing the workforce. "We're no longer on the edge of the retirement bubble," says James Honchar, deputy secretary of human resources and management in Pennsylvania. "We're in the midst of it." In Pennsylvania, about a third of the workforce is eligible to retire in the next five years.

Similar numbers crop up in other states. In Nevada, 44 percent of employees will be eligible to retire in the next three to five years; a third will be in that position in Mississippi in the next five years.

Not only does turnover leave states and cities scrambling for people to fill mid-level positions, it's also a very expensive phenomenon. According to a recent auditor's report to the city council in San Jose, Calif., 16 percent of new hires left the police department within two years in the 2005–2007 time period. That number climbed to nearly 25 percent in 2012–2014. Given the significant amount of money a city spends to train police—in San Jose it's roughly $200,000 per recruit—that hike in turnover is costly.

Unsurprisingly, much of the challenge on retention as well as hiring comes down to money. Uncompetitive compensation is one of the biggest issues confronting states in search of new hires. "Starting salaries are too low, and we can't compete in the market," IPMA-HR's Reichenberg says. "We all hear, 'It's the people who matter'—until budget time and then the people fall to the bottom of the heap."

In Minnesota, a compensation study found that the 2014 salary for agency heads was $119,517, which was 35 to 69 percent below similar base salaries for the private sector. The state raised salaries in early 2015, but compensation for many agency heads still remained far below market rates. The salary for the commissioner of human services, for instance, was 60 percent below 2014 median private-sector salaries in comparable positions. As a 2013 study on compensation in Minnesota reported, "The bigger the job, the bigger the pay gap with the private sector."

Beyond a restructuring of the pay scales, states and cities face problems of internal equity. When an entity increases salaries to attract new employees, old employees with the same level of experience end up demoralized if they're being paid less. But the better new-hire salaries are part of the new competitive environment state and local human resources directors face. "The competition today is a lot greater than it was five years ago," says Neal Alexander Jr., the state human resources director in North Carolina. "We've got to figure out how we can be more flexible in attracting and retaining people."

That's certainly true in Pennsylvania: If you're an agency manager and you want to recruit candidates for a particular job, you can't. Instead, candidates must first come in and take an examination to get on a general statewide employment list. Then the agency that wants to fill a vacant job must pore through the list and reach out to applicants to see if they're interested in that particular position. Not only is it a cumbersome process, the lists can hopelessly get out of date; sometimes the applications are as much as four years old. "You can literally get halfway through a list and still not have enough candidates to have a decent interview process," Honchar says, adding that some of the candidates either "have another job already or they're not interested in the job you're hiring for."

Pennsylvania, along with New Jersey, has among the most stringent civil service regulations in the country. Such rules are a hurdle in other places, too, including California and Illinois. "We have a very antiquated civil service system," says Honchar. "That's our biggest impediment at this point. We can't compete against a noncivil service process that can literally hire on the spot."

The impact on hiring can be disastrous. Hiring in San Jose, for example, can take as much as 10 months for hard-to-fill positions and an average of six months if the city hasn't already assembled a list of readily available candidates. Though the city has begun to ease the process, historically it's taken 53 different steps from the approval of being able to fill the position to hiring the person.

There's also the simple matter of job descriptions and titles. They're often hard to understand or simply sound uninteresting—and certainly unenticing. Only a few years ago, Connecticut and other states finally stopped using common business-oriented language (COBOL) to describe their jobs. They also stopped overdescribing the duties and requirements of the position. As Connecticut's Regan puts it, "They typically had the kitchen sink written in."

So what are states and localities to do? One commonsense solution is workforce planning. States and cities that make careful predictions of their employment needs in the future have the opportunity to get ahead of the game through heightened recruitment, optimized retention programs and even enhanced compensation where that's possible. In Nevada, for example, agency directors are notified when someone on their staff is eligible to retire within the next five years. Armed with that information, they can begin to consider the best route to replacing them, says Lee-Ann Easton, administrator of Nevada's Division of Human Resources Management.

In Denver, data analysis of retirement and other turnover has been very helpful for some departments, says David Edinger, chief performance officer for the city and county of Denver. By making the budget case that upcoming vacancies will create high overtime costs, departments have been given permission to hire a replacement before someone leaves. That is, they can hire on the statistical probability that the person will be heading out the door in the near future. "This smooths the curve out so as to avoid drops in service levels and overtime," says Edinger. It's a particularly effective strategy for a service-oriented department such as motor vehicles.

Having a better idea of what future workplace needs are going to be is a great first step. But actually filling those positions is a different matter. As state and local governments have worked to reform their approaches to hiring, some best practices have emerged. Here are 10 recommendations:

Enhance your benefits. With many pension plans struggling to make sure future benefits will be available, there hasn't been much talk about enhancing the income employees will get upon retirement. But softer benefits can be very attractive. Nevada's Easton takes note of a guidance resource program her state offers employees. It's a form of an employee assistance program. People get free counseling, health advice, legal advice and even help with more mundane services. Easton says she can call the assistance office and tell them she's having a party for her 75-year-old mom and needs some ideas. "They will research everything and put a package together," she says. The idea behind it is that it serves the state well to take care of outside challenges that might take an employee away from concentrating on their work.

Loosen civil service requirements. Ranked lists based on testing is fading as a hiring practice, and other inflexible civil service rules are withering away as well. Despite central control of its hiring system, Alabama

recently allowed selected agencies to do their own hiring without any state-prepared list. After the direct appointment tool was provided to the state Alcoholic Beverage Control Board, there was a 25 percent reduction in that agency's overtime costs. "Now it's so much easier for them to hire," says Jackie Graham, director of the Alabama State Personnel Department. "They have a pool of applicants and on short notice they can bring them in."

Kansas is moving even further. Last spring, the legislature gave agencies the authority to hire some people as unclassified—that is, not subject to civil service rules. In agencies that are taking advantage of various aspects of the new law, employees can elect to forgo civil service protection, often in exchange for a potential increase in pay or a change in job duties. As John Milburn, director of legislative and public affairs for the Kansas Department of Administration, says, "That gives them much more flexibility to utilize their human and monetary capital to carry out their mission."

Reexamine minimum qualifications. Minnesota's O'Brien reports that she is looking at the minimum qualifications to make sure that they haven't gotten out of date. For example, some Minnesota jobs had physical requirements that are no longer necessary, such as the requirement that tax auditors be able to lift boxes of documents. That was important back when tax auditors hefted heavy files to take with them in order to do an audit. Now those documents are available online.

Change your own expectations. Rather than fight the trend among young employees to leave after a short time, there's a way to embrace it. Denver's new branding campaign emphasizes the variety in city and county jobs and the idea that working for the city-county exposes people to a variety of different careers.

Grow your own. When there aren't enough qualified applicants available for a particular job category, governments can start out with unqualified men and women and help them learn the necessary skills. Michigan has a "grow your own" approach in the IT area. Normally an applicant would have to have at least a minimum of a bachelor's degree for an IT job. Under Michigan's approach, someone with an associate degree and no experience can be hired in an entry-level professional position. Then, as Matthew Fedorchuk, deputy director of the Michigan Civil Service Commission, explains it, "after two years, they become a fully functioning journey-level professional and if they then finish getting a bachelor's degree they'll move to a higher level."

Recruit online (and not just on your website). "Public-sector HR practitioners consider their own organization's website the most effective tool for recruiting both millennials and military personnel," according to the IPMA-HR's 2014 Talent Management Benchmarking Survey. But Internet tools can go further. The association's Reichenberg reports that he's seeing an increase in the use of social media—recruiters who are on LinkedIn, for instance, and able to go after candidates they spot there. In Denver, recruiters now all have LinkedIn recruiting access.

Another Internet approach that's catching on: posting short videos that showcase what a hard-to-recruit for job would be like. Louisiana's civil service, which uses job preview videos, has one where Shalenia Reed, who works as a residential services specialist at a developmental disability center, describes her typical morning. She also adds: "I know I'm touching their lives. I'm making a difference in their lives. I know they love me. I love them."

Beef up your technology. Not long ago, hiring systems in many states and cities were still fundamentally paper-based. This is precisely the kind of government operation that can be improved dramatically with technology. For example, Minnesota has a new applicant processing tool that will notify people when their application has been received. "Before, they never heard anything, so they felt like [the application] went into a black hole. Now they know where they stand," O'Brien says. Applicants will also be able to see where their application is in the review stage, and they'll receive notification if they don't meet minimum qualifications. The system also asks questions that signal to an applicant that they don't qualify for a job—for instance, it might ask, "Do you have a commercial driver's license?" If the applicant doesn't, they'll immediately know that this is not a job they should apply for.

Get serious about interns. Historically, internships have been loosely run programs aimed primarily at offering young people in universities an opportunity to gather public-sector experience. But a growing number of cities and states are now using internships as training grounds for new employees. Jim Smith, Maine's CIO, has been revamping his intern program so that interns will be chosen as if they were being selected for employment after graduation. "We give them mentors when they come in," he says. "We make sure they have meaningful work." The state has been doing this for about two years and over 70 percent of its interns are now going on to become full-time employees.

In Pennsylvania, college students who have completed their sophomore year can do six-month internships (for example, two summer internships or a six-month stint after graduation). "Based on their work experience, they can move right into an entry-level position," Honchar says.

Focus on military vets. "If there's an area where governments ought to be developing some sort of strategy, it's really there," says Reichenberg of the potential pool of veterans and military personnel as qualified applicants. To tap into that source, Michigan translates how military experience can provide sufficient experience for state jobs.

The question, "Are you a veteran?" is asked on every application. Even if an applicant doesn't strictly meet minimum qualifications, the agency attempts to find a combination of prior military experiences that would indicate the person could do the job. "You might want someone with a bachelor's degree, but if we find a military veteran who has 10 years of that experience in the military, they can probably do the job and should be interviewed," says Fedorchuk. "We're not guaranteeing a job, but we're making sure their qualifications are reviewed."

Change the conversation. Governments offer a valuable opportunity for people who want to make a difference, for those employees who want to make their community a better place to live. But too often, public servants get branded as bureaucratic cogs in the government machine. Hiring can reinforce that impression.

24

States Employ Temporary Workers, but Often Know Little about Them

By Sophie Quinton

Steve Howard, the head of Vermont's state employees union, says that temporary jobs are among the fastest-growing in state government. But Vermont's Human Resources Department wasn't sure.

Many states don't publish records of their short-term and contract hires. Even states that do, like Vermont, have to do a little research to determine how that share of the state workforce may be changing over time and why.

"We probably have that data," said Thomas Cheney, deputy commissioner for the Vermont Department of Human Resources on investigating Howard's claim. He can say that when the state has experienced increases in temporary staffing in recent years, it's been because of an emergency, such as Tropical Storm Irene.

A small but growing body of research suggests that work arrangements other than full-time jobs are more common across the economy, including in government. It's hard to tell, however, how much states contribute to the so-called 1099 economy through their hiring and contracting.

States have long hired short-term workers for seasonal jobs, to fill emergency vacancies, or to serve as outside advisers. Such arrangements allow agencies to staff up during busy periods and give workers more flexibility.

But temporary jobs also can leave workers without benefits such as unemployment or health insurance. And agencies may end up spending more money on outside help than they would if they brought people on full-time. There's no way for states to weigh costs and benefits if they don't track their employees.

From *Stateline*, a project of the Pew Charitable Trusts, April 2016.

A few states, such as Hawaii and Vermont, are taking a closer look at their short-term positions to make sure they're being used appropriately. Georgia's one state that has been prompted by federal health care reform to keep a closer eye on short-term jobs.

"I think at just a strategic level, it makes business sense to really understand what it takes for us to deliver services to the state of Georgia," said Candy Sarvis, the deputy commissioner of human resources administration for the Georgia Department of Administrative Services.

A LACK OF DATA

Positions that are neither permanent nor full-time could employ as many as 40 percent of Americans, according to a 2015 study from the U.S. Government Accountability Office.

Lawrence Katz of Harvard University and Alan Krueger of Princeton University published survey data last month that showed more people are working as freelancers, on an on-call basis, for temporary help agencies or for contract firms across all industries and occupations. In 2005, about 10 percent of jobs fit those definitions. Last year, 16 percent did.

The increase was so significant that it might account for all the job growth over the past decade, the economists said.

Public administration experienced a jump from about 2 percent of workers in temporary arrangements to 10 percent, they found. In education and health service, which include many public sector jobs, 16 percent of jobs now fit their definition of alternative work arrangements.

Across all industries, the arrangement that increased the most was workers hired through contract firms.

It's hard to tell if—or how—state workforces have been shaped by the trend. Many states only keep close track of their core civil servants, who are still overwhelmingly full-time, permanent employees. State agencies track their spending on contracts, not the number of jobs those contracts create.

Colorado, for example, defines as state workers those employees of the executive, judicial and legislative branches, as well as most employees in higher education. But the state's Human Resources Division only oversees full-time and part-time workers in executive branch

agencies. So those workers, who comprise a third of the state's workforce, are the ones included in annual workforce reports.

The state's human resources team doesn't track how many people are employed through personal services contracts, said Michaela Turner, the communications manager who puts the reports together.

A public records request revealed that state agencies, the governor's office and the judicial branch employed about 4,000 temporary workers last year, 100 fewer people than two years before.

Federal health care reform has pushed states to keep better data. Georgia started including nonpermanent employees in its workforce reports in 2013, and started tracking the share of employees that qualified for health insurance in 2014. The Affordable Care Act requires large employers to provide health insurance to workers who log at least 30 hours a week.

"I wanted to get a better handle on how many people were actually working for the state," Sarvis said.

Eighty percent of the state's 71,000 employees worked full time and were eligible for benefits in 2015, a slight decrease from the year before. Sixteen percent were considered short-term hires, not including independent contractors and people employed by temporary staffing firms.

Sarvis' office is planning to more closely manage temporary staffing, too, because the state may have to offer those employees health insurance under some circumstances. "The IRS may consider them our employees instead of the temp staffing agency's employees," she said.

Most Georgia agencies employ a small number of short-term workers, usually 6 percent of their employees. The state's technical colleges are an outlier: about 56 percent of their 13,000 jobs are short-term, including 4,000 adjunct faculty positions.

That's typical. About half of college faculty nationally now work on a part-time basis.

ENSURING TEMPS AREN'T ABUSED

Nonstandard jobs give state agencies hiring flexibility, but positions that fly under the radar can be easily abused.

In 2013, a Massachusetts investigation found some state agencies had held on to temporary workers for years—including, in one case, a temporary employee who worked in accounting for the State Police for over a decade.

Outside workers can also cost taxpayers. Nonpartisan evaluators for the North Carolina Legislature found last year that state agencies were hiring consultants and contractors improperly and paying some of them more than what the state's top executives earn.

In Vermont, one challenge is that the Legislature sets the total number of state jobs. When state agencies need more workers than they've been allocated, they may hire temps instead. There are about 2,000 temporary workers in the state, and Howard says some departments rely too heavily on them.

In its 2014 budget, the Legislature approved a pilot program that allows some agencies to use their existing funding to add full-time positions.

About 175 positions have been created to date, Cheney said. In some cases, state agencies have converted temporary and contract positions to full-time positions. Cheney's office hasn't calculated whether the changes have saved or cost the state money.

"What the position pilot allows us to do is to refocus on ensuring that our programs are achieving the goals that we set out for them, and they're operating within their means," Cheney said. The Legislature is considering extending the pilot.

In Hawaii, a House bill would limit temporary workers to serving two 89-day terms, with certain exceptions.

Converting the state's 300 temporary employees to full-time workers would add $3 million to $4 million a year to the state pension fund, according to the Department of Budget and Finance.

State agencies say that, for various reasons, some jobs are impossible to fill with full-time workers. Georgia's Sarvis said many workers don't want nine-to-five jobs anymore. "We've got several examples in Georgia where we've offered full-time positions to individuals and they've said 'no, thank you,'" she said.

The investigative division at the Hawaii Attorney General's Office relies heavily on retired law enforcement officers hired as temps. "The compensation, benefits and career opportunities for an investigator is not competitive when compared with other law enforcement opportunities in the State," the agency explained in written testimony to the Legislature.

Temporary jobs aren't going anywhere, but federal rules and regulations will push all employers—including states—to devote more attention to the people they hire. The Department of Labor called for employers to make sure they weren't misclassifying employees as independent contractors last year, and is preparing a rule that would extend overtime pay to more white-collar workers.

"Regardless of sort of the nudge that we got from a federal level, I think you'll find that leaders across the state just think that this is the right thing to do anyway," Sarvis said of her office's efforts to track temporary workers.

25

What Does It Take to End a Teacher Shortage?

By Sophie Quinton

K elci Gouge teaches third-graders at a summer reading academy in Oklahoma City. Oklahoma is one of several states grappling with a severe teacher shortage.

Prairie View Elementary School doesn't usually have trouble attracting new teachers. It's one of the more affluent schools in rural Enid, Oklahoma, housed in the district's newest building, which looks out on to wheat fields.

"When I started having trouble hiring teachers—I can only imagine what the other principals are doing," said Prairie View's principal, Clark Koepping.

Schools nationwide are reporting teacher shortages that go beyond the chronic struggle to fill positions at low-income schools and in subjects such as science and special education. Oklahoma, where education funding has been slashed, may be the hardest hit state.

Like many of her counterparts, Republican Gov. Mary Fallin has focused on one solution: giving teachers a raise. Her latest budget proposal finds money for teacher pay increases despite declining revenue and a projected $1.3 billion deficit for fiscal 2017.

In South Dakota this week, the House approved Republican Gov. Dennis Daugaard's plan to raise the state sales tax to fund teacher pay increases. New Mexico's Republican Gov. Susana Martinez has proposed raising entry-level teacher salaries and expanding student loan repayment and scholarships. Washington's Democratic Gov. Jay Inslee has also called for increasing teacher compensation.

From *Stateline*, a project of the Pew Charitable Trusts, February 2016.

Raising teacher pay is a simple policy lever for lawmakers to pull—most states have increased K-12 spending in recent years, including spending on teacher compensation. But there are other things states can do to close the gap, such as establishing residency programs, akin to those for young doctors, to give new teachers more support.

"The solution is to improve the job," said Richard Ingersoll, a professor at the University of Pennsylvania Graduate School of Education. Some approaches, such as raising teacher salaries and reducing class sizes, cost a lot of money. Others, such as giving teachers a bigger role in how classrooms are run, do not.

IS LOW PAY A DRIVING FACTOR?

When this school year started, about 1,000 teaching positions across Oklahoma weren't yet filled. Schools there have canceled courses, crammed more children into classrooms, and hired more teachers on emergency licenses as the shortage has worsened over the past few years.

Enid's hiring problems now go beyond a longtime difficulty finding math, science, foreign language and special education teachers, said Amber Graham Fitzgerald, director of human resources for the school district.

To Shawn Hime, head of the Oklahoma State School Boards Association, the reason is clear: Oklahoma teachers haven't had a pay raise since 2008. Oklahoma teachers new to the profession earn about $31,600 a year, less than they could earn in cities in neighboring states.

Although $31,600 is higher than the average private sector salary for a new college graduate in Oklahoma, after 10 years private sector workers earn 37 percent more than teachers do, according to an analysis commissioned by the School Boards Association and the Oklahoma Business and Education Coalition.

Fallin's budget would spend $178 million to raise every teacher's salary by $3,000. "The education of our students remains my biggest priority in my budget, even in fiscal climates like this," she said in her State of the State address this month.

State legislators have put forward their own proposals for raising teacher pay. Meanwhile, David Boren, president of the University of Oklahoma and a former Democratic governor and U.S. senator, is leading a drive for a ballot initiative that would raise money for schools (including teacher salaries) through a $0.01 sales tax increase.

The ballot initiative could also fund additional pay for highly skilled teachers and science, technology, engineering and math teachers, Boren says.

Many Oklahoma teachers are already eligible for additional compensation, in the form of federal loan forgiveness for working in a designated shortage area. Last year, the Legislature passed bills that allow districts to offer one-time bonus payments to attract rookie teachers.

A BROADER FOCUS ON RECRUITMENT AND RETENTION

Low pay may not be Oklahoma's only problem, however. Teacher shortages involve many factors, including teacher retirements, a growing school-age population, and efforts to reduce class sizes. Educators, advocates and researchers nationwide have different theories about why schools may have trouble recruiting qualified teachers.

Koepping, the elementary school principal, said he thinks there's a supply problem: Fewer young people are getting bachelor's degrees in education. Nationally, college education programs are producing fewer graduates than they used to, and it's not clear why.

But Ingersoll says that focusing on college graduates misses the point. Public schools hire teachers of all ages, including people who enter the profession through an alternate route, such as the Teach for America program. In any case, students will return to education programs once the economy improves and teacher hiring picks up, he said.

"The problem isn't shortages, so much as it is too much turnover," he said. The latest federal survey data shows that 17 percent of new teachers leave the profession in five years or less.

New teachers are more likely to stay in the profession if they're connected with mentors and additional training, Ingersoll said. As of 2012, a majority of states required such a program; Oklahoma suspended its statewide mentoring program in 2010 but reinstated it in 2014.

In California, a Senate bill would put a twist on the idea by giving money to districts, counties and charter school operators to establish a residency program for trainee teachers working toward their teaching credentials.

Lawmakers also are removing regulatory barriers that keep out some qualified teachers. In Oklahoma, a 2015 law made it easier for teachers certified elsewhere to work in the state. Lawmakers are considering a bill that would allow retired teachers to return to the classroom and earn $18,000 a year without losing their retirement benefits.

Lawmakers can also consider scaling back the bureaucratic rules and paperwork that teachers find frustrating once they're in the classroom. The latest federal K-12 education law, which gives states more control over their schools, could provide an opportunity for rethinking requirements placed on teachers, Hime said.

ENID'S PATH FORWARD

Schools and districts can also take steps to address local teacher shortages. Enid matched new teachers with mentors even when the state didn't require it. The high school offers a teaching career training course. A partnership with a local university helps get student teachers into Enid's pre-K classrooms.

But all those efforts are up against years of education funding cuts. Since 2008, Oklahoma has cut per-pupil education funding by 24 percent, the deepest reduction in the country, according to the Center on Budget and Policy Priorities.

The Enid school district anticipates a 15 to 18 percent reduction this year, and eliminated 20 positions last year to get ready. "The crisis that we're facing is so large—it's hard to be prepared for it," Fitzgerald said.

With schools under so much stress, teacher salary increases aren't enough, education advocates say. The ballot initiative in Oklahoma would create a constitutionally protected education fund for schools, higher education, career education and early childhood education. According to organizers, the proposal would raise about $615 million per year.

Further funding cuts aren't inevitable, said Republican state Sen. David Holt. He has proposed raising teacher pay by $10,000 over several years, by eliminating tax breaks and funneling new revenue into education— once the state budget recovers.

Oklahoma lawmakers have to find a way to protect education funding and deal with teacher pay, Holt said. "If we don't figure out this issue this year, even with the budget shortfall, I think Republicans will pay a political price—and deservedly so."

26

Wisconsin Tenure Fight Likely to Spread to Other States

By Karen Herzog/Tribune News Service

With more voices joining the highly charged debate over tenure protections in the University of Wisconsin System, it has become increasingly clear that at least in education circles, what's happening here is perceived as a bellwether for public universities across the country.

And as the national fervor rises, two assumptions are meriting a closer look.

The first assumption is that the proposed changes are drawing concern only from educators who are part of an entrenched liberal elite that exasperates the political leadership in Madison.

Last week, two conservative educators—both University of Wisconsin-Madison professors—echoed much of what many of their liberal-leaning colleagues have been saying for weeks, albeit with a twist.

Changing tenure rules would put their viewpoints at risk, too, Donald Downs and John Sharpless wrote in a Politico piece.

"As far as college campuses go, we're a rare, endangered species: two long-tenured professors who lean right and libertarian," the political science professor and history professor, respectively, wrote. "But we're increasingly worried that in trying to take up another conservative crusade, our governor, Scott Walker, is going to silence the very voices he claims to support."

Without strong tenure protections, they wrote, "professors like us who fight for free speech and liberty—values Walker himself espouses—could be even more at risk of being targeted on college campuses for our beliefs."

Sharpless was a Republican candidate for Congress in a tight race with Democrat Tammy Baldwin in 2000; Downs served on

From *Governing*, July 2015
©Tribune News Service

his campaign strategy and finance committees. Both were leaders of the free speech/academic freedom movement at UW-Madison in the 1990s, when conservative and liberal professors with tenure protection stood together against speech codes that were perceived as censorship.

The second assumption in the national debate is that Wisconsin Gov. Scott Walker—a certain presidential candidate in 2016—is the behind-the-scenes architect of the provisions in the GOP plan put forward by the Legislature's budget-writing Joint Finance Committee on May 29.

It's unclear what role the governor played, if any, in the layoff language that faculty are most upset about. Walker has been noticeably silent on the matter.

Several key Republicans on the Joint Finance Committee have said they want to give the UW System more flexibility to manage personnel—including layoffs—given tight economic times and fast-changing educational demands in which some academic programs may lose their appeal and others need to be ramped up.

Asked whether Walker supports the more permissive layoff language for tenured faculty, and whether he played a role in developing that language in the GOP plan, his spokeswoman Laurel Patrick said in an email: "The specific provision you're referencing was introduced by and approved by members of the budget committee and was not proposed by the governor. Gov. Walker will review the budget in its entirety when it gets to his desk."

Pressed about the governor's position on the layoff language, Patrick would only restate that it "is different from his original budget proposal."

While the intent of tenure is to give scholars freedom to express unpopular opinions and pursue controversial research, critics in the Legislature argue it also has become ironclad job security for some professors to coast through the years to retirement.

The governor's original budget proposal re-imagined the whole structure of the UW System, removing most of the state statute governing the system and creating a more autonomous public authority that would set its own governing policies.

Tenure wasn't explicitly targeted, but the proposal did remove it from the state statute.

That idea fizzled, but in a revised plan now being considered by the GOP, tenure would be removed from state statute and placed under the control of the Board of Regents. Further, layoffs no longer would be a last resort response to a campuswide financial emergency. Tenured faculty instead could be laid off or terminated "when such an action is deemed necessary due to a budget or program decision requiring program discontinuance, curtailment, modification, or redirection." The language is identical to parameters for academic staff layoffs.

The GOP plan does not specify a process for determining when faculty terminations are "deemed necessary" due to a budget or program decision. It also doesn't specify who would be responsible for making such determinations, according to a memo from the nonpartisan Legislative Fiscal Bureau, which advises the Joint Finance Committee and analyzes proposed legislation.

"If the provisions approved by the Joint Finance Committee were to become law, the Board of Regents would have the authority to adopt policies or promulgate rules regarding when and how faculty terminations would be deemed necessary due to a budget or program decision," the memo says.

A regents-appointed task force that includes faculty members already is drafting a new tenure policy, and UW-Madison is working on one, too. Republican Sen. Sheila Harsdorf, who co-sponsored the controversial Joint Finance Committee plan for the UW System, said the layoff provisions have been "very misrepresented" in public discussions.

"The reality is we are not eliminating tenure," she said. "The Board of Regents will establish a tenure policy that will be comparable to other states and other institutions. That would be my expectation."

The senator from River Falls said she understands, however, that "any time you have change, it's difficult and people have fear of what that change is going to entail."

So why did the Republican-led Joint Finance Committee quietly insert layoff provisions for tenured faculty in its biennial budget plan?

"It's important we give our campuses and the UW System the flexibility to make the decisions they face to provide an affordable and competitive education,"

Harsdorf said. "It is about giving them the tools they need in the marketplace."

That's exactly the kind of language that makes tenured faculty so wary—and it's also why what's happening in Wisconsin has caught the attention of the rest of the country, and even an international audience. No other state has broad layoff provisions for tenured faculty in statute, according to national higher education associations, which are rallying support behind UW System faculty.

Words like "flexibility" and phrases like "giving them tools" are the same as what Walker used over and over in explaining Act 10, the legislation that eviscerated the power of public employee unions. And in these hyperpolitical times, educators perceive themselves as under siege, particularly by the political right.

Just a couple of weeks ago, during budget deliberations, a last-minute amendment by GOP Senate leaders in North Carolina docked the University of North Carolina School of Law $3 million. Democrats alleged it was political payback for the school's employment of Gene Nichol, a frequent and outspoken critic of Republican legislative leaders.

Earlier this year, the GOP-appointed UNC Board of Governors ordered the closure of the think tank Nichol used to lead, the privately funded Center on Poverty, Work and Opportunity. Because he has tenure, Nichol is still employed. But one Democratic legislator, blindsided by the law school budget cut, said, "This feels like the Gene Nichol transfer amendment."

UW-Madison Chancellor Rebecca Blank is trying to move the discussion to the bigger picture of what is needed to keep a highly regarded public university system strong.

In an op-ed piece published last week by the *Chronicle of Higher Education*, Blank said two key points in the debate over tenure have been misunderstood.

"First, the University of Wisconsin hasn't abolished tenure," she wrote. The second misunderstanding, she said, is about what tenure is and why it matters.

"Critics dismiss tenure as 'a job for life,'" the chancellor wrote. "Tenure, however, is not about protecting people but rather about protecting open conversation and debate. It is about academic freedom—the ability to research and teach on all topics, without fear of reprisal."

Wisconsin may be the first state, but it won't be the last to take up this issue, Blank predicted in her op-ed piece: "I expect this same debate to play out in other states and on other campuses over time."

Blank said in a statement to the *Milwaukee Journal Sentinel* that her broader concern is "how we can ensure that Wisconsin maintains a world class public research university and the substantial benefits that brings to the state."

A university's reputation rests on the quality of its faculty, "so we're very concerned about anything that makes it harder to recruit and retain top talent," the chancellor said.

©2015 *Milwaukee Journal Sentinel*

VIII

Local Government

In many ways, these are good times for local governments, or at least good times compared to most recent years. The Great Recession hammered local governments and even today many are still dealing with the devastating financial consequences of the worst economic dislocation in five generations. Still, revenues have generally stabilized and the wave of municipal bankruptcies that made headlines over the past years—notably those of Detroit, Michigan, and Stockton, California—seem to be in the past.

That doesn't mean, though, that all is financially rosy for local governments. Many have gone through years and years of painful penny pinching, balancing budget cuts, and increases in taxes and fees. Long term financial stress takes a toll, even though the economic recovery has been more or less in full swing for years.

The general theme of the readings in this chapter is "What next?" Local governments have toughed out through the hard-times. So, now what? Have lessons been learned, are cities better prepared now for an economic downturn, are there things they can do to be more resilient to the slings and arrows of economic misfortune?

The first essay, by Zach Patton, brings back a mixed report from the front lines of local government. Cities like Colorado Springs, Colorado, at least on the surface, look healthy. Colorado Springs is well-known for the anti-tax sentiments of its citizens, and when the city was hitting the financial doldrums, they balked at a proposed property tax hike to help fill the city coffers. The basic message is we'll make do with less rather than increase our taxes. This seems to have worked; taxes didn't increase and citizens just got by with fewer public services and programs. As the economy got going again, the city finances started look rosier. All's well that end's well, right? Well, not quite. The roads and bridges have not been maintained in Colorado Springs, and that lack of investment might have saved money in the short term, but the bill to fill the potholes and crumbling infrastructure is getting bigger.

The second reading is an academic study by Amy Uden that takes an in-depth look at city-county consolidation. Merging city and county governments has made sense to a lot of people over the years, especially in large urban areas. The basic idea is that city-county consolidation will be more efficient, reduce redundancy, and generally make it easier to have coherent governance. Despite these claimed advantages, city-county consolidations are rare. This study looks at the assumptions underlying arguments for consolidations and synthesizes a checklist for thinking about a path to consolidating.

The final essay, by Sophie Quinton, takes a look at the "smart city." An increasing number of municipalities are designating themselves as smart cities, the implication being that they are deploying technology to make public programs and services faster and more efficient. But what does it really mean to be a "smart city"? As Quinton explains, it means different things to different people.

27

The Illusion of Cities' Recovery from the Recession

By Zach Patton

The lights are back on in Colorado Springs.

Five years ago, in the immediate aftermath of the Great Recession, Colorado Springs, Colo., became a poster child for municipal service cuts. Because the majority of its revenue comes from sales taxes, the city was hit hard—and particularly early—by the economic downturn. After its revenue plummeted in 2009, Colorado Springs slashed many core public functions in an effort to make ends meet. One-third of the city's streetlights were turned off to save money. Swimming pools and community centers were shuttered. The city stopped collecting trash from parks and ceased mowing the grassy medians in downtown streets. Buses quit running on nights and weekends; some routes were terminated altogether. City jobs went unfilled, including firefighters, beat cops, drug investigators and other essential positions. The police department auctioned off its three helicopters online. Infrastructure spending fell to zero.

The sweeping cuts gained international attention, including a cover story in this magazine five years ago this month. But it wasn't just the cutbacks that drew focus to Colorado Springs. It was the way citizens responded to them. In November 2009, with the looming service reductions already announced, local voters overwhelmingly turned down a proposed property tax increase. The message from residents was clear: We'd rather suffer the cuts than spend more to avoid them.

From *Governing,* September 2015

111

Thus the already libertarian-leaning city became an extreme experiment in limited government. "People in this city want government sticking to the fundamentals," City Councilmember Sean Paige told *Governing* in 2010. "I think the citizens have made it clear that this is the government people are willing to pay for right now. So let's make it work."

In many ways, that's exactly what happened. The bare-bones budget went mostly to fund fire and police services, along with some money for parks and public works. Citizens and private groups filled in the gaps. Neighborhoods chipped in to pay for their own streetlights. Churches ran some of the community centers that had been slated to close. Volunteers helped out with back-office police functions. Some outsourcing was more formal: A city-owned hospital was sold off to the University of Colorado health system, and the YMCA formally took over the public swimming pools. The city even privatized its entire fleet of vehicles.

By late 2011, things started looking up. Sales taxes began to rebound, and the city restored many of the services that had been cut. The lights came back on, trash pickup resumed, more cops were hired. By the next year, Colorado Springs' reserve funds were at their highest levels ever, a fact that helped the city cope with a couple of devastating floods and wildfires, including the 2012 Waldo Canyon fire that killed two people and destroyed nearly 350 homes in the area. By 2013, the city's revenue was already back to pre-recession levels.

It's easy for Colorado Springs residents today to feel as if the city has fully recovered from the recession. "There's this sense that everything's back to normal," says Daphne Greenwood, an economics professor at the University of Colorado at Colorado Springs. "But just like the rest of the country, we're not really back to where we were."

What's happened in Colorado Springs has played out in municipalities across the country. Revenues are back up and jobs are returning. Many cities, in fact, are thriving. But there are worrisome cracks in the foundation—structural imbalances that go beyond the cyclical churn of the economy. "Compared to 2010, obviously cities are much better off—at least in the short term," says Kim Rueben, a senior fellow at the Urban-Brookings Tax Policy Center who focuses on state and local economies. "But there are still

fundamental problems. Things are getting better, but I wouldn't necessarily say it's all sunshine and roses. This is really just a time for people to catch their breath."

Nationwide there's a lot to be optimistic about when it comes to local government finances. Property values, after bottoming out in 2012 and 2013, have bounced back. The National League of Cities' (NLC) most recent *City Fiscal Conditions* report, published last fall, showed that property tax collection was at 90 percent of pre-recession levels, and NLC economists say they expect to see higher numbers in next month's report. Just in the past year, it seems cities have turned a corner. That 2014 NLC report showed the first positive growth for city revenues in five years, and for the first time since the downturn, a majority of local officials surveyed in the report said they were optimistic about their cities' fiscal health.

There are other positive indicators. Last year, more cities increased the size of their municipal workforce than decreased it, something that hasn't happened since 2008. In fact, this past May marked six consecutive months of job growth for cities—a first in several years. And in the first quarter of 2015, Moody's credit rating upgrades for cities finally outpaced downgrades.

But every silver lining has a cloud. Take the employment numbers. Despite those six months of sustained growth, cities are still about 195,000 jobs below the peak employment levels they saw at the end of 2008.

Or consider the Moody's upgrades. It's an important sign, says Tom Kozlik, an expert on local finances and a municipal strategist with PNC Bank. "On the other hand, it took several years for that to happen, and there are still a number of downgrades happening." Many of those downgrades are occurring because of multiyear fiscal structural imbalances. Lots of municipalities are still dipping into their reserves as a way to balance the budget year to year. "That tells me it's going to be really difficult to turn this trend around," says Kozlik. "If local governments don't really sit down and recognize this new financial reality—budgeting conservatively and managing expenditures—then their credit will deteriorate and they'll continue to face downgrades."

Overall the recovery has been markedly uneven for localities. An NLC report released in late July laid out some of the frustrating inequalities of "an economy defined as much by job gains as by slow productivity growth, suppressed wages and stubborn unemployment." In the report, which surveyed more than 250 municipal officials from across the country, nearly all cities reported a rosier economic picture, with 28 percent reporting a "vast improvement' in their economy and 64 percent citing a "slight improvement." But smaller cities of under 100,000 residents haven't seen the same rates of economic growth that larger cities have, and some of those smaller localities actually reported worsening conditions over the past year. Rising demands in all cities for assistance in areas such as food and housing indicate that not everyone has shared in the strengthening economy. "Even those cities that are emerging as post-recession leaders still have a long way to go in terms of low- and middle-class residents," says Christiana McFarland, co-author of the NLC report. "You see conflicting storylines within the same city."

The recovery has been a mixed bag in Colorado Springs as well. On the one hand, revenues are at 10-year highs. But the city's population has also risen, meaning per-capita revenue and expenditures have actually fallen sharply since 2007. And while police and fire positions have almost inched back up to where they were before the downturn, other departments are still stretched thin. The number of nonemergency civilian positions is down 24 percent today compared to 2008. "Of course we're in a better place now than we were," says Kara Skinner, the city's chief financial officer. "But we're still super, super lean." City departments like parks and public works want to add back some of the staff they've lost, she says, "but the funds are just not there to meet those requests. Realistically that's just a new normal for us."

Drive around Colorado Springs today and there's one thing you can't help but notice: "Potholes," says Greenwood, the economics professor. "It's hard to keep your eye on traffic because of having to dodge all the potholes." Colorado Springs is spread out over 195 square miles, with 5,600 miles of roads, and most of them are in disrepair. Sixty percent of the city's roadways have gone more than a decade without being repaved, and the pothole problem has become severe. The city's roads are "rapidly deteriorating, and we need to deal with it," says Mayor John Suthers, who took office this June. "That's definitely a product of the recession. There's still essentially no money for road improvement or maintenance."

Suthers is backing a slight increase in sales taxes for five years, which would give the city about $50 million a year solely to fix its roads. Residents will vote on the proposal in November. Suthers says he's "incredibly optimistic" that it will pass, despite the strong antitax sentiment in his city. Residents, he says, are keenly aware of the poor state of the city's roadways.

Infrastructure investment is not a problem unique to Colorado Springs, of course. During the recession, one of the first places cities reduced their spending was on the maintenance of roads and bridges and other facilities. Most haven't restored that funding even now. But as the nation's infrastructure continues to deteriorate, localities will have no choice but to spend money to repair it. As early as next year, "growing capital demands will force local governments to significantly increase investment in infrastructure," one Moody's analyst said in a report earlier this year.

"Cities are disinvesting—you're not even maintaining the value of the infrastructure you have," says Michael Pagano, dean of the College of Urban Planning and Public Affairs at the University of Illinois at Chicago and co-author of NLC's *City Fiscal Conditions* report since 1991. "We've postponed repair and maintenance for so long that we've now got to decide what to address, what to abandon and what to sell off." Public-private partnerships are one way to help finance projects, and cities are increasingly utilizing them as an important tool. But many of cities' most pressing infrastructure needs—alleys, sidewalks, school facilities and bridge maintenance—might not be attractive to corporate partners.

If infrastructure is one looming crisis for localities, the other is certainly pensions. While a few cities have initiated some retirement benefit reforms in the past five years—around 20 percent of localities, according to NLC—pensions remain a major fiscal problem for municipalities. Pension burdens increased for 31 of the 50 largest local governments in fiscal 2013, the most recent year for which data is available, according to a recent Moody's report. And in general, required pension contributions are growing faster—in some cases much faster—than local government revenues. As aging public employees retire in the next decade, those pension obligations will continue to gobble up an increasing share of city expenditures, crowding out spending on other services.

The twin crises of infrastructure investment and pension burdens represent deeper structural problems that cities must confront. The good news, says Pagano, is that cities are at least talking about their pension and infrastructure needs. But talk doesn't always translate into appropriate action. "Yes, cities are having serious conversations" about these topics, he says. "But are they adequately addressing the long-term liability issue? That's something we don't have an answer to yet."

The underlying question, in Colorado Springs and elsewhere, is whether cities are any better equipped to handle the next fiscal downturn. If history is any guide, an economic contraction will happen within a few years. Are cities ready? In one aspect, they may be. "If the Great Recession taught cities anything," says Pagano, "it taught them not to believe in overly optimistic forecasts in their pension systems. Maybe that's a good thing."

In Colorado Springs, leaders say they're definitely better prepared. The city's reserves today are $10 million higher than they were in 2007. And Suthers says that if voters pass his tax increase for road repairs, the city will be on even surer footing. "We're in a better place than we were," he says. While Suthers doesn't question the cuts that were made in 2010 because they were "philosophically consistent" with the views of Colorado Springs residents, he acknowledges that they remain an issue. "I'm still dealing with many of the cuts we made five years ago and trying to get back to square one."

For the most part, though, cities continue to face those entrenched, longer-term trends that will make it much harder to weather future fiscal storms. In addition to unmet infrastructure and pension needs, cities are bridled with an increasingly outdated sales tax system that doesn't reflect the shift to a service economy. "I had hoped the Great Recession would cause cities to really examine the adequacy of their fiscal architecture," says Pagano. "But for the most part, that hasn't happened."

Without some sort of action on taxes, infrastructure and pensions, he says, cities won't be able to withstand the next downturn any better than the last. "I'm not sure they're any more prepared for a recession in the next five to seven years than they were in 2008," Pagano says. "The future isn't going to be too much different from the past."

28

A Checklist for Alternatives in City–County Consolidation Decisions: From Separation to Unification

By Amy B. Uden

INTRODUCTION

If commentators are correct, local jurisdictions with "too many" smaller units of government present a problem. They are barriers to a manageable system of local government that inspires citizen trust and creates a strong business climate (Indiana Commission on Local Government Reform 2007). Thinking about local government administration typically links these "fragmented" units of government to public sector inefficiency, administrative excess, and an inward-looking parochialism (Maciag 2012). This thinking rests on two assumptions: (1) local fragmentation leads to negative outcomes for efficient and effective governance and (2) consolidation is the best way to address these negative outcomes.

This article sets out to do four things. First, it explores the two assumptions given above. Second, it looks at cases of city–county consolidation in midsize jurisdictions with an urban–rural mix. Third, based on the "takeaways" from these cases and other agreed-upon findings, it presents a checklist tool to assist practitioners in thinking through the important underlying factors in their jurisdiction. Fourth, it applies an interpretive guide to the checklist to

From *State and Local Government Review,* March 2016

help select among the contingent paths toward jurisdictional unification. In doing so, it is hoped it will assist practitioners in thinking through these issues and also contribute to a literature that typically deals with larger, more urbanized areas.

ANALYTICAL FRAMEWORK

Given the recent economic recession, public administrators have stressed the importance of a regional basis for economic efficiency (Barnes 2010). There is a perceived excess of local government units, which is at odds with an increasingly favorable disposition toward regional unification (Maciag 2012). Accordingly, practitioners' conversations on streamlining local government are often framed in sweeping generalizations about local spending and the number of jurisdictions. Likewise, these conversations admit a perception of consolidation as a panacea for the perceived harms of fragmentation, perhaps because it is easy to understand and intuitively appealing to reformers (Savitch and Vogel 2000b, 162). Nonetheless, it is difficult to quantify either the effects of fragmentation or the need for increased collaboration or consolidation created by it (Maciag 2012). In spite of these ambiguities, however, the scholarly literature points to three chief considerations for efforts in government integration: public sector efficiency (an improved ratio between services received and tax burdens), taxation transparency (clarity for citizens regarding amount and purposes of taxation), and taxation equity (a distribution of the tax burden deemed just across varying groups of citizens).

PUBLIC SECTOR EFFICIENCY

Most authors agree that fragmentation seldom happens through institutional design. Home rule restrictions, tax and expenditure limitations, and similar limitations on local autonomy can lead to increased proliferation of units of government (Bowler and Donovan 2004; Carr 2006; Joyce and Mullins 1991; McCabe 2000). Local officials use new districts as a tool to circumvent state constraints when they run into revenue limitations. Studies lend support to these ideas as motivators for fragmentation (Berry 2008; Bowler and Donovan 2004; Boyne 1992b; Campbell 2004; Dolan 1990; Farmer 2010; Schneider 1986), but with some disagreement about their effects. In addressing effects of fragmentation, Jimenez and Hendrick (2010) link regional integration to increased responsiveness and service efficiency, though others suggest that the opposite effect occurs (Tiebout 1956). Most studies of regional fragmentation take one or the other of these positions (Berry 2008; Boyne 1992a; Campbell 2004). Hendrick, Jimenez, and Lal (2011) conclude that local government fragmentation leads to reduced spending among general purpose units and increased spending among special purpose units.

The effects of these efforts on government efficiency and spending are ambiguous. Complete consolidation and other forms of government and functional integration have been distinguished from each other, but little can be said about their comparative efficiency (Rosenbaum and Henderson 1972). In many cases, expenditures continue to increase after consolidation, in spite of preconsolidation arguments to the contrary (Selden and Campbell 2000).

TAXATION TRANSPARENCY

Alongside the efficiency literature, some scholars focus on features of tax structure as most important to unification efforts. Defenders of local control argue that fragmentation is beneficial, as it increases public choice in arrangements for taxation and service delivery. Tiebout (1956) argues that local government fragmentation is favorable, because multiple units compete to have lower tax rates to attract residents. Campbell (2004), in contrast, sees any taxation advantages in fragmentation as a "fiscal illusion," noting that increased complexity in units of government leads to diminished accountability for raising taxes. Complex integrated structures arguably can result in scenarios where taxpayers have little awareness, or associated control regarding how and why they are taxed. While differing on the benefits, these scholars' arguments focus on transparency as a key value for taxpayers.

TAXATION EQUITY

Likewise, other scholars focus on the degree to which tax burdens are evenly distributed among varying service recipients. Berry (2008) demonstrates how overlap between jurisdictions is detrimental because it leads to "overfishing" of the same tax base, which can disadvantage groups living in the overlapped areas. This is echoed by Farmer (2010) and McCabe (2000) in their studies of special districts that "vertically" overlap within a single region. Consolidation literature highlights areas of tax disparity across racial and cultural groups, as well as situations in which sharing debt burdens proved challenging to these efforts (Leland and Thurmaier 2004). As such, although conclusions about the impact of efforts to more closely integrate jurisdictions are somewhat confusing, there does seem to be agreement that efficiency, transparency, and equity are important considerations, though just how and why is unclear.

CITY–COUNTY CONSOLIDATION CASES

As the foregoing indicates, consolidation is often assumed as the default approach to counter the assumed negative effects of fragmentation. This article will attempt to identify factors that have played an important role in city–county consolidation in midsized jurisdictions with an urban–rural makeup. The analysis is limited to cases of attempts to reduce fragmentation through formal city–county consolidation referenda since 1990 (Murphy 2012): these include both successful and failed consolidation attempts and a range of service alternatives. Table 1 depicts attempts with a city population of 100,000 or greater and a countywide population between 100,000 and 300,000: these resulted in four successful and four unsuccessful consolidations.

CASE BY CASE REVIEW: COMPARING CONSOLIDATION EFFORTS

Following is a brief examination of the case histories of the jurisdictions in Table 28.1. Successful consolidations have been well documented and, where available, this article relies on peer-reviewed secondary case studies, particularly Leland and Thurmaier (2004).

Table 28.1 City-County Consolidation Attempts since 1990, Small-to-Midsized Cities

City—County	Year	City-Only Population (Balance)	County Population	Population Density (City, County; per square mile)	Consolidation Achieved?
Athens—Clarke County, Georgia	1990	115,452	116,714	992 979	Yes
Lafayette—Lafayette Parish, Louisiana	1992	120,623	221,578	2,450 826	Yes
Augusta—Richmond County, Georgia	1995	195,844	200,549	648 618	Yes
Kansas City—Wyandotte County, Kansas	1997	145,786	157,505	1,168 1,039	Yes
Wilmington—New Hanover County, North Carolina	1995	106,476	202,667	2,068 1,058	No
Clarksville—Montgomery County, Tennessee	1996	132,929	172,331	1,362 320	No
Topeka—Shawnee County, Kansas	2005	127,473	177,934	2,119 327	No
Evansville—Vanderburgh County, Indiana	2012	117,429	179,703	2,660 770	No

Sources: Murphy (2012); U.S. Census Bureau (2010).

Unsuccessful consolidation attempts have received less attention in the literature on consolidation, but primary sources helped fill these gaps. Comparing the successful and unsuccessful cases illustrates the recurrence of several important factors in analyzing consolidation prospects: the proposed government structure (the organization and distribution of services and fiscal benefits and burdens anticipated by consolidation efforts), the surrounding demographic context (population density, ethnic, and cultural factors faced by consolidation efforts), the legal context (constitutional, statutory, and legislative framework encountered by consolidation efforts), catalyzing conditions (assumed conditions of government or economics that motivate consolidation efforts), and perceived future opportunities (assumed benefits and other results from consolidation efforts).

SUCCESSFUL CONSOLIDATIONS

Athens–Clarke County, Georgia (1990). Motives for this consolidation included "good government" and service distribution arrangements. It was the product of three prior attempts at consolidation since 1969 (Durning, Gillespie, and Campbell 2004). By 1990, population growth in Clarke County outside of the City of Athens led to considerable demographic change. Throughout the 1980s, the two governmental entities squabbled about service provision in the unincorporated fringe, so the governmental structure in the proposed 1990 consolidation charter addressed high water rates and other fiscal inequities for county residents (Durning, Gillespie, and Campbell 2004). Also, proposed structural changes included both spending limits and an assurance that local government workers would not lose employment under consolidation. The potential for controversy over government structure associated with combining law enforcement organizations was minimal because the elected Clarke County Sheriff had responsibility only for the court system. Clarke County's small geographic size may have contributed to a sense among voters that a single unit of government could provide adequate service.

Lafayette–Lafayette Parish, Louisiana (1992). The Lafayette consolidation was motivated by prior success in professionalizing government, rather than a reaction to concerns about corruption or inefficiency like many efforts (Bacot 2004). Successful reform in the 1970s resulted in the professional manager form of government in both the city and parish, which assisted in the consolidation study and promotion. The local chamber of commerce and newspaper were enlisted to promote the consolidation as well. Demography played a role as in most Southern consolidation efforts with a principal concern of ensuring that minorities were not disadvantaged. To address these issues acceptably under federal restrictions, the proposed structure of the consolidated council districts mirrored existing school board districts. Likewise, to address concerns that the city was "bailing out" the parish, the proposed Lafayette consolidated government assumed control of all special districts in the parish, including assets and liabilities, but Lafayette City debt was to be paid off by only those living within what had been the city's boundaries. Other structural changes such as unified planning were acceptable given the small geographic area of the region and resulting economies of scale.

Augusta–Richmond County, Georgia (1995). After a failed effort in 1988, Augusta's consolidation with Richmond County was motivated predominantly by demographic change. Due to both "white flight" and long-standing African American distrust of local government, Augusta's population was declining (Campbell, Gillespie, and Durning 2004) and Augusta's deepening revenue shortfalls were a strong motive for the consolidation. In the 1988 consolidation attempt, representation concerns were the sticking point for African Americans who largely opposed consolidation. The proposed 1995 charter provided for equitable racial representation and greater limitations on the new entity's chief executive. The successful 1995 consolidation effort had local media support.

Kansas City–Wyandotte County, Kansas (1997). Kansas City–Wyandotte County is one of the few Midwestern cases of consolidation in recent decades. It was motivated by two factors that often typify successful consolidation (Rosenbaum and Henderson 1972): major economic deterioration and lack of confidence in government (Leland 2004). To address the former, the city and county collaborated to create incentives (Moline 2005) to address the future economic opportunity of having a stadium located in the area. This cooperation and the perceived benefits eased consolidation. On the second factor, Wyandotte County lacked a professional government. It had neither a county administrator nor a functioning personnel classification system. Given these circumstances, consolidation was backed by business leaders and the newspaper. The legal context proved important as well with the Kansas legislature playing an active role by setting up the county's Consolidation Commission. Structural and demographic factors were minimal in this case: the consolidation left separate the law enforcement entities of the County Sheriff and City Police, and neither race nor population changes were important contextual factors (Moline 2005).

Unsuccessful Consolidation Attempts

Wilmington and New Hanover County, North Carolina (1995). Wilmington and New Hanover County, North Carolina, have been unsuccessful in four city–county consolidation attempts, evidencing contentment with the status quo (G. A. Johnson 2004). Largely, this is due to a lack of catalyzing conditions, some doubts about restructuring, and the legal context. Concerns about taxation levels in the areas outside the city were the driving force behind the consolidation's failure. Proconsolidation forces in New Hanover County have been concentrated largely within the city of Wilmington, whereas anticonsolidation forces have generally come from the county jurisdictions outside the city. Also, the legal context presented some challenges as North Carolina state statute requires that the city be "abolished" into the county: the vagueness of this mechanism has made consolidation more challenging. Liberal annexation laws in North Carolina played a role as well: Wilmington reduced the potential benefits of consolidation by annexing much of the area that experienced growth and development before 1995 (G. A. Johnson 2004), reducing the need for consolidation.

Clarksville and Montgomery County, Tennessee (1996 attempt). Clarksville and Montgomery County's 1996 referendum represented its second unsuccessful attempt

at consolidation in the last two decades. In this instance, the legal context took center stage. Tennessee state statute requires city–county consolidation referenda to pass not only at large, but in each involved jurisdiction. In the 1996 attempt, residents of the City of Clarksville passed the referendum, but it was unsuccessful in the outlying county mostly due to the structural concerns about local representation (V. Coleman, personal communication, April 23, 2013). Likewise, the proposed roles of the City Police Department and County Sheriff were a factor, and rural residents were concerned about tax increases. Generally, the Clarksville–Montgomery County community remained unengaged in the reorganization debate (Cook 2007).

Topeka and Shawnee County, Kansas (2005). Topeka and Shawnee County's consolidation attempt occurred after the successful Kansas City–Wyandotte County consolidation (Myers 1999) and may have been motivated by it. A Shawnee County consolidation study referendum passed in 2005, and a consolidation study commission released a plan for voter review (Consolidation Commission of Topeka 2005; The *Topeka Capitol-Journal* 2005; Hrenchir 2005). However, the referendum for approving this plan ended in the consolidation failing with 60 percent of the voters opposed (Consolidation Commission of Topeka 2005). Opposition was largely on structural grounds: given the absence of any genuine catalyst, current activity indicates that the incremental and specific changes may be preferable to the jurisdiction's residents rather than full consolidation. Following the unsuccessful referendum, Topeka and Shawnee County have combined limited services, in keeping with a report issued prior to the consolidation attempt (The *Topeka Capitol-Journal* Editorial Board 2004; Hrenchir 2012). This has achieved expanded rural services and reduced urban–rural service differences. There continues to be dialogue about combining law enforcement agencies in the city and county (The *Topeka Capitol-Journal* 2012).

Evansville and Vanderburgh County, Indiana (2012). Voters in the City of Evansville and surrounding Vanderburgh County faced a consolidation referendum in 2012. The referendum was defeated with 67 percent opposed (Vanderburgh County Clerk 2012). In large part, this case demonstrates how perceptions about opportunity can affect the consolidation outcomes. In early 2010, both the city and county legislative bodies adopted resolutions in support of a consolidation plan (City of Evansville 2011). The consolidation debate in the region had a lengthy history (Coures 2011). In the public debate, however, perceptions of expected fiscal impact were somewhat ill-defined (Mattingly 2012). Reduced financial pressures and increased governmental efficiency were touted as benefits of consolidation, along with accountability and transparency, professionalism in elected and appointed officials, and an improved urban–rural cost distribution (City of Evansville 2011). Immediate structural changes were not a factor as most county-wide elected offices were to remain in existence in the plan (City of Evansville 2011). Tax rate changes were to be phased in over three years. The consolidation plan did not address the combined law enforcement (Langhorne 2012), but the result was that the County Sheriff was a consolidation supporter (Mattingly 2012), while the local law enforcement union opposed consolidation (Langhorne 2012). Although elected officials in both units supported the consolidation (Mattingly 2012; Citizens Opposed to Reorganization in Evansville 2012), they met resistance from union members unsure of the economic impact on them. Urban versus rural differences on representation impacted residents' perception of the proposed charter as well.

CASE TAKEAWAYS

The cases presented provide a resource for practitioners in peer comparisons for small to midsized cities. As the cases illustrate, initial success in consolidation has a very low likelihood (Murphy 2012). Each case illustrates to some degree the recurrence and interaction of the several important factors noted above for analyzing the consolidation prospects: *proposed government structure; demographic context; legal context; catalyzing conditions; and perceived future opportunities.*

Proposed Government Structure. The structure and functional relations of the proposed new entities is greatly influential—what is in or what is out can make

or break a consolidation effort. Even in successful consolidation cases, full consolidation is not always achieved. The intentional exception of some municipalities outside of the central city was a condition for success in nearly all the city–county consolidation cases. Likewise, chief executive powers, voter representation provisions, or the inclusion of a single entity, jurisdiction, or function can play a role.

Demographic Context. Of the eight cases above, the consolidation attempts that succeeded had an average difference in population density of just under 450 persons per square mile between the city and county. In contrast, the failed consolidation attempts had an average difference of over 1,430 persons per square mile. Several of the failed consolidation attempts point to urban–rural differences or distinctions in city–county service levels as important contextual components for the "fit" of their consolidation goals. In addition, racial equity served as a motivator for consolidation efforts in some cases. Particularly in the south, racial concerns heavily influenced whether consolidation plans were appropriate to their jurisdictions.

Legal Context. State legal institutions can also play a key role in the context of local consolidation efforts. States legislatures can support consolidation, set referendum thresholds, or create incentives for local governments to combine services, functions, or units of government. State constitutional frameworks are the context in which local governments become more or less fragmented (Stephens 1974; Krane, Rigos, and Hill 2001; L. S. Johnson 2004; Stephens and Wikstrom 2007).

Catalyzing Conditions. A perceived crisis of confidence is often required to catalyze the support for successful consolidation through the referendum process. For example, in Kansas City–Wyandotte County, concerns about patronage generated support for reform. Citizen distaste for perceived mismanagement in both the city and county governments provided a large base of support for reform of both jurisdictions. In cases where the consolidation referenda failed initially, perceptions of worsening crises served to catalyze the support in each following referendum. The progressive image that the city–county consolidation provides for a region incentivizes efforts from reformers, business leaders, and academics (Feiock and Carr 2000; Savitch and Vogel 2000a)—they are strongly rationalizing constituencies with much to gain from reform through consolidation.

Perceived Future Opportunities. One important ingredient in selling consolidation is the perception of future opportunities from reduced fragmentation through consolidated government. Economies of scale in economic development projects, service unification, and grant applications are purported benefits of consolidation (Indiana Commission on Local Government Reform 2007). While the prospect of future economic development opportunities contributes to the success of consolidation campaigns, actual gains provided by proffered opportunities are difficult to measure.

EIGHT FACTOR CHECKLIST: SEPARATION TO UNIFICATION

The checklist below is a tool to assist practitioners in applying these factors to their own jurisdictions and priorities. Although practitioners may have an intuitive sense of what will and will not work in their region, the checklist offers a way to systematically weigh the factors. It can provide practitioners with a way to present items that go beyond the often politically charged rhetoric of "too many units" or "power grabbing" that can occur in the political dialogue.

THE CHECKLIST

Value Section. Items 1–3 below are the potential outcomes of greater unification drawn from the research presented. These items are related to the "values" of a jurisdiction as expressed in the priorities it seeks in reducing separation. The elements, A through E, under each numbered item represent options and benefits associated with that item in the order of their strength of association with unified government. For each set of elements below, please rank the responses from one to five (using each number only once) in order of your greatest priority to least priority for your jurisdiction.

1. Public sector efficiency:

_____ A. Reduced transition costs for policy and service change
_____ B. Reduced inefficiency in service delivery
_____ C. Flexibility in handling services
_____ D. Improved case-by-case cooperation
_____ E. Clear service distinctions provided to taxpayers

2. Taxation transparency:

_____ A. Reduced/eliminated tax overlap
_____ B. Taxation for only those receiving services
_____ C. Minimized number of tax-sharing arrangements
_____ D. Reduced complexity for taxpayers
_____ E. Straightforward marketplace for taxpayers

3. Taxation equity:

_____ A. Complete equality in taxation
_____ B. Redistribution for most needed services
_____ C. Debt paid by those who incurred it
_____ D. Resources stewarded on behalf of taxpayers
_____ E. Taxpayers choose their own tax burden

Fit Section. Items 4–8 below are contextual factors that influence efforts to achieve greater unification drawn from the research presented. These items are related to the fit between a jurisdiction's current situation and the feasibility of a successful effort to reduce separation. The elements under each numbered item, A through E, represent situational elements associated with each factor in order of their strength of association with unified government. For each set of responses below, please rank the responses from one to five (using each number only once) in order of most accurate to least accurate in describing your jurisdiction.

4. Perceived future opportunity:

_____ A. Improved prospects on state and federal grants
_____ B. Progressive image for local government
_____ C. Better project development and planning
_____ D. Coordination on special projects
_____ E. Incentives for the creation and implementation of new policies

(Continued)

(Continued)

5. Proposed government structure:

_____ A. Straightforward solutions are important to local officials

_____ B. Sufficient political capital to get through challenging restructuring

_____ C. Willingness to experiment with new service delivery arrangement

_____ D. Desire for intergovernmental cooperation

_____ E. Preference for competitive and clear choices for taxpayers

6. Legal context:

_____ A. Referendum required for local consolidation

_____ B. Challenging to change local tax rates

_____ C. Low thresholds for local annexation

_____ D. Intergovernmental agreements provide flexibility

_____ E. Referendum campaigns costly

7. Demographic context:

_____ A. Population density similar across jurisdictions

_____ B. Racial equity

_____ C. Low suspicion of local "power grabs"

_____ D. Local boards and commissions work well together

_____ E. Constituents understand the government services they receive

8. Catalyzing conditions:

_____ A. Strong consolidation champions present in community

_____ B. Crisis conditions (e.g., corruption and lack of professionalism)

_____ C. History of racial tensions

_____ D. History of power grab concerns

_____ E. Much of citizen population is highly informed

USING THE CHECKLIST FOR DECIDING ON CONTINGENT PATHS

In addition to providing a way to check off the important goal and situational factors for a jurisdiction, by applying the interpretive guide found below, the checklist can help analyze contingencies for decisions about the best paths to follow to achieve the desired outcomes and address the strengths and weaknesses of jurisdictional situations. The guide helps to fit the factors above with five different contingent paths (unified government, blended systems, shared services, intergovernmental cooperation, and separate governance) that range from partial to full integration of jurisdictions (Savitch and Vogel 2000b; see Table 28.2).

These paths demonstrate the range of options available to local practitioners. The guide scores some of the goals and situational factors of the subject jurisdiction from the checklist tool to fit potential paths for the locality to achieve greater integration. With these possible outcomes in mind, practitioners can use the checklist tool to test which path might be the most desirable and practical fit for their jurisdiction.

Five alternative paths to integration that range in formality and intensity of cooperation are summarized in Table 28.2 (Savitch and Vogel 2000b). The five paths are arranged from most (unified government) to least (separate government) intense. The paths combine different degrees of formal, structural integration with informal, service integration, allowing for a more comprehensive array of alternatives for local governments considering opportunities for integration.

SCORING AND INTERPRETING THE CHECKLIST

For each of the two sections (Value and Fit) of the checklist above, count how many first, second, and third rankings were given to each letter A through E, respectively. Then, multiply the count for each letter's first, second, and third rankings by the value shown below in the associated column on the grid below (by 3 for first rankings, by 2 for second rankings, and by 3 for third rankings). Afterward, transfer the counts for each section to the appropriate letter on the grid in Table 28.3. Finally, total these counts in the appropriate cell under the column total, to the right.

Higher totals indicate a better situational fit with a particular contingent path toward integration (from formal to informal ranging from full consolidation—unified

Table 28.2 Contingent Paths: From Unified to Separate Government

Contingent Path	Overview	Benefits	Challenges
Unified government	Full consolidation, single metro government	Straightforward, distributes benefits equally	Focuses on institutional structures, making unification difficult
Blended system	Tiered partial consolidation with more labor-intensive services in narrower units	Flexible, deals with both structures and services	Can be confusing or result in identity loss
Shared services	Provides some functions on unified basis without combining the structures	Flexible, provides some cost efficiencies	Less progressive image, power grab perception issues
Intergovernmental cooperation	Networked cooperation through overlapping agreements	Allows voluntary cooperation in limited format	Little clear accountability or scope for ongoing cooperation
Separate government	Completely distinct units and services	Presents clear alternatives to taxpayers	May reduce the individual governments' capacities

Source: Savitch and Vogel (2000b); terminology modified.

Table 28.3 Guide for Checklist Interpretation

Response Alpha Order	Number of First Rankings (x 3)	Number of Second Rankings (x 2)	Number of Third Rankings (x 1)	Total	Contingent Paths
Value section: How desirable is this path, given my jurisdiction's priorities?					
A.					Unified government
B.					Blended system
C.					Shared services
D.					Intergovernmental cooperation
E.					Separate government
Fit section: How likely is this path to succeed, given current situational factors of my jurisdiction?					
A.					Unified government
B.					Blended system
C.					Shared services
D.					Intergovernmental cooperation
E.					Separate government

government—to no consolidation—separated government). The first section (Value) of the guide scores the desirability of a path in respect to priorities for consolidation and the second section gives a rough estimate of the likelihood of the political success (Fit) of that path given jurisdictional characteristics.

One potential result is a match or near match between the scores for the contingent paths in each section. In this case, a jurisdiction's circumstances are clear: taking the path indicated can both meet the goals of the jurisdiction and give them a good chance of being achieved. A second potential scoring result, opposed or nearly opposed scores for contingencies in each section, is clear as well, but somewhat more problematic. This scoring result may occur with some frequency because, as noted above, unified government (city–county consolidation) is a kind of default position for reform and improvement in local governments. In this case, the jurisdiction has three options: first, it can decide not to act at all and see whether priorities or situational factors change over time; second, it can attempt to shape public opinion to fit goals; and third, it can try to influence internal priorities to fit the political realities. Either undertaking will take some time, and the latter may wind up emphasizing political reality over operational efficiency. A third potential scoring result is that of a roughly equal distribution of scores for the contingent paths on the grid in one or both sections. In this case, action is inadvisable: the jurisdiction has a multiplicity of priorities, they are unclear, or the situation is politically divided or chaotic. In such a case, at the very least, priorities need to be worked on before any action can be taken.

CONCLUSION

This analysis has developed a practical checklist tool to assist practitioners in considering alternative approaches to local consolidation. The balance between the viability of the alternatives and the desirability of the outcomes of these alternatives needs to be considered for an optimum outcome. Since city–county consolidation efforts rarely succeed and efforts to pass major restructuring referenda are seldom without cost, smaller and midsized regional governments in particular may benefit from something other than the default approach of full consolidation.

The current literature on local governance emphasizes the importance of administrative efficiency and regional governance to combating the challenges in local public administration (Barnes 2010). It also emphasizes cases from high-population regions and most frequently explores full, structural consolidation efforts. A focus on how local governance can utilize degrees of structural or functional change provides local governments of varying sizes with options beyond a simple "yes" or "no" to full consolidation. The checklist developed in this piece above can assist local governments of diverse sizes in reviewing these options. Every tool used to apply theories to local realities has its limits. Future research could benefit from additional review of larger consolidations and from further applications of the checklist. Ultimately, though, looking past the too many units conversation allows local governments to focus on service efficiency. By considering coordination both within and across existing jurisdictional lines, this analysis expands practitioners' tools for addressing alternatives beyond consolidation.

REFERENCES

Bacot, Hunter. 2004. City-parish consolidated government: Lafayette Parish and the City of Lafayette, Louisiana. In *Case studies of city-county consolidation: Reshaping the local government landscape*, ed. Suzanne M. Leland and Kurt Thurmaier, 129–54. Armonk, NY: M. E. Sharpe.

Barnes, William R. 2010. Governing cities in the coming decade: The democratic and regional disconnects. *Public Administration Review* 70: S137–44.

Berry, Christopher. 2008. Piling on: The fiscal effects of jurisdictional overlap. *American Journal of Political Science* 52: 802–20.

Bowler, Shaun, and Todd Donovan. 2004. Evolution in state governance structures: Unintended consequences of state tax and expenditure limitations. *Political Research Quarterly* 59: 189–96.

Boyne, George A. 1992a. Local government structure and performance: Lessons from America. *Public Administration* 70: 333–57.

Boyne, George A. 1992b. Is there a relationship between fragmentation and local government cost? *Urban Affairs Quarterly* 28: 317–22.

Campbell, Rebecca J. 2004. Leviathan and fiscal illusion in local government overlapping jurisdictions. *Public Choice* 120: 301–29.

Campbell, Richard W., William Gillespie, and Dan Durning. 2004. Financial crisis, racial accommodation, and the consolidation of Augusta and Richmond, Georgia. In *Case studies of city-county consolidation: Reshaping the local government landscape*, ed. Suzanne M. Leland and Kurt Thurmaier, 193–222. Armonk, NY: M. E. Sharpe.

Carr, Jered B. 2006. Local government autonomy and state reliance on special district governments: A reassessment. *Political Research Quarterly* 59: 481–92.

Citizens Opposed to Reorganization in Evansville. 2012. Merger defeat oversimplified. CORE2012, November 11. http://www.c or e2012.net/? p¼2786 (accessed April 18, 2013).

City of Evansville-Vanderburgh County, Indiana. 2011. Plan of reorganization. http://www.evansvillegov.org/Modules/ShowDocument.aspx?documentid¼-11499 (accessed April 2, 2013).

Consolidation Commission of Topeka, Kansas and Shawnee County. 2005. Summary of Activities and Events. Consolidation Commission of Topeka, Kansas and Shawnee County.

Cook, Charles. 2007. Friends of Clarksville in 2007. Clarksville Online, January 18. http://www.clarksvilleonline.com/2007/01/18/friends-of-clarksville-in-2007 (accessed April 23, 2013).

Coures, Kelley. 2011. The consolidate debate: A his- tory lesson for the proposed, hotly contested merger of city and county governments. Evansville Living. http://www.evansvilleliving.com/articles/the-consolidate-debate (accessed April 19, 2013).

Dolan, Drew. 1990. Local government fragmentation: Does it drive up the cost of government? *Urban Affairs Quarterly* 26: 28–45.

Durning, Dan, William Gillespie, and Richard W. Campbell. 2004. "The better way": The unification of Athens and Clarke, Georgia. In *Case studies of city-county consolidation: Reshaping the local government landscape*, ed. Suzanne M. Leland and Kurt Thurmaier, 103–28. Armonk, NY: M. E. Sharpe.

Farmer, Jayce L. 2010. Factors influencing special purpose service delivery among counties. *Public Performance & Management Review* 33: 535–54.

Feiock, Richard C., and Jered B. Carr. 2000. Private incentives and academic entrepreneurship: The promotion of city-county consolidation. *Public Administration Quarterly* 24: 223–45.

Feiock, Richard C., Jered B. Carr, and Linda S. Johnson. 2006. Structuring the debate on consolidation: A response to Leland and Thurmaier. *Public Administration Review* 66: 274–78.

Hendrick, Rebecca M., Benedict S. Jimenez, and Kamna Lal. 2011. Does local government fragmentation reduce local spending? *Urban Affairs Review* 47: 467–510.

Hrenchir, T. 2005. Consolidation commission advances city/county merger plan. The *Topeka Capitol-Journal*, November 2. http://cjonline.com/stories/110205/loc_consolidate.shtml (accessed March 16, 2013).

Hrenchir, T. 2012. County OKs management merger. The *Topeka Capitol-Journal*, July 28. http://cjonline.com/news/2012–07–26/management-jobs-reorganized-2-county-departments (accessed March 16, 2013).

Indiana Commission on Local Government Reform. 2007. *Streamlining local government: We've got to stop governing like this*. Bloomington: Center for Urban Policy and the Environment, Indiana University.

Jimenez, Benedict S., and Rebecca Hendrick. 2010. Is government consolidation the answer? *State and Local Government Review* 42: 258–70.

Johnson, Gary Alan. 2004. City-county consolidation for Wilmington and New Hanover, North Carolina. In *Case studies of city-county consolidation: Reshaping the local government landscape*, ed. Suzanne M. Leland and Kurt Thurmaier, 223–37. Armonk, NY: M. E. Sharpe.

Johnson, Linda S. 2004. Tallahassee/Leon consolidation referenda. In *Case studies of city-county consolidation: Reshaping the local government landscape*, ed. Suzanne M. Leland and Kurt Thurmaier, 60–78. Armonk, NY: M. E. Sharpe.

Joyce, Phil G., and Daniel R. Mullins. 1991. The changing fiscal structure of the state and local public sector: The impact of tax and expenditure limitations. *Public Administration Review* 51: 240–53.

Krane, Dale, Platon N. Rigos, and Melvin B. Hill, Jr., eds. 2001. *Home rule in America: A fifty-state handbook*. Washington, DC: Congressional Quarterly Press.

Langhorne, Thomas B. 2012. Law enforcement a key issue in city-county consolidation. *Evansville Courier & Press*, November 5. http://www.courierpress.com/news/2012/nov/05/no-headline—consol-no_cops/ (accessed April 19, 2013).

Leland, Suzanne M. 2004. Reforming politics through reorganization: Consolidation in Wyandotte/Kansas City, Kansas. In *Case studies of city-county consolidation: Reshaping the local government landscape*, ed. Suzanne M. Leland and Kurt Thurmaier, 261–71. Armonk, NY: M. E. Sharpe.

Leland, Suzanne M., and Kurt Thurmaier, eds. 2004. *Case studies of city-county consolidation: Reshaping the local government landscape*. Armonk, NY: M. E. Sharpe.

Leland, Suzanne M., and Kurt Thurmaier. 2005. When efficiency is unbelievable: Normative lessons from 30 years of city-county consolidations. *Public Administration Review* 65: 475–89.

Maciag, Mike. 2012. Which states have most fragmented local governments? Governing: By the numbers, August 20. http://www.governing. com/blogs/by-the-numbers/local-government-consolidation-fragmentation.html (accessed February 1, 2013).

Mattingly, Kara. 2012. Both sides debate on city-county consolidation. 14 News WFIE, October 17. http://www.14news. com/story/19849207/both-sides-debate-on-city-county-consolidation (accessed April 21, 2013).

McCabe, Barbara Coyle. 2000. Special-district formation among the states. *State and Local Government Review* 32: 121–31.

Moline, Matt. 2005. KCK area: Merger led to growth. The *Topeka Capitol-Journal*, May 19. http://cjonline.com/stories/051905/loc_kckmerger.shtml (accessed March 29, 2013).

Murphy, Kathryn. 2012. *Reshaping county government: A look at city-county consolidation*. Washington, DC: National Association of Counties.

Myers, R. 1999. City-county consolidation bill tentatively approved by senate. The *Topeka Capitol- Journal*, February 25. http://cjonline.com/stories/022599/cyb_consolidation bill.shtml (accessed March 16, 2013).

Rosenbaum, Walter, and Thomas Henderson. 1972. Explaining comprehensive governmental consolidation: Toward a preliminary theory. *The Journal of Politics* 43: 428–57.

Savitch, H. V., and Ronald K. Vogel. 2000a. Metropolitan consolidation versus metropolitan governance in Louisville. *State and Local Government Review* 32: 198–212.

Savitch, H. V., and Ronald K. Vogel. 2000b. Introduction: Paths to new regionalism. *State and Local Government Review* 32: 158–68.

Schneider, Mark. 1986. Fragmentation and the growth of local government. *Public Choice* 48: 255–63.

Selden, Sally C., and Richard W. Campbell. 2000. The expenditure impacts of unification in a small Georgia county: A contingency perspective of city-county consolidation. *Public Administration Quarterly* 24: 169–201.

Stephens, G. Ross. 1974. State centralization and the erosion of local autonomy. *Journal of Politics* 36: 44–76.

Stephens, G. Ross, and Nelson Wikstrom. 2007. *American intergovernmental relations: A fragmented federal polity.* Oxford, UK: Oxford University Press.

The *Topeka Capitol-Journal*. 2005. Final consolidation plan unveiled. November 6. http://cjonline.com/stories/110605/loc_consplantext.shtml (accessed March 16, 2013).

The *Topeka Capitol-Journal*. 2012. Poll: Should the police merge with the Sheriff's office? September 2. http://cjonline.com/news/2011–09–02/poll-should-police-merge-sheriffs-office (accessed March 16, 2013).

The *Topeka Capitol-Journal* Editorial Board. 2004. Consolidation—Already begun: The city-county consolidation commission could begin with Ernie Mosher's study. The *Topeka Capitol-Journal*, November 4. http://cjonline .com/stories/110404/ opi_eddy.shtml (accessed March 16, 2013).

Tiebout, Charles. 1956. A pure theory of local expenditures. *Journal of Political Economy* 44: 416–24.

U.S. Census Bureau. 2010. Census state area measurements. http://www.census.gov/geo/www/2010census/statearea_intpt.html (accessed February 3, 2013).

Vanderburgh County Clerk. 2012. Canvass reports: 2012 general election. http://www.evansville.in. gov/index.aspx? page11812 (accessed April 20, 2013).

29

What Is a Smart City?

By Sophie Quinton

On the new streetcars that will start running in Kansas City next week, there's a decal that says "KC is a smart city." As the streetcars clang through the downtown business district on trial runs, pedestrians can watch the sentence slide by.

Along the 2-mile streetcar line, Kansas City is installing video sensors to spot badly parked cars, traffic lights that are programmed to keep traffic flowing and digital kiosks that serve as city guides. All this, the city says, helps makes it smart.

But the truth is that there's no clear definition of a smart city, a label that many cities are grabbing onto by integrating some information technology into some city services.

"The concept of a smart city is somewhat amorphous, but it's focused on cities leading with technological innovation," said Brooks Rainwater of the National League of Cities.

"It's just using digital technology to improve community life," said Jesse Berst of the Smart Cities Council.

"It's a paradigm shift in the way we think," said Kate Garman, the innovation analyst for Kansas City.

Some smart city advocates emphasize efforts to engage and connect with residents, others emphasize infrastructure. But the general goal—something no city has yet achieved is to collect immediate data on everything from traffic patterns to home water use, analyze it, and use that information to make the city work better.

"We have some cities moving in that direction, but a lot more doing little one-offs, really," said Stephen Goldsmith of the Harvard

From *Stateline*, a project of the Pew Charitable Trusts, April 2016.

127

Kennedy School of Government, a former mayor of Indianapolis and former deputy mayor of New York.

Advocates say smart city technology will save cities money and energy, while better connecting cities and citizens. The White House announced $160 million in spending to research and develop smart city technology. British government researchers estimated in 2013 that the global market for such technology would reach $408 billion by the end of the decade.

But as cities like Kansas City are finding, being smart doesn't just mean installing new gadgets. It really means changing the way city agencies operate and learning to balance that against security and privacy concerns.

KANSAS CITY'S SMART CORRIDOR

Kansas City has already installed two digital kiosks, the first of 25, near the streetcar line. "They're in beta testing, so they might not work," Garman warned recently as she approached a 7-foot unit on the wide and empty sidewalk.

She touched the icons on the kiosk's touch screen—it worked. They opened to offer information about local news, attractions and public transit. A related smartphone app will push restaurant deals and other promotions to users.

A few blocks away, sensors wired on top of energy-saving LED streetlights will alert the city to cars parked in the streetcar's path and brighten lights automatically when more than six people pass by.

Modems clamped to lampposts will provide free wireless internet. Updated traffic lights will use advanced computing to keep vehicles moving to avoid congestion.

The features along the streetcar line aren't revolutionary. The kiosks mostly serve as a high-tech visitor's guide. In a metropolitan area that sprawls across two states, a few miles of programmable lights and Wi-Fi seem very small.

But Kansas City's latest smart city efforts, to be launched along with the streetcars, could grow into something bigger. "What you see now is technically called phase one. What phase two is, we still don't know," said Garman, a part-time law student and half of the city's two-person innovation staff.

Kansas City will truly become a smart city when it starts using all this technology to find problems and fix them, she said.

The streetcar corridor isn't the city's first investment. In 2010, the state-run police department bought scanners that automatically collect license plate data from passing cars. In 2011, the local electric utility finished installing over 14,000 smart meters in homes and businesses. And in 2012, Google installed internet cables with speeds up to 1 gigabit here.

Kansas City is a finalist for the U.S. Department of Transportation's $40 million Smart City Challenge, which will fund investments in driverless cars, connected vehicles and sensors. If it wins, the city will develop a self-driving shuttle from the international airport to downtown and expand the kiosks and sensors to other parts of the city, among other initiatives.

As part of its streetcar corridor, Kansas City has also issued an open invitation to entrepreneurs who are developing technologies that could improve city services. A few cybersecurity companies and a drone company are already interested in testing their products here, according to Herb Sih of Think Big Partners, a startup accelerator.

Drones, for example, could help the city save money on searching for an elderly person with a mental disability who goes missing, Sih said. He described a California company that's developing drones that connect to wristbands; when an alert is issued, a drone can find and hover over the missing person.

THE CITY AS A CUSTOMER

Getting city bureaucracies to think creatively, using data, is the biggest obstacle aspiring smart cities face, Goldsmith said. "Government is highly mechanistic in how it's organized."

To aid with the transition, the Kansas City Council last year established a chief data officer position and designated contacts in charge of data in every branch of city government.

Like most cities, Kansas City will rely on outside contractors to build its smart city infrastructure. It has had to figure out how to vet vendors—who, in some cases, are hawking technology that seems straight out of science fiction—and think carefully about security and privacy.

"We get approached by vendors constantly," Garman said. "There's so much out there, it's crazy."

Kansas City didn't plan to add sensors, kiosks and Wi-Fi along its streetcar line until it was approached by Cisco Systems Inc., a multinational technology company looking for a city to debut its smart cities software.

Cisco and Think Big Partners researched city agencies to find areas where technology could improve services. The companies and the city agreed on the streetcar corridor as a starting point. Cisco helped identify subcontractors who had the kind of technology the city wanted.

The result is a patchwork of technologies run by corporate partners: a Wi-Fi network run by Sprint Corp., video sensors run by Sensity (a lighting technology company), kiosks run by Smart City Media (a company that makes interactive signs for cities), and—as part of a separate contract—traffic lights run by Rhythm Engineering (a traffic management company).

Cisco made sure Kansas City installed the newest and best technology, Garman said. All told, the city has only had to allocate $3.7 million toward the projected $15.7 million cost of the 10-year partnership, and will share with Smart City Media some of the money raised by advertising on the kiosks.

Not all cities are becoming partners with big corporations. Boston's innovation office is a little more leery of buying software from them. Often, software engineers at such companies don't know what problems cities actually face, said Nigel Jacob, co-chair for the Boston mayor's Office of New Urban Mechanics.

Jacob's team has worked on research projects for the city since the office was set up in 2010. In the process, it has learned that new technology doesn't fix every problem.

For example, almost half of requests for city services now come through an app Jacob's team built. But the app hasn't engaged new groups of people. Homeowners, the group most likely to call in a problem, are also the most likely to use the app.

SMART CITY OR SURVEILLANCE CITY?

As cities add more sensors, analyze more data, and use advanced computer programming to run traffic lights and even vehicles, they're increasingly confronting new ethical, legal and policy questions.

Smart city technology exposes infrastructure and potentially personal data to computer malfunctions and hackings. The more data cities collect, the easier it'll be to aggregate a detailed picture of an individual's life.

What smart city advocates call data collection their critics call surveillance.

"From an ideal privacy perspective, much of this technology is a bad idea," said Jeffrey Mittman, head of the American Civil Liberties Union of Missouri. But technologies such as license plate scanners and drones exist, and are being used. So the question becomes how to manage the data collected, he said.

Kansas City has tried to address privacy concerns in a few ways. In April 2015, the City Council passed a resolution that laid out a number of basic data privacy principles, including a promise to consider public well-being before collecting, using and disclosing personal information.

Kansas City contractually owns all the data collected by Cisco, Sensity and Smart City Media, such as the most popular time of day for accessing a certain kiosk in a certain location. The companies can't sell or use the data without permission. The kiosks will be able to use the interactions between users and devices to sell advertising. That's how they'll raise revenue.

Sprint owns the Wi-Fi data, and will follow the usual industry practice of having users click yes on a user agreement.

The city is choosing to collect less data than it could, Garman said. Her office will receive only bulk data, although cameras in the kiosks and lights will record video footage. The city will only request that footage in an emergency, such as a terrorist attack. Because it won't have the footage, it won't have to release it in response to a public information request.

Garman said that some potential uses of the light sensors will require users to opt in—for example, to get a text message alert when their car is parked in the streetcar's path.

Although Kansas City's innovation office holds periodic events to educate the public about its projects, Mittman thinks the city should do more. "The average Kansas Citian likely doesn't know how they're being tracked," he said.

Chances are, the average Kansas Citian is already being tracked by private companies. Think of how Google saves everyone's search history, or how retailers can now use video cameras to track customers through the store or use Bluetooth beacons to send customers promotions.

"This is the future, and as a city government we need to be responsive to our citizens' expectations," Bennett said. "And as we move toward the 22nd century we need to be a data-driven organization, we need to be connected."

IX

Budgets and Taxes

Fiscally speaking, it has been a horrible decade for state and local governments. The Great Recession put the economy into freefall in 2008 and the associated job losses, plunging property values, and belt tightening by consumers scythed into income, property, and sales taxes, the three main revenue streams of sub-national governments. In the ten years since, there has been a string of municipal bankruptcies and budget cuts and freezes at all levels.

True, the financial picture looks much rosier now than it did in the depths of recession. The contemporary state of government budgets, though, is a long way from stable and settled. The recession may have ended, but conflict on how to deal with its aftermath is still very much at the heart of often bruising political battles over state finances.

This mixed story—the bottom line is slowly healing while partisan conflict opens new financial wounds—is the theme underpinning the readings selected for this chapter. The first two readings are basically examinations of state ledgers, and the news there is, if not great, then certainly not bad. The second two readings are examinations of the budget battles at the center of a good deal of partisan friction in the states. These are less about the economic bottom line than ideological red lines.

The first reading is an overview of the fiscal health of the states by the National Association of State Budget Officers (NASBO). In this report, NASBO documents moderate but steady improvement in state finances. More than forty states are planning on increasing expenditures, and fewer states are reporting the need to cut budgets.

Embedded in this report, however, is also a hint of the political battles brewing over state budgets. Some states are increasing taxes and fees to generate revenue, other states are cutting taxes and fees in hopes of economic stimulation.

The second reading is an analysis by the Pew Charitable Trusts that reports that tax revenues in a majority of states have finally bounced back to their pre-recession levels. True, that majority was not huge—only 29 states notched this milestone—but it is nonetheless an important benchmark that points toward a broad economic recovery and increasing health in state budgets.

The third essay, by Liz Farmer, focuses less on bottom line numbers and more on the underlying specifics. As Farmer details, there has been a fundamental shift in revenue streams for state governments. Leading the way is a shift away from relying on corporate income taxes. Adjusted for inflation, for example, corporate tax collections in Michigan have fallen by nearly three-quarters in less than a decade. This is not simply a side effect of tough economic times, but of deliberate policy decisions made by state government.

The final reading, by Charles Chieppo, reports on Kansas's decision to hire a consulting firm to perform a comprehensive review of the state budget with the explicit aim of trying to find efficiencies. The report finds that accounting and purchasing practices could be altered to save Kansas taxpayers millions. This effort is being driven mainly by a budget crisis precipitated by an aggressive tax cutting agenda advanced by Kansas Gov. Sam Brownback. After adopting these tax cuts, revenues in Kansas plummeted and forced the state into a series of painful budget cuts. Given what the consulting firm is finding in the budget, Chieppo suggests, states would be well advised not to await on a budget crisis to start searching for hidden budget efficiencies.

30 Summary: Fall 2015 Fiscal Survey of States

OVERVIEW: MODERATE BUDGET GROWTH CONTINUES FOR STATES IN FISCAL 2016

State budgets continue to grow at a moderate pace after several years of slow recovery in the national economy following the Great Recession. According to states' enacted budgets, general fund spending is projected to grow 4.1 percent in fiscal 2016. This growth rate falls below the historical average, though the current inflation rate remains low as well. Forty-three states enacted spending increases in fiscal 2016 compared to fiscal 2015 levels, helping to bolster core services such as K-12 education and health care. At the same time, progress is slow for a number of states and structural issues remain. States vary in their fiscal health due to a combination of economic, demographic and policy factors. Long-term spending pressures in areas such as health care, education, infrastructure, and pensions continue to pose challenges for many states that will require difficult budgetary decisions. General fund revenue growth was solid in fiscal 2015, helping to strengthen states' ending balances and bringing total balance levels to an all-time high in actual dollars, though not as a percentage of expenditures. However, revenues are expected to grow more modestly and total balances are projected to decline in fiscal 2016.

STATE GENERAL FUND SPENDING EXPECTED TO INCREASE 4.1 PERCENT IN FISCAL 2016

In fiscal 2016, general fund expenditures are projected to increase by 4.1 percent, a slower rate of growth than the estimated

From the National Association of State Budget Officers, December 2015

133

4.6 percent increase in fiscal 2015. Enacted budgets show general fund spending increasing to $790.3 billion in fiscal 2016, compared to $759.4 billion in fiscal 2015. General fund spending in fiscal 2014 reached $725.7 billion, a 4.5 percent increase over general fund spending in fiscal 2013.

Enacted budgets in 43 states call for higher general fund spending levels in fiscal 2016 compared to fiscal 2015. However, new spending is expected to be limited, with few additional budget dollars available to address competing spending demands. A majority of states (30) enacted budgets with modest positive spending growth of less than five percent in fiscal 2016, while 13 states project growth of five percent or more. Among the remaining states, four enacted budgets that decrease spending in fiscal 2016, one enacted a budget with no net change in spending, and two states have yet to finalize their budgets for fiscal 2016.[1]

Despite five consecutive years of budget growth and the low inflation environment, state general fund spending for fiscal 2015 for the 50 states combined remains below the fiscal 2008 pre-recession peak, after accounting for inflation. Aggregate spending levels would need to be at $789 billion, or 3.9 percent higher than the $759.4 billion estimated for fiscal 2015, to be equivalent with real 2008 spending levels.[2]

STATE BUDGETS DIRECT MOST ADDITIONAL SPENDING TO K-12 EDUCATION AND MEDICAID IN FISCAL 2016

Once again, state budgets in fiscal 2016 directed most additional dollars to boost funding for K-12 education and Medicaid, the two largest areas of state general fund expenditures. Forty-one states enacted spending increases for K-12 education and 31 states enacted increases for Medicaid, for net increases of $14.7 billion and $9.2 billion, respectively. K-12 education and Medicaid together comprise a majority of state general fund spending, according to NASBO's State Expenditure Report.

Spending increases were enacted for all other areas of the budget in fiscal 2016, with the exception of transportation. However, since most states primarily rely on other fund sources to finance transportation spending, general fund spending adjustments are not necessarily indicative of overall enacted state spending changes for transportation in fiscal 2016.

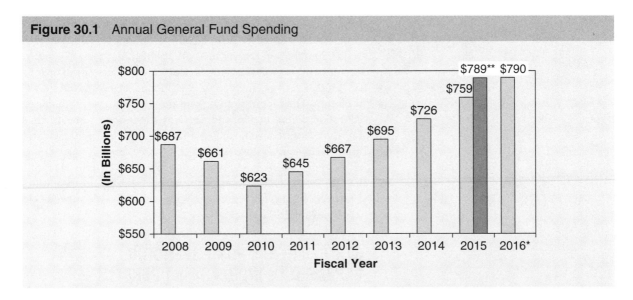

Figure 30.1 Annual General Fund Spending

* Fiscal 2016 spending is based on states' enacted budgets.

** Aggregate spending levels would need to total $789 billion in fiscal 2015 to be equivalent with real 2008 spending levels.

Figure 30.2 Enacted Budget Adjustments, Fiscal 20116

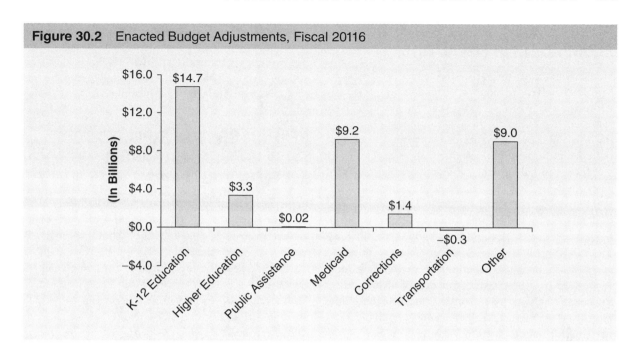

Figure 30.3 General Fund Expenditures by Function

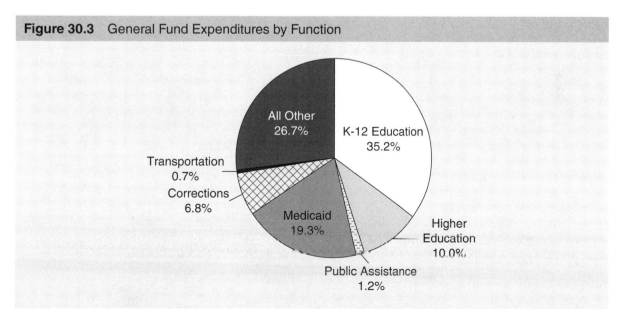

Source: NASBO State Expenditure Report

STATES MADE MINIMAL MID-YEAR BUDGET CUTS IN FISCAL 2015

State budget gaps that arise during the fiscal year are primarily solved through a reduction in previously appropriated spending. Mid-year budget cuts have subsided compared to the years immediately following the recession, when states had to make substantial cuts and take other actions, such as expend rainy day funds, to balance their budgets. Similar to recent years, mid-year budget reduction amounts were minimal in fiscal 2015, with 14 states making net mid-year budget cuts totaling $999 million. While the number of states with net mid-year budget cuts in fiscal 2015 is a bit higher than has been observed in recent years, most of these reductions were relatively small in value. Also, these reductions do not always reflect fiscal stress or even true spending cuts, but sometimes are the result of technical or accounting changes. At the time of data collection, only two states reported making net mid-year budget reductions so far in fiscal 2016 totaling $63 million. However, since the fiscal year was just underway when data were collected, the number of mid-year budget reductions is likely to increase as the year progresses. In sharp contrast

to fiscal 2009, 2010 and 2011, states have enacted minimal mid-year cuts over the last several fiscal years, indicating that states' fiscal situations have stabilized, and budgets are successfully adapting to the current economic and budgetary environment.

REVENUE GROWTH EXPECTED TO SLOW IN FISCAL 2016 AFTER ACCELERATING IN FISCAL 2015

Aggregate general fund revenues are projected to modestly grow in fiscal 2016, marking a sixth consecutive annual increase. Enacted budgets show revenue collections are projected to increase by 2.5 percent in fiscal 2016—a significantly slower growth rate than the estimated 4.8 percent gain in fiscal 2015. The general fund revenue growth rate in fiscal 2015 can be partially attributed to the strong stock market performance in calendar year 2014, which helped to bolster income tax collections; personal income tax collections increased 8.0 percent in fiscal 2015.

Most states are expecting more modest revenue growth in fiscal 2016, with 28 states projecting positive growth below five percent. Nine states enacted

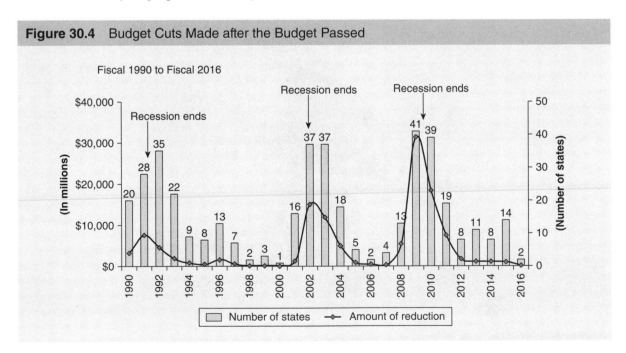

Figure 30.4 Budget Cuts Made after the Budget Passed

fiscal 2016 budgets with general fund revenues growing more than five percent, while 11 states project negative revenue growth this fiscal year. Overall, most states show signs of returning to more stable, steadier revenue growth, though certain energy-producing states are seeing some negative impact on their revenues and economies from the recent decline in oil prices.

Enacted budgets project total general fund tax revenues of $784.7 billion in fiscal 2016, compared to the estimated $765.4 billion collected in fiscal 2015. Despite five years of consecutive growth, aggregate revenues are still 2.0 percent below fiscal 2008 levels after accounting for inflation. Fiscal 2015 revenues would have needed to reach $781 billion, rather than the estimated $765.4 billion, to be equivalent with inflation adjusted 2008 levels.[3]

Personal income tax collections are expected to grow 3.3 percent in fiscal 2016, while sales tax collections are projected to increase by 3.9 percent and corporate income tax collections are projected to decline slightly by 0.5 percent. At the time of data collection, 16 states reported fiscal 2016 general fund revenue collections from all sources to date coming in higher than projections used to enact the budget,

20 states reported that collections are on target, and six states reported collections coming in below budget estimates.[4]

STATES ENACT A MIX OF TAX INCREASES AND DECREASES IN FISCAL 2016

Twenty-two states enacted net tax and fee increases in fiscal 2016, while 18 states passed net decreases in fiscal 2016, resulting in an aggregate net increase of $545 million. States with the largest increases in taxes and fees in fiscal 2016 include Connecticut and Louisiana, both of which modified certain provisions and reduced tax breaks across a number of revenue categories, Georgia, which increased taxes and fees to fund transportation projects, and Nevada, which enacted various tax increases to enhance funding for K-12 education. Texas enacted the largest tax decrease with its property tax relief and reduction in the business franchise tax rate (which both fall under the "other taxes" category), followed by Ohio's personal income tax cuts. Tax changes on sales, corporate income, cigarette and tobacco products, and motor fuel all contributed to the net increase in taxes and fees. Meanwhile, states enacted a significant net decrease in personal income

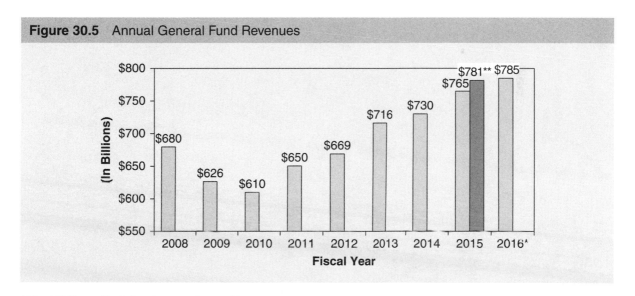

Figure 30.5 Annual General Fund Revenues

* Fiscal 2016 spending is based on states' enacted budgets.

** Aggregate spending levels would need to total $789 billion in fiscal 2015 to be equivalent with real 2008 spending levels.

Summary of Enacted State Revenue Changes for Fiscal 2016

Revenue Type	# of States Enacting Increases	# of States Enacting Decreases	Net Change ($ in Millions)
Sales Tax	9	7	+$494
Personal Income Tax	9	15	−$1,264
Corporate Income Tax	4	10	+$576
Cigarette/ Tobacco Tax	8	0	+$535
Motor Fuel Tax	8	1	+$472
Alcohol Tax	1	3	−$9.3
Other Tax	11	5	−$239
Fees	13	3	−$19

taxes, as well as very small net decreases in fees and alcohol taxes. A number of states also enacted a mix of increases and decreases in the other taxes category. In addition, states enacted $351 million in new revenue measures in fiscal 2016.

TOTAL BALANCES EXPECTED TO DECLINE IN FISCAL 2016 AFTER REACHING ALL-TIME HIGH IN ACTUAL DOLLARS IN FISCAL 2015

Total balances include both ending balances and the amounts in states' budget stabilization funds (rainy day funds). Total balances reached a recent low in fiscal 2010 due to the severe decline in revenues and rise in expenditure demands tied to the recession. Since that time, states have made significant progress rebuilding budget reserves. In fiscal 2015, total balances amounted to $73.3 billion, representing an all-time high in actual dollars and 9.6 percent of general fund expenditures. Total balances are projected to decrease in fiscal 2016 to $61.0 billion or 8.8 percent of expenditures, resulting from an anticipated decline in ending balances. However, rainy day funds or

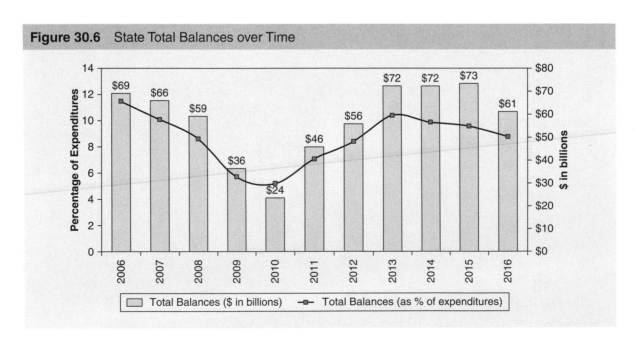

Figure 30.6 State Total Balances over Time

budget stabilization funds, which tend to fluctuate less year-to-year than ending balances, are projected to increase to $43.5 billion in fiscal 2016.[5]

CONCLUSION: MODEST GROWTH TO CONTINUE IN FISCAL 2016 BUT CHALLENGES REMAIN

Enacted budgets for fiscal 2016 represent a sixth consecutive year of spending and revenue growth for states. Most states continue on a path of steady, modest budget increases, though some states face significant fiscal challenges that will need to be addressed going forward. Spending pressures on K-12 education, health care, pensions and other critical areas continue to increase, while state revenue growth is expected to remain limited. Overall, state fiscal conditions continue to be stable, but fiscal 2016 budgets remain cautious as they plan for modest revenue growth and seek structural balance.

NOTES

1. Illinois and Pennsylvania have not yet enacted operating budgets for fiscal 2016. In order to allow for year-over-year comparisons of aggregate state spending and revenue data, fiscal 2016 general fund 50-state totals in this report include the general fund amounts for Illinois and Pennsylvania reported in NASBO's Spring 2015 Fiscal Survey of States, which were based on governors' recommended budgets for fiscal 2016. These amounts are being used as placeholders in this report; NASBO plans to update this report with final enacted fiscal 2016 amounts for both Illinois and Pennsylvania once these states enact budgets.

2. The state and local government implicit price deflator cited by the Bureau of Economic Analysis National Income and Product Account Tables, Table 3.9.4, Line 33 (last updated on October 29, 2015), is used for inflation adjustments. Quarterly averages are used to calculate fiscal year inflation rates.

3. See Bureau of Economic Analysis National Income and Product Account Tables, Table 3.9.4, Line 33 in April 2015, which provides state and local government implicit price deflator. The fiscal 2015 inflation rate is determined based on the average of first three quarters.

4. Not all states were able to compare actual collections to-date to original projections at the time of data collection.

5. Fiscal 2016 figures for total balances and rainy day fund balances exclude Georgia, Oklahoma, and Wisconsin, due to complete balance data being unavailable for these states, as well as Illinois and Pennsylvania, which had not yet enacted budgets for fiscal 2016 as this report went to print.

31

For First Time, Tax Revenue Has Recovered in Majority of States

By the Pew Charitable Trusts

State tax revenue has passed a milestone on the road to recovery. Adjusted for inflation, tax receipts in 29 states had bounced back by the second quarter of 2015 from drops during the Great Recession. This is the first time recovery has widened to a majority of states.

Nationally, total state tax revenue recovered more than two years ago from its plunge in the Great Recession. In mid-2015, states collectively took in 5.6 percent more tax revenue than they did at the 50-state peak in the third quarter of 2008, after accounting for inflation and seasonal fluctuations.

But the total masks how widely recovery has varied across the states. In five of the 29 states in which tax revenue had recovered by the second quarter of 2015, receipts were more than 15 percent higher than at their inflation-adjusted peak before or during the recession. Conversely, collections in three of the 21 states with below-peak tax revenue were down 15 percent or more, after adjusting for inflation.

State results vary dramatically because of differences in economic conditions as well as tax policy choices since the recession. Among states in which tax revenue has recovered, some such as California and Minnesota raised taxes after the recession, contributing to gains spurred by economic growth. Not all states with tax increases have regained their prior revenue peaks. Among states in which receipts remain below their previous peaks, some such as Kansas and Ohio chose to cut taxes since the recession.

STATE HIGHLIGHTS

A comparison of each state's tax receipts in the second quarter of 2015 with its peak quarter of revenue before the end of the

From *States' Fiscal Health*, a project of the Pew Charitable Trusts, December 2015.

Figure 31.1 Real Tax Revenue in 29 States Has Recovered from Recession

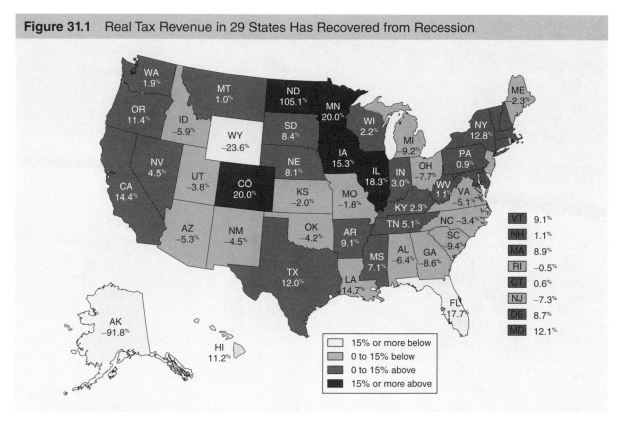

Source: Pew analysis is based on the U.S. Census Bureau's quarterly tax revenue data, as adjusted by the Nelson A. Rockefeller Institute of Government. © 2015 The Pew Charitable Trusts

recession, averaged across four quarters and adjusted for inflation, shows:

- For the first time, Montana (1.0 percent), New Hampshire (1.1 percent), and Pennsylvania (0.9 percent) moved onto the list of states in which tax revenue has recovered. Three other states returned to the list after falling off in previous quarters: Connecticut (0.6 percent), Indiana (3.0 percent), and Wisconsin (2.2 percent).

- North Dakota, buoyed by an oil boom, continued to outpace all states, with tax receipts 105.1 percent above their highest point during the recession, although revenue has slipped over the past two quarters as crude prices have fallen.

- The next largest rebounds were in Minnesota (20.0 percent), Colorado (20.0 percent), Illinois (18.3 percent), and Iowa (15.3 percent). Illinois' level has edged down since the January 2015 expiration of a temporary income tax increase.

- Alaska was furthest from its peak, down 91.8 percent. This was its lowest point since a short-lived windfall in 2008, when a new state oil tax coincided with record-high crude prices. As oil production has waned, the state has seen revenue decline for the past 10 quarters, even before a steep drop in worldwide crude prices.

- Also down more than 15 percent from their prior peaks were Wyoming (−23.6 percent) and Florida (−17.7 percent).

- Amid falling oil prices, six of the top 10 oil-producing states registered a decline from last quarter's tax revenue levels: Alaska, New Mexico, North Dakota, Oklahoma, Texas, and

Wyoming. Two other states also saw declines from last quarter: Illinois and Michigan.

- Two states with receipts well above peak—Colorado (20.0 percent) and Oregon (11.4 percent)—may not keep all of the tax revenue they collected in fiscal year 2015. Both have constitutional caps on tax revenue growth that can trigger refunds to taxpayers.

TRENDS

The increasing number of states to regain their tax revenue levels shows that the effects of the Great Recession are receding—but slowly. As recently as last quarter, the tax collections of just 23 states were back to prior peak levels. By this time after the 2001 recession, which was shorter and less severe, tax collections had rebounded in all but one state—Michigan.

North Dakota in 2010 was the first state to surpass its recession-era peak, followed by Vermont, Arkansas, and New York by mid-2011. Tax receipts were above peak in nine states at the end of calendar year 2011; 16 states at the end of 2012; 23 states at the end of 2013; and 21 states at the end of 2014.

Combined, the 50 states now have the equivalent of about 6 cents more in purchasing power for every $1 they collected at their 2008 peak. For most states, current tax revenue levels are providing less or only a little extra purchasing power than they had more than six years ago, even as they face pressure to catch up on deferred spending or meet new needs for schools, safety-net programs, corrections, employee salaries and pensions, and road maintenance and construction. Since the end of the recession, for example, state populations have grown by more than 12 million people and millions more have enrolled in the state and federally financed Medicaid health care program.

REVENUE OUTLOOK

Looking ahead, state tax revenue is expected to continue growing, though at a slower pace. Low oil prices and stock market volatility could impinge on growth in certain states. Preliminary figures show a "significant softening" in growth rates for the third quarter of 2015 compared with the first half of 2015, particularly in corporate and personal income tax receipts, according to the Nelson A. Rockefeller Institute of Government. States have also forecast slower growth in sales and personal income taxes this fiscal year compared with last, Rockefeller reported.

Figure 31.2 Number of States in Which Tax Revenue Has Recovered, after Inflation

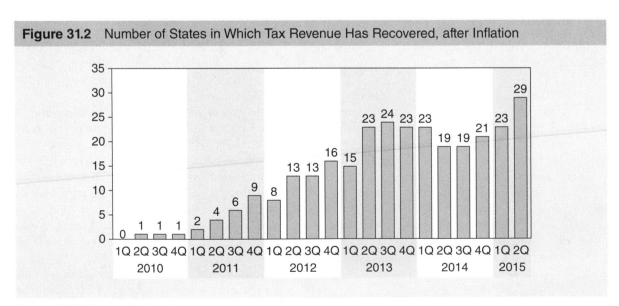

Source: © 2015 The Pew Charitable Trusts

State budgets do not adjust revenue for inflation, so states' own documents may show tax collections closer to pre-recession totals. Without adjusting for inflation, 50-state tax revenue was 16.8 percent above peak and tax collections had recovered in all but four states—Alaska, Florida, Louisiana, and Wyoming—as of the second quarter of 2015. Unadjusted figures do not take into account changes in the price of goods and services.

32

The Curious Case of Disappearing Corporate Taxes

By Liz Farmer

When Rick Snyder became governor of Michigan in 2011, his state had been on a 10-year economic slide—businesses were leaving and so were people. Where the rest of the country saw growth in the first two-thirds of the 2000s, Michigan's fiscal health was slip-sliding away.

Reversing a slide is difficult, and Michigan's governor and legislators focused a good chunk of their turnaround efforts on taxes. They wanted to reform the tax code so that it would lure businesses and generate the revenue needed to underwrite the kind of quality services that make people want to live there. Snyder's first step was to ask the legislature to slash business taxes. Within months, lawmakers repealed the unpopular and complicated Michigan Business Tax—though businesses could opt to stay with parts of the old system and its arcane web of credits and rebates. That isn't all the legislation did. The new tax law created a flat 6 percent tax that only certain types of corporations paid on their income. Talk about simplification: Nearly 100,000 businesses no longer had to file corporate returns.

Michigan has made economic progress since the 2011 tax reforms were passed. The population has stabilized, and the state ranks fifth in the country in job creation. Earlier this year, Michigan's bond rating was upgraded, an affirmation of a more stable fiscal environment.

But tax policy changes don't happen in a vacuum. It's difficult to tell whether the state's upturn is a result of the national economy recovering from the 2008 recession or from changes to Michigan's business taxes. What is certain, however, is that the

From *Governing*, January 2016

tax reform is bringing in less money. Before the 2008 recession, Michigan was collecting more than $2 billion annually in business taxes; in 2013, collections were less than $1 billion. That fall-off is in keeping with an in-state trend that had been building for two decades: Michigan corporate tax collections, adjusted for inflation, have fallen by 72 percent. Meanwhile, perhaps counterintuitively, total state revenues over that period grew by 56 percent.

Michigan is just one of a handful of states that has seen corporate tax revenue drop sharply, but it is one of many that has watched that tax base shrink while overall tax revenue grows. Nationally, real net corporate income revenues have grown on average at about half the pace of total revenues in states collecting the taxes over the past two decades, according to a *Governing* analysis of financial data reported to the U.S. Census Bureau. This weak growth of corporate taxes took place despite rising corporate profits, which more than doubled in the same time period, according to the St. Louis Federal Reserve Bank.

State tax policy clearly played a role in the diminishment of corporate tax revenue. As Greg LeRoy notes in his book *The Great American Jobs Scam*, federal corporate income tax revenues grew annually by 6 percent in the second half of the 1990s; state corporate income tax revenues grew by just half that rate. "Same companies, same profits, same years—half the tax," says LeRoy, who is also executive director of Good Jobs First, which tracks corporate tax giveaways.

The bottom line for states is that over the past three years, corporate income tax has represented 1.9 percent of total annual revenues. That's down significantly from an average of 2.7 percent over the decade of the 1990s and 3.5 percent over the decade of the 1980s.

Michigan's corporate tax reforms required sacrifice, especially in the form of a revenue hit. The reforms called for the state to continue to pay out any remaining tax credits under the old system. In fact, the state gave out nearly as much in rebates as it received in corporate tax revenue in 2015, according to Michigan Treasury spokesman Terry Stanton. Over the next few years, however, those credits are expected to decline to $600 million annually. Stanton also notes proprietorships no longer subject to the old business tax are

reporting their business earnings as personal income. About $900 million in income tax revenue this year is due to that shift.

The positive news for Michigan is that the downturn in corporate revenue is about to end. The 2011 reforms eliminated a number of loopholes and ended preferential treatment for some industries, such as tax credits to woo the filmmaking industry and to keep automobile manufacturers in the state. The state's treasury office expects corporate tax revenue will total more than $1 billion this year and the next.

But critics of the 2011 tax program point out that Michigan now ranks near the bottom in corporate income tax revenue per capita among the states that levy such a tax, according to the Michigan League for Public Policy. The state paid for part of the corporate cuts by eliminating most individual income tax deductions and credits, and by partially taxing retiree incomes, which had been exempt. "We cut taxes on businesses by a lot, but in reality we just shifted it on to individuals under the guise of a simpler tax system," says the policy league's Rachel Richards.

While Michigan's case is more extreme, most states have lackluster corporate revenue growth compared with other revenue streams. Colorado, however, is one of the 10 states where corporate income tax revenue has increased at a faster pace than total revenue. This may be due in part to several decades of economic growth. The state has added 2 million people since 1990, a population increase of 60 percent. Colorado has consistently ranked among the top states for business, not necessarily because of its business environment but because of its economic climate and educated labor force. "We're very much on the cutting edge of the creative economy," says Carol Hedges, executive director of the Colorado Fiscal Institute. "Increasingly, it's about lifestyle—those intangibles. People are flocking here."

In short, there's no cookie-cutter solution that can be applied from one state to the next to attract businesses, people and jobs. Business tax breaks are no panacea. Policymakers need to study economic trends in their region to understand what is actually helpful to companies, says Zach Schiller, executive director of Policy Matters Ohio. He points to one of Ohio's recent gross receipts tax adjustments that allows sole proprietors to exempt some of their business income. Set up as an incentive for small businesses, the change nets small businesses just several hundred dollars, yet will cost the state hundreds of millions of dollars. "The idea that we're doing small businesses a favor with this is ill-conceived," he says. "It's like flying an airplane over Ohio and throwing money out the window."

When it comes to tax incentives, LeRoy would like to see states ask more of corporations in return for the tax favor. So-called community benefits agreements, for instance, often include local hiring requirements, job quality standards and affordable housing set-asides. A broad coalition of labor and community-based organizations negotiated such an agreement with the developers of Los Angeles' downtown sports and entertainment complex in 2001.

Businesses that refuse to make any trade-offs should make lawmakers wary, LeRoy adds, pointing to a recent experience in Illinois. In 2013, the head of Decatur-based Archer Daniels Midland announced he wanted to relocate to Chicago but needed a tax credit to help pay for the cost—otherwise he might have to move out of state. Legislators balked at the threat, called it blackmail and did nothing. In December of that year, Archer Daniels Midland announced where it had decided to open new offices: Chicago—no incentives required.

The slashed business taxes, the incentives and assorted rebates that woo corporations aren't the only reason corporate tax revenue is down. There is a growing sophistication in the ability of big corporations to shelter profits in offshore tax havens. The Institute on Taxation and Economic Policy (ITEP) estimates that Fortune 500 companies reporting profits pay an average of 3.5 percent in state corporate taxes. The average state corporate income tax rate, however, is about 6 percent nationwide.

The sheltering of profits got a boost from computerization, which made it easier for companies to move profits around on paper, notes ITEP's Executive Director Matthew Gardner. He says states can close a key loophole in their corporate tax laws by requiring companies to report their income from overseas. This move—known as combined reporting—effectively treats a parent and its subsidiaries as one corporation for state tax purposes. About half the states have implemented combined reporting, which discourages companies from using noncorporate income tax states as tax havens. But few states expand that requirement to international holdings.

"Thirty years ago," Gardner says, "the cutting edge in income shifting was moving profits to Delaware or Nevada [states that have significant tax advantages for corporations]. Now they're shifting them out of the country entirely."

Data reporting by Mike Maciag

33

State Spending and the Search for Hidden Efficiencies

By Charles Chieppo

After years of dealing with budget crises that followed the major tax cuts pushed through by Gov. Sam Brownback in 2012, Kansas is proving that necessity is indeed the mother of invention. With all of the easy spending cuts—and a number of hard ones—already made, the state commissioned a study to determine how it can achieve money-saving efficiencies. A preliminary draft includes 105 recommendations that would save an estimated $2 billion over five years.

The need to find more ways to save money couldn't be clearer. The state faces an estimated $354 million two-year shortfall in its current $15.4 billion budget. Last spring, budget woes caused some Kansas schools to close early.

A number of the recommendations made by the consulting firm of Alvarez & Marsal certainly make sense. Shifting school district employees to the state health insurance and benefit plan and consolidating school purchasing would save an estimated $600 million over five years. Changing the way the state bids and administers insurance policies and creating a central office of risk management is projected to save another $170 million over that time. On the income side, the estimated five-year yield from filling vacant revenue officer and auditor positions is $381 million.

Other recommendations, however, represent the kinds of bad choices that cash-strapped state and local governments often face. For example, high-deductible health insurance plans are appealing to many younger, healthy employees, but making it the only option for an aging state workforce would create a significant obstacle to attracting and retaining quality employees.

From *Governing*, February 2016

How Kansas got itself into its present fix is no mystery. The tax cuts the legislature enacted three years ago included reducing the top income tax rate from 6.5 percent to 4.9 percent and eliminating the income tax entirely for small businesses that file as an individual. In arguing for the cuts, Brownback said they would "be like a shot of adrenaline into the heart of the Kansas economy." But it hasn't worked out that way.

It's true that since 2012 Kansas has seen more migration from neighboring Missouri and that most counties have seen a net increase in wealth. But the state's gross domestic product is growing more slowly than the national rate and, while unemployment is down, the decrease is smaller than in neighboring states. Deficits and insufficient reserves led to a 2014 downgrade in the state's bond rating, and last year state leaders resorted to raising the sales tax from 6.15 percent to 6.5 percent.

There are a number of lessons state and local government leaders can draw from Kansas' experience. One is that while tax cuts can be good policy, they rarely pay for themselves and must usually be accompanied by spending reductions to avoid deficits. And there is the fact that federal taxes account for by far the biggest part of the overall tax burden, so the economic impact of changing state tax policy is always going to be limited.

A different kind of lesson public officials around the country can learn from their Kansas counterparts is that seeking expert outside advice on how to achieve efficiencies is something that should routinely be done on a periodic basis. Efforts to find ways to be more efficient with taxpayer dollars should be continuous, not an option employed only in times of crisis.

Policy Challenges

S tate and local governments are tasked with addressing a staggering variety of social and economic problems. Name pretty much any problem on the public agenda—from filling potholes to regulating pot—and chances are that people are demanding that state and local governments do something about it. It makes for a very long list, and even a cursory examination of that list would require a book in itself, and a fairly lengthy book at that.

Rather than trying to comprehensively cover all the policy challenges state and local governments are grappling with, in this chapter we are going to focus on three big issues that pretty much all states are dealing with in some form or another. Specifically, the readings dip into the challenges related to education, health care, and the environment.

The first reading, by Alan Greenblatt, examines school choice. Though school choice takes many forms, the basic idea is to offer alternatives to the traditional public school system where school assignments are based on residential address and schools are uniformly regulated by a central authority. Advocates of school choice argue a more market-based approach to education can effectively address many issues plaguing K-12 education. It is not clear, though, that school choice is actually delivering on those promises.

The second reading, by Sophie Quinton, stays with education but shifts the focus to universities and colleges. It is no secret that college is expensive—both to students and parents paying tuition bills, and to taxpayers who are subsidizing public systems of higher education. State governments are experimenting with placing conditions on those subsidies, tying funding to performance on a range

149

of evaluation metrics. The idea is to create meaningful financial incentives to increase the performance of public institutions of higher education.

The third reading, by Chris Kardish, shifts from education to the environment. Specifically, Kardish investigates a growing battle over Louisiana wetlands. These wetlands play an important role in limiting flooding and other damage from hurricanes. They are also disappearing at an alarming rate, leaving parts of Louisiana more vulnerable to the effects of natural disasters. Local governments are responding by starting to legally target those seen as having an outsized role in the disappearance of wetlands—oil companies. That sets up a battle pitting the interests of a state economic mainstay against the long-term future of its environment.

The final reading, by John Daley and Jeff Cohen, looks at state healthcare cooperatives. These cooperatives help provide health insurance at reasonable costs in a lot of states and a key component in making Obamacare work. The problem is that a number of these cooperatives are in trouble—a dozen are folding and more are in trouble. Yet in other states, co-ops are thriving. This essay looks at what explains the difference between success and failure.

34

Has School Choice Been All It Set Out to Be?

By Alan Greenblatt

Kasey Locke has been diagnosed with autism. When her parents enrolled her in the public school in her town in Arizona, she had a hard time communicating, let alone learning. The Lockes, however, took advantage of an education savings account (ESA) program to sign their daughter up at a private school. ESAs work like vouchers, with one difference: The funds can be used not just for tuition but for other expenses, such as tutoring. For Kasey, the new school and continuing educational therapy did the trick. "With the ESA, the parents were able to put her in a private school that specializes in autism," says Debbie Lesko, the majority whip in the Arizona Senate. "The child is not only learning, but thriving."

Lesko thinks a program that has worked so well for a family like the Lockes should be available to any Arizona resident who wants to use it. Five years ago, she sponsored legislation that made Arizona the first state to offer ESAs, which it calls empowerment scholarship accounts. Since then, Arizona has repeatedly expanded the pool of eligible residents to include groups such as foster children, Native Americans and the children of military veterans.

No state has embraced school choice ideas with the fervor of Arizona. It has the nation's highest percentage of students enrolled in charter schools—14 percent, which is roughly three times the national average. The state Department of Education itself runs an office of school choice.

At the start of this year, the time seemed right in Arizona to expand the ESA program to take all comers. Neighboring Nevada enacted the nation's first statewide ESA program last year, freeing up

From *Governing*, May 2016

151

state money for students to use regardless of geographic location, or educational or family status. Thousands of families immediately signed up and the idea of copying Nevada became the ambition of state legislators across the country.

Lesko got her version through the Arizona Senate in February. But that was as far as it has gotten. The bill was twice pulled from the House floor due to a lack of support. Even some Republicans, who hold the majority in both chambers, were nervous that universal ESAs would drain too much money from traditional public schools. Meanwhile, Nevada's universal ESA program has been put on hold due to a court challenge.

School choice is having its glass-half-full moment. On the one hand, the various choice options—vouchers, charter schools, home schooling, tuition scholarship programs, open enrollment within districts—have grown enormously over the past decade. Once choice is available, there's no denying its popularity. Waiting lists for charter schools are common. Parents who want their kids to study Mandarin or engineering can find charter schools that cater to such ambitions.

On the other hand, proponents of choice say that the better they do in terms of improved test scores, high enrollment and reducing long waiting lists, the more pushback they encounter. People who run and support charter schools contend that traditional school districts and teachers unions use every tactic at their disposal, from political and legal battles to simply hogging school buildings and buses, as part of the ongoing effort to beat them down. "A lot of our friends feel like charters are getting their butts kicked," says Charles Barone, policy director of Democrats for Education Reform.

As a generation's worth of momentum toward school choice begins to slow a little, policymakers have the opportunity to explore whether school choice is doing what it was supposed to do in the first place: offer not just an alternative to public schools, but new methods that improve education and can be widely replicated elsewhere.

While charter school operators feel embattled, the reality is that charters and other choice options have become a structural part of the education landscape. That wasn't a sure thing even a few years ago. Obituaries were being written about school choice at the beginning of the Obama administration, given Democratic opposition to vouchers and the lack of love for charter schools among teachers unions. As the current administration starts to wind down, though, school choice is more popular than ever, embraced not only by conservative Republicans eager to inject competition into any state-run system, but by many Democrats as well. Even traditional school administrators now must accept the language of choice. "I don't think anybody is arguing that we should just have traditional public schools and we shouldn't have these options," says Thomas Gentzel, executive director of the National School Boards Association.

The first charter school law passed 25 years ago. There was scarcely any enrollment even at the dawn of the century. Today, charters—which receive public funding but are mostly run independently of school districts—educate more than 2 million students. "It's no longer niche programs just in cities," says Patrick Wolf, an education policy professor at the University of Arkansas. "It's risen above a critical mass."

Choice may continue to rise, but that doesn't mean its growth will continue at a rate that seriously erodes the dominance of the traditional public school model. Cities such as New Orleans and Washington, D.C., where majorities of kids are educated outside the traditional school district, will remain what they are now—outliers. This year, Florida's budget provides equal amounts of money for construction of both charters and traditional public schools. But that's unusual. The vast majority of the nation's schoolchildren still attend traditional public schools in their neighborhoods.

School districts and unions are doing everything they can to maintain their market dominance. A superintendent who has graduated from a foundation-sponsored training program such as the Broad Academy is sure to be confronted with angry accusations that he or she is a corporate sellout. "The rule is, it's still a street fight," says Michael Petrilli, president of the Fordham Institute, a conservative think tank that supports school choice. "They basically hassle and harass the charter schools at every opportunity."

Most dramatically, teachers in both Chicago and Detroit recently staged walkouts and strikes, in part to protest encroachment from charters and other choice options. Both city systems have deficits reaching well into the hundreds of millions of dollars, leading many to worry that support for the traditional system will continue to erode in favor of charters and other newer models. "You can't overstate what bad shape we're in because of charters and choice decimating a public school district and running it into the ground," says Margaret Weertz of the Detroit Federation of Teachers.

It's true that in terms of actually delivering education that's measurably better than traditional public schools, vouchers and charters continue to have a mixed record. School reformers have consistently overpromised the effects their bright new ideas would have. In the face of ongoing political opposition, it may no longer be enough to slap the name "charter" on a school and convince parents it's going to be a better place for their children.

As to measuring the record of accomplishment, it's not a simple matter. Choice supporters and opponents continually accuse the other side of cherry-picking numbers that overstate the benefits or drawbacks of their own approach. It's easy to find a study showing that vouchers, for instance, have no effect on test scores, or that kids in voucher programs end up doing worse in reading or math. You can also find a study that demonstrates the exact opposite.

In February, Don Coberly, the superintendent of schools in Boise, Idaho, put out a public memo accusing a foundation of presenting college admission tests in misleading ways to make his schools look bad. "At a recent downtown Rotary Club meeting, the executive director of the Albertson Foundation stated that the goal of the foundation is to increase charter school seats by 20,000 in the next few years," Coberly wrote. "That will only happen if Idahoans lose faith in their public schools."

In response to complaints that people have already lost faith, public school supporters respond that charters and other choice options are being pushed by big-money foundations, as well as corporations out to make money by siphoning off per-pupil spending. Programs such as ESAs are seen as giveaways to parents who would be sending their kids to private schools anyway. Private schools and charters can "cream" off their choice of applicants, while old-fashioned neighborhood schools—which have to keep their doors open to all comers—are left to deal with a population of less-motivated parents and often struggling students. "If a charter program fails to deliver, those kids come back into the traditional public schools," says Gentzel, the school boards association official. "Often, they need remediation and end up costing the taxpayer more."

But in a consumer culture where the Internet makes shopping for any conceivable item easy and your corner bar may stock 20 different kinds of craft beer, parents are clamoring for choice when it comes to something as essential as their kids' education. Every parent who has the chance exercises school choice, if only by picking neighborhoods that boast strong schools, says Doug Lemov, managing director at Uncommon Schools, which runs urban charters. "For most of the 20th century, if you were poor, you were forced by law to send your child to a dysfunctional school that was probably dangerous," he says. "There was hidden choice for other families. Now, for the first time, there is a conversation about whether we can make choice available to others."

Aside from that fairness argument, school choice has something else major going for it: true believers. Families such as the Lockes in Arizona become fierce partisans of their preferred flavor of choice and the institutions that support them. Active and avid supporters make a big difference. So-called reform programs such as Common Core and standardized testing have their adherents, but they won't inspire 20,000 people to march across the Brooklyn Bridge. That happened back in 2013, when Bill de Blasio was running for mayor of New York and threatened to make charter schools pay rent. He might have sounded pretty hostile to charters back then, but his administration has ended up approving most charter school applications. Thousands again rallied in Brooklyn last October in support of charter schools.

De Blasio himself notes that more than 90 percent of kids in New York are still being taught in traditional public schools. The focus, he argues, should be on creating greater educational outcomes for them. All over the country, it's clear that traditional public schools still do the bulk of the work of educating kids. The choice movement, for all its success, is a long way from scaling up and demonstrating that its approaches guarantee greater performance. "Successful districts feel they have no trouble retaining students in their systems," says Sasha Pudelski, assistant policy director for the American Association of School Administrators. "They don't see vouchers or charter schools as a threat."

Traditional public schools should be able to retain market share, if only by borrowing ideas from the most successful charters, whether it's individualized instruction or longer school days. Some states have made the mistake of assuming that charter schools, ESAs or tuition scholarship programs should be encouraged because they beat the stagnant alternative of the status quo. But that's not necessarily so. It's important to look at how particular options are working on the ground in particular places. "It's not just about having choices, but good choices," says Barone, the Democrats for Education Reform policy director. "The states that let a thousand flowers bloom tend not to do as well as states where there's an emphasis on both choice and quality."

Finding out what works and weeding out the programs that don't is something that both choice advocates and supporters of traditional public schools should be able to get behind. Gentzel makes a fair point, noting that when tax dollars are paying for charters and other programs there needs to be accountability. "There's not adequate oversight and expenditure of the funds and performance of the schools," he says.

The idea of having a "harbormaster"—one entity with oversight over all schools that receive public funding within a city—is gaining some currency. One good thing that can come out of the endless political and legal battles over the very existence of school choice is a growing insistence on accountability.

Maybe much of the work of education can be contracted out, but that doesn't mean there shouldn't be oversight of finances, governance and results. Every school that's publicly funded should not only strive to do well, but use comparable data for measuring success, Barone suggests.

One Florida family sought to use ESA money for an "educational vacation" in Europe. They were turned down, but making sure public education dollars are being spent as intended—providing the best possible schooling for the nation's kids—could prove one of the most profitable of the many growing pains school choice is still experiencing.

35

States to Colleges: Prove You're Worth It

By Sophie Quinton

N ew College of Florida, a liberal arts school, must demonstrate it is graduating students on time and helping them find jobs or risk losing some state dollars. Florida is one of 26 states that now apply performance-based funding formulas to their colleges and universities.

New College of Florida doesn't offer pre-professional degrees, like nursing or engineering. Students choose the public liberal arts college because they want an intellectual experience. Many take a year off after graduation to pursue research or community service.

Yet last fall, New College opened a flashy new career center on its Sarasota campus. It needed to prove to the state that it was helping students find jobs and graduate on time, or risk losing $1.1 million in state aid. "That's a big deal for us," David Gulliver, media relations coordinator for New College, said of the money.

This fiscal year, Florida was one of 26 states to fund their two- or four-year college systems (or both) partly based on outcomes such as graduation rates, according to HCM Strategists, a consulting firm. Mississippi, Nevada, North Dakota, Ohio and Tennessee all spent over half their higher education budgets that way.

The idea of using outcomes—not enrollments—to guide public funding of higher education has so much bipartisan backing that both President Barack Obama and Florida's Republican Gov. Rick Scott support it. In July, the Florida Board of Education approved a performance-funding system for state colleges, adding to its existing system for state universities.

From *Stateline*, a project of the Pew Charitable Trusts, December 2015.

It's too early to say whether performance-based funding will drive the changes lawmakers want. But the policy so aligns with national concerns about the cost and payoff of a college education that it's likely here to stay.

THE COMPLETION CRAZE

Tennessee started giving state colleges and universities bonus payments for meeting goals in certain categories, such as student performance on national exams, in 1979. In the 1990s, a handful of states set aside a small percent of funding to reward outcomes, such as degree completion. Those programs typically didn't last long.

Then the Great Recession happened. As the economy tanked, so did state tax revenue. Almost every state cut higher education funding between 2009 and 2014, and many colleges and universities raised tuition to compensate.

College became less affordable even as Obama and governors emphasized how important it was for Americans to go. "Education is an economic issue when nearly eight in 10 new jobs will require workforce training or a higher education by the end of the decade," Obama said in 2010.

To get the economic benefit of a college degree, the president emphasized, students have to graduate. Fifty-nine percent of first-time college students, studying full time, who started a bachelor's degree program in 2007 graduated in six years from that institution, according to federal statistics.

The Lumina Foundation and the Bill and Melinda Gates Foundation have added to the sense of urgency over the past few years by spending millions of dollars on developing and promoting strategies for raising graduation rates. One strategy is performance-based funding, also known as outcomes-based funding.

The men and women who oversee Florida's 12 state universities started developing a performance funding model in 2012. "We knew we needed to come up with a different approach to get additional state support [for state universities]," said Tim Jones, chief financial officer for the State University System of Florida Board of Governors.

The Florida Legislature wanted more accountability for money spent on higher education. Both lawmakers and the board wanted to push colleges to become more efficient.

Here's the formula they came up with: Starting in 2014, a small portion of every university's base funding—plus any additional state money—has to be distributed according to the university's performance on 10 metrics. Metrics include the average wages of graduates, the six-year graduation rate, the second-year retention rate and the share of undergraduates who come from families with incomes low enough to qualify for a federal Pell Grant. In 2012–13, the vast majority of Pell Grant recipients had a family income of $40,000 a year or less, according to an analysis of federal data by the nonprofit College Board.

Universities are scored between 0 and 5 points on each metric, once based on performance and again based on improvement. The board takes the higher of the two numbers for each metric and adds them up. If the university scores less than 25 points overall, it risks losing the performance portion of its base funding. If it scores above, it's eligible to get new money. The three institutions with the highest scores get additional funds.

Other states have put much more money at stake and have built much more comprehensive formulas. While performance-based funding made up 8.8 percent of Florida's spending on state universities this year, Tennessee allocates almost 100 percent of its higher education funding—for both community colleges and universities—through an outcomes-based formula.

"For every degree you award, it counts. For every student that accumulates 12 hours, they count. And we just simply count those up, and those are your outcomes for that funding year," said Crystal Collins, a director at the Tennessee Higher Education Commission. "You don't have to perform at a higher rate than you did last year; you just have to perform."

The formula involves multiple calculations (you can check them out on the commission's website). But basically, the state decides how much it wants to spend on higher education and parcels the money based on certain factors. A big one is whether students are progressing and graduating.

Tennessee's model also takes into account basic operating costs and adjusts its formula based on each institution's mission. Research universities are rewarded for spending money on research, for example, while community colleges are rewarded for connecting students with jobs.

SO FAR, SO GOOD?

So is performance funding making a difference? "Yes—incredibly, actually," said Joe DiPietro, the president of the University of Tennessee. The university system has beefed up academic advising and started stressing that students should take a full course load each semester, he said.

Graduation rates have risen across the university system since the outcomes-based formula was implemented in 2010. And they're improving across the state, Collins said.

Yet researchers say it's unclear whether performance funding is pushing up graduation rates. "We do not have as yet conclusive evidence that performance funding does indeed improve student outcomes in any significant way," Columbia University researchers wrote in a 2014 working paper that reviewed models in Indiana, Ohio and Tennessee.

More statistical analysis needs to be done before researchers can disentangle performance funding from everything else that affects colleges. Decisions made by presidents and faculty, requests by accrediting agencies, grants from foundations or the federal government and public pressure can all push colleges to change. Other factors affect whether students graduate in two or four years, such as the availability of financial aid.

So far, studies haven't found a strong link between performance funding and graduation rates. A recent analysis of Washington state's model for community colleges found that it hadn't much affected retention or the number of associate's degrees awarded. Institutions were awarding more short-term certificates, credentials that don't always have much labor market value.

The results suggest, the researchers wrote, that it may be more difficult for institutions to retain students from year to year than the designers of Washington's formula thought.

Kevin Dougherty, the lead author of the Columbia working paper, thinks states should pay more attention to what he calls "the issue of creaming." An easy way for colleges to improve their metrics is to raise admissions standards, potentially pushing out disadvantaged students.

About 30 percent of administrators interviewed by Dougherty and his fellow researchers for the study said restricting admissions was already happening or could happen. Colleges can also game performance-funding systems by shifting recruitment to better-prepared students, including from out of state, or by making it easier to pass classes, the administrators said.

States such as Tennessee try to address this concern by weighting the success of low-income students and other subpopulations more heavily in their formulas. But it's not clear how well that works, or what the right weight should be. This year, in response to campus officials' concerns, Tennessee raised the premium it places on low-income and adult students' progress.

Performance-based funding has caught on at a moment when colleges are less reliant on state money than they used to be. State funding now makes up just 29 percent of revenue for Tennessee's universities and about 41 percent of revenue for its community college system, according to Collins.

Sean Tierney, a strategy officer for the Lumina Foundation, says the states' growing shift to tuition to fund higher education—which rises with enrollment—strengthens the case for rewarding outcomes. "It makes more and more sense for the state to fund on a different variable, in order to help these students," he said.

In a different world, you might imagine policymakers figuring out how much it would cost to raise graduation rates by a certain amount and funding institutions that way, says Robert Bradley, a professor at the Institute for Academic Leadership hosted by Florida State University.

Instead, performance-funding formulas take the money states want to spend and divvy it up based on productivity. And that's exactly how lawmakers like it.

Gov. Scott wants to spend $500 million on performance funding for the State University System, half of which would come from universities' base budget.

"The fact that we've gotten $220 million over the past two years, three years, shows the belief that our policymakers and the Legislature and the governor's office have in what the board is doing," Jones, the State University System's CFO, said of Florida's formula. "It's very likely that we wouldn't have gotten the money without this model. So I think folks are happy, because they are getting funding for this."

36

Southern Louisiana Picks a Fight with Big Oil to Save the Wetlands

By Chris Kardish

In the middle of Lake Hermitage, about 30 miles south of New Orleans, there used to be a marsh about a mile long. There also used to be, amid the grasses, dozens of wells tapping oil and gas deposits below. Dave Marino, a charter captain who grew up nearby, scans the coast from his boat. Down the road, closer to the Gulf of Mexico, he says, "it's all gone." Marino is talking about the marsh. While there are a few wells still standing, the marsh itself has vanished. "When you kill the vegetation," he says, "the rest of it just melts away."

Louisiana's wetlands were once considered more of a nuisance than an environmental blessing. But that was before people understood they served an important purpose: They formed a natural barrier against hurricanes, which lose strength as they travel over land. In other words, the longer the coastline, the greater the protection. With the loss of mile upon mile of wetlands, the threat of severe flooding has intensified. Flooding here could disrupt an economic corridor of national importance, an area that's home to the nation's largest commercial port, that refines a quarter of the country's crude oil and that brings in more than half of its foreign supplies. But it could also further wreak havoc on coastal life. The local government here blames the energy companies for the damage, and it wants them to pay.

Lake Hermitage is just one waterway named in 21 lawsuits filed by the government of Plaquemines Parish against many of the energy companies that have helped pay its bills and employ its people for decades. There are other suits from governmental groups as well. They're all different, but at bottom they want

From *Governing*, August 2015

the same thing: to force oil and gas companies to pay for wetland destruction that has made the area more vulnerable to storms.

The stakes are enormous. Louisiana has lost about 1,880 square miles of coastal land in the last 80 years, and official estimates predict the loss of another 1,750 in the next half-century if the state doesn't take drastic engineering measures to stem the erosion and recreate land. Studies by the U.S. Geological Survey have concluded that the energy industry is responsible for at least 36 percent of the damage; other estimates put the number much higher. But the politics of the oil and gas industry in Louisiana is a tricky business. At one point, that industry contributed 70 percent of state government revenue—today, it's about 14 percent—and still supports close to 300,000 jobs in the state, according to a study commissioned by oil and gas interests. Critics contend that industry influence has led regulators and elected officials to take a loose approach that allowed the damages to mount.

Once consigned to the op-ed pages, these critics are now turning to the courts. Growing awareness of the coastal crisis has prompted the most significant legal action in the state's 100-year relationship with the oil industry. But it's happening without the blessing of state leaders, who argue litigation isn't the best way to get the industry to help with a restoration effort that most agree is essential. Support for the legal action is far from universal in the coastal parishes, where the influence of the energy companies remains potent, but the lawsuits demonstrate that a vocal contingent of Louisiana residents is demanding relief, no matter how crucial the industry is to local commerce and day-to-day living.

The lawsuit that has attracted the most attention is the one that was first out of the gate: The Southeast Louisiana Flood Protection Authority-East, charged with protecting the New Orleans area from the kind of flooding that followed Hurricane Katrina, argues in its suit against 97 oil and gas companies that their exploration and extraction undermined the authority's mission. It wants them to pay billions in damages, and the money would go to fortifying levees and shoring up the state's coastal restoration plan, which is far from fully funded.

In the flood protection authority's view, the single biggest contributor to wetland loss has been the network of canals forged out of the marshes surrounding New Orleans over the past 80 years or so. There are at least 10,000 miles of canals cut across coastal Louisiana to access rigs, navigate barges and construct pipelines. But the canals disrupt the natural process that replenishes wetlands with sediment and allows saltwater intrusion that corrodes freshwater vegetation. The flood protection authority says the canals should have been backfilled and restored to their previous condition under coastal regulations.

The opposition to the authority's lawsuit has been fierce. Gov. Bobby Jindal opposes the suit and has fought to reassert state control over the flood protection authority, whose members he appoints. The legislature passed a bill trying to preempt the lawsuit. And in February, the federal judge presiding over the case ruled that the authority doesn't have standing to sue oil interests for coastal damage. An appeal is expected to be heard in the coming months by the U.S. Court of Appeals for the Fifth Circuit, which has a history of backing the business side in environmental cases.

Chip Kline, the Jindal-appointed chairman of the state's coastal restoration fund, acknowledges oil industry involvement in coastal destruction, but says that state litigation isn't the way to negotiate over damages. He and others say the authority's lawsuit overstates the industry's responsibility compared with other drivers of erosion, particularly the leveeing of the Mississippi River that contributed to flood protection but deprived wetlands of the sediment they needed to maintain themselves. Under Jindal, the state has launched a $50 billion, 50-year restoration plan that, among other things, is creating new barrier islands off Plaquemines Parish. But independent experts argue that it will cost at least double that price tag. Currently, the plan has enough funding to stay on schedule for about seven years, and much of the revenue over that time depends on settlements from the 2010 BP oil spill that will gradually thin out. The state has nowhere near $50 billion committed after that. As for the oil and gas industry, Kline says, "they're absolutely hesitant to come to the table and discuss anything until the lawsuit is 102 percent put to bed."

But Kline takes no issue with the local lawsuits, of which there are now 28 in total, seven from Jefferson Parish and 21 from Plaquemines. It's expected that two more parishes will file suits as well. The parish litigation may face fewer questions about the right to sue because of state law giving coastal governments some influence over their wetlands. The energy companies, however, are not conceding this.

Plaquemines Parish is more dependent on oil jobs and money than Jefferson, which makes the Plaquemines council's unanimous decision to sue such a bold one. Two-thirds of government revenue comes from oil and gas companies. But Plaquemines Parish is also a critical front in the fight to save Louisiana's coast. It actually accounts for nearly 10 percent of the entire nation's wetlands, and it's right at New Orleans' back.

The Jefferson and Plaquemines lawsuits could come to trial sometime next year. In addition to canal dredging, the parish cases focus on industry techniques for disposing of saltwater that bubbles up from oil and gas wells. Lawyers for Plaquemines argue that oil companies discharged their saltwater directly into the wetlands or through pits dug into the marsh, usually without getting a permit. Louisiana didn't officially outlaw the waste pits until 1986, however, decades after other oil-producing states, according to attorneys.

Many of those pits, like the marsh, have washed away. "The oil industry knew going back to the '30s that if you put water in these pits that are unlined, you're kidding yourself if you think it's going to stay there," says John Carmouche, whose law firm is taking the lead in the Plaquemines and Jefferson suits. The firm is still fleshing out the level of damages it will ask for and ironing out the responsibility of individual companies, but one partner at Carmouche's firm said the number they're thinking of for both parishes "will have to have a 'b' in front of it."

Despite the unanimous vote in favor of litigation in 2013, the resolve of Plaquemines Parish government is in question. The former parish council president who became synonymous with the suit, Byron Marinovich, lost his re-election bid in 2014 to a gas company administrator bankrolled by energy interests. Despite some grassroots sentiments in favor of killing the suits, however, the councilwoman who replaced Marinovich has failed to rally a majority so far.

The only coastal parish that has publicly refused to file a suit is nearby Terrebonne, one of the hardest-hit in terms of land loss. A quarter of the 1,880 square miles of Louisiana coastal land that has disappeared over the last 80 years has come from the Terrebonne Basin, eliminating an amount of land roughly the size of New York City. One council member said last year that the parish's crest bears a fishing boat and an oil rig for good reason. "Without the two there is no Terrebonne," she said. "There is no good earth, no good people and no good economy."

The oil companies have said little publicly in their defense, instead arguing that the flood protection authority and the parishes have no legal right to sue. A spokeswoman for BP, Shell and Chevron declined to make company officials available for an interview. "While there may be isolated exceptions," she said in a statement, "we believe that the vast majority of the industry complied with these permits, which were regulated and monitored by the agencies that issued and managed them, including the Corps of Engineers and the Louisiana Department of Natural Resources. These agencies also had the authority to enforce these permits, and that includes the authority to bring suit, which they have not done."

It's impossible to read the lawsuits and the mountain of work on Louisiana coastal erosion without asking one simple question: Where were the state regulators? The Department of Natural Resources has issued oil and gas permits in Louisiana's coastal zone since 1978 and is also charged with enforcing them. The department defends its record by pointing out that canal dredging is now relatively rare and takes place on a smaller scale. When the department does allow larger-scale dredging, it requires operators to use the proceeds to offset damage through a state program. "What you're trying to do is balance economic benefit without sacrificing too much environmental impact," says Patrick Courreges, a department spokesman.

The question for critics is whether the balancing act has been achieved. Development has clearly won out, even in some of the most environmentally sensitive areas. The state has the legal authority to establish special zones to minimize it, but so far only two of these zones have been created. Backfilling canals is also within the department's enforcement powers, but a survey by Louisiana State University scientist Gene Turner has found only 10 miles of backfilled canals in the state, compared to at least 10,000 that were dredged. Alternative methods for accessing wells, such as requiring air-cushioned vehicles that would minimize the need for dredging, have been rejected by state regulators even though they are commonly used in other places, according to Oliver Houck, a Tulane University environmental law professor who's written a history of energy regulation in the state.

State regulators argue that Plaquemines' claims of improper waste disposal should come to them—not to the courts. But without legal intervention, there's little parishes can do to enforce environmental law or get compensated for damages, especially from activities that are decades old. The state's Oilfield Site Restoration Program has a long waiting list and only about $4 million in funding a year. If the state really wanted to monitor waste disposal properly, critics contend, it would need a small army of watchdogs. According to Courreges, there are about 20 on patrol in the coastal zone at any given time.

On the issue of canal dredging, arguably the biggest sore spot for environmentalists, the Department of Natural Resources says much of the damage came so long ago that requiring restoration isn't possible. But about 70 percent of the more than 200 dredging permits listed in the flood authority's lawsuit came from the state under the coastal zone program after 1978. The state just doesn't view backfilling canals as a good

policy, as they've publicly said, because operators may need to reaccess a well at some later date. Paul Templet, who helped to write Louisiana's environmental law and has also worked in other states, says Louisiana could set tougher standards for companies that claim they'll need to reuse the canals and press far harder for efforts to mitigate damage. "If you put pressure on oil and gas companies, they'll find ways to do things and money to do it with," he says.

That's essentially the lesson of Long Beach, Calif. That city stands on a bounty of fossil fuels; drilling was so heavy in the 1930s that the area began to sink at a rapid clip. That was because sucking up oil from reservoirs below the earth without replacing it creates a vacuum that leads to subsidence, or sinking land. Officials in California were so alarmed that they put a halt to most drilling in the 1960s. But five major oil companies formed a consortium to construct manmade islands that allow for drilling away from population centers, along with replacements that maintained pressure in oil reservoirs to prevent subsidence. "In the 1960s, Long Beach said, 'Fix it or leave,' and they fixed it," says Brandon Taylor, a lawyer representing the Plaquemines plaintiffs. "I guess the question I have is, why couldn't they do the same things they were doing in Long Beach in Lake Hermitage?"

37

Why Colorado's Obamacare Co-op Is Falling, and Connecticut's Isn't

By John Daley and Jeff Cohen/Kaiser Health News

Thousands of Americans are again searching for health insurance after losing it for 2016. That's because health cooperatives—large, low-cost insurers set up as part of Obamacare—are folding in a dozen states.

The failure of Colorado's co-op has hit Rick and Letha Heitman hard. They are currently customers of the Colorado HealthOP, which is closing up shop at the end of the year. The couple, who own a contracting business, say the co-op proved to be a life-saver when Rick was diagnosed with aggressive prostate cancer last spring.

"I owe them for taking care of me. They helped me at a time when I needed it a lot," he says.

About 80,000 people are in the same boat as the Heitmans, on the hunt for new insurance plans on Colorado's exchange. HealthOP's CEO Julia Hutchins says the co-op got walloped by the equivalent of a fast-moving tornado after the federal government said it wouldn't be paying co-ops millions in subsidies they had expected.

"We were really blindsided by that," she says. "We felt like we'd done our part in helping serve individuals who really need insurance and now we're the one left holding the bag."

And, she insists the co-op was on track to be profitable. Colorado HealthOp is one of 23 nationally in 22 states that opened after Obamacare was enacted. The startups were supposed to shake up the traditional marketplace by being member-owned and non-profit, but it was tough to figure out how much to charge. They needed to estimate how much medical care their customers would use, and they had to do that without data from previous years and without the cushion of a reserve fund. Established insurers can use reserves and experience to recover if they underestimate premium prices in a given year.

Many co-op plans were priced low, and customers poured in. But these new customers had high health costs, so the co-ops had to start paying a lot of bills. The math didn't add up. On top of that, they were counting on a variety of funding streams from the federal government, and not all of them materialized.

Linda Gorman, with the Independence Institute, a conservative-leaning Colorado think tank, says the new co-ops were in over their heads.

"You shouldn't go into business counting on federal subsidies," she says. "The notion that you should beat up on for-profit entities and then form these nonprofits and everything will be magically OK is unfortunate to begin with. We've wasted a lot of taxpayer money on that."

But the HealthOP's senior IT manager Helen Hadji, a Republican, blames conservatives in Congress for not authorizing the money needed to keep the cooperatives afloat.

"This is a federal failure," she says. "This is all a political battle to dismantle Obamacare."

Colorado's co-op captured 40 percent of the individual market on the state's exchange. Now as customers, like the Heitmans, hunt for new insurance, they are finding higher prices: They paid about $500 a month last year. Next year, it could be double or triple that.

"You know, that's a big 'owee!'" says Letha Heitman.

But it's the price they'll pay to keep Rick with the doctors who are treating his cancer.

In Connecticut, the opposite story is playing out. If Colorado saw an early surge in membership because of low prices, Connecticut's co-op nearly priced itself out of the market in its first year. With rates much higher than its competitors, HealthyCT only got 3 percent of the state's business under the Affordable Care Act.

"In that first year, the reason we had such low market share was that consumers—new to the industry, new to insurance—most of those individuals bought on price," says Ken Lalime, who runs the co-op.

And, he says, starting it was hard.

"Nobody's built a new insurance company in the state of Connecticut in 30 years," he says. "There's no book that you pull off the shelf and say, 'Let's go do this.'"

Lalime faced the same problem as insurers across the country: He didn't know who his customers would be, he didn't know whether they'd be sick or healthy, and he didn't know how much to charge. It turns out he ended up charging too much.

But even though that meant relatively few signups in year one, the slow ramp-up actually helped. He didn't have a huge number of claims to pay right out of the gate, and the ones he did pay didn't break the bank.

"Hindsight, yes, that didn't hurt us. To be able to take it slowly," he says.

In year two, he had more competitive average premiums—and his company went from 3 percent market share to 18 percent. For 2016, HealthyCT and the state—after some back and forth—settled on a 7 percent premium hike for customers.

Paul Lombardo is an actuary for the state. He says that bouncing around is an indicator that setting premiums under the Affordable Care Act is still a bit of a gamble. That's in part because there's still no good data. So few people signed up with HealthyCT in the beginning that they didn't have enough information to help set 2016 premiums.

"There wasn't a lot of data to say, OK, we can use 2014 experience to project forward," Lombardo says.

For now, at least, Lombardo says HealthyCT is holding its own.

"They're in good standing," he says. "The premium we think that we're setting for 2016—albeit a little bit higher than they wanted it to be on the revision—is appropriate."

Enrollment for health insurance in the co-ops runs through Jan. 31 with just 11 of the original 23 co-ops still in business.

Text Credits

1. Kettl, Donald F. "Are States Still 'Labs of Democracy'?" *Governing*, April 2015. Accessed May 18, 2016. http://www.governing.com/columns/potomac-chronicle/gov-states-still-labs-of-democracy.html.

2. Kettl, Donald F. "Is Federalism Breaking Down?" *Governing*, February 2015. Accessed May 18, 2016. http://www.governing.com/columns/potomac-chronicle/gov-bad-intergovernmental-relations.html.

3. Greenblatt, Alan. "Beyond North Carolina's LGBT Battle: States' War on Cities." *Governing*, March 25, 2016. Accessed May 18, 2016. http://www.governing.com/topics/politics/gov-states-dties-preemption-laws.html.

4. Bowser, Jennie Drage. "Constitutions: Amend with Care." *State Legislatures*, September 2015. Accessed May 18, 2016. http://www.ncsl.org/research/elections-and-campaigns/constitution-amend-with-care.aspx.

5. Levitt, Justin. "Voter Identification in the Courts." *The Book of the States 2015*. http://knowledgecenter.csg.org/kc/system/files/Levitt%202015.pdf.

6. National Conference of State Legislatures. "Voter ID History." NCSL.org, January 4, 2016. Accessed May 18, 2016. http://www.ncsl.org/research/elections-and-campaigns/voter-id-history.aspx.

7. Norden, Lawrence, and Christopher Famighetti. "Aging Voting Machines Are a Threat to Democracy." Brennan Center, September 28, 2015. Accessed May 18, 2016.

http://www.brennancenter.org/blog/aging-voting-machines-are-threat-democracy.

8. Greene, Sean, and Kyle Ueyama. "Vote-by-Mail Rates More Than Double since 2000." *Stateline*, April 29, 2015. Accessed May 18, 2016. http://www.pewtrusts.org/en/research-and-analysis/blogs/stateline/2015/4/29/vote-by-mail-practices-more-than-double-since-2000.

9. Weiner, Daniel I., and Ian Vandewalker. "Stronger Parties, Stronger Democracy: Rethinking Reform." Brennan Center, September 16, 2015. Accessed May 18, 2016. http://www.brennancenter.org/publication/stronger-parties-stronger-democracy-rethinking-reforming.

10. Greenblatt, Alan. "Rex Sinquefield: The Tyrannosaurus Rex of State Politics." *Governing*, June 2015. Accessed May 18, 2016. http://www.governing.com/topics/politics/gov-rex-sinquefield-missouri.html.

11. Jacobson, Louis. "Why Democratic Governors and Republican Mayors Have Become Rare." *Governing*, July 16, 2015. Accessed May 18, 2016. http://www.governing.com/topics/politics/gov-political-party-success-president-governor-congress-mayor.html.

12. Kurtz, Karl. "Who We Elect: The Demographics of State Legislatures." *State Legislatures*, December 1, 2015. Accessed May 18, 2016. http://www.ncsl.org/research/about-state-legislatures/who-we-elect.aspx.

13. Beitsch, Rebecca. "Stalled Progress for Women in State Legislatures." *Stateline*, December 8, 2015. Accessed May 18, 2016. http://www.pewtrusts.org/en/research-and-analysis/blogs/stateline/2015/12/08/stalled-progress-for-women-in-state-legislatures.

14. Weiss, Suzanne. "Birds of a Feather." *State Legislatures*, October/November 2015. Accessed May 18, 2016. http://www.ncsl.org/legislators-staff/legislators/legislative-leaders/birds-of-a-feather.aspx.

15. Jacobson, Louis. "Experience Preferred." *State Legislatures*, January 2016. Accessed May 18, 2016. http://www.ncsl.org/bookstore/state-legislatures-magazine/experience-preferred.aspx.

16. Jacobson, Louis. "Rocky Roads Ahead for Governors with Failed Presidential Bids." *Governing*, January 2016. Accessed May 18, 2016. http://www.governing.com/topics/politics/gov-governors-post-presidential-careers.html.

17. Wogan, J. B. "Scott Pruitt Will See You in Court." *Governing*, September 2015. Accessed May 18, 2016. http://www.governing.com/topics/politics/gov-oklahoma-scott-pruit-feature.html.

18. McGaughy, Lauren. "After Spending Millions Suing Obama 39 Times, Has Texas Seen a Return on Investment?" *Governing*, November 2015. Accessed May 18, 2016. http://www.governing.com/topics/finance/tns-texas-lawsuits-federal.html.

19. Soronen, Lisa. "Cases with Consequences." *State Legislatures*, September 2015. Accessed May 18, 2016. http://www.ncsl.org/research/civil-and-criminal-justice/cases-with-consequences.aspx.

20. Beitsch, Rebecca. "States at a Crossroads on Criminal Justice Reform." *Stateline*, January 2016. Accessed May 18, 2016. http://www.governing.com/topics/public-justice-safety/sl-criminal-justice-states-crossroads.html.

21. Chang, Cindy, Marisa Gerber, and Ben Poston. "The Unintended Consequences of California's New Criminal Justice." *Governing*, November 2015. Accessed May 18, 2016. http://www.governing.com/topics/public-justice-safety/unintended-consequences-of-prop-47-pose-challenge-for-californias-criminal-justice-system.html.

22. Clark, Maggie. "Legislators Attempt to Strip Courts of Power." *Stateline*, January 23, 2012. Accessed May 18, 2016. http://www.pewtrusts.org/en/research-and-analysis/blogs/stateline/2012/01/23/legislators-attempt-to-strip-courts-of-power.

23. Barrett, Katherine, and Richard Greene. "Can Government Hiring Get Out of the Stone Age?" *Governing*, February 2016. Accessed May 18, 2016. http://www.governing.com/topics/mgmt/gov-government-hiring-best-practices.html.

24. Quinton, Sophie. "States Employ Temporary Workers, but Often Know Little about Them." *Stateline*, April 13, 2016. Accessed May 18, 2016. http://www.pewtrusts.org/en/research-and-analysis/blogs/stateline/2016/04/13/states-employ-temporary-workers-but-know-little-about-them.

25. Quinton, Sophie. "What Does It Take to End a Teacher Shortage?" *Stateline*, February 25, 2016. Accessed May 18, 2016. http://www.pewtrusts.org/en/research-and-analysis/blogs/stateline/2016/02/25/what-does-it-take-to-end-a-teacher-shortage.

26. Herzon, Karen. "Wisconsin Tenure Fight Likely to Spread to Other States." *Governing*, July 2015. Accessed May 18, 2016. http://www.governing.com/topics/education/tenure-battle-in-wisconsin-seen-as-bellwether-by-educators-across-us.html.

27. Patton, Zach. "The Illusion of Cities' Recovery from the Recession." *Governing*, September 2015. Accessed May 18, 2016. http://www.governing.com/topics/finance/gov-recession-recovery-cities-colorado-springs.html.

28. Uden, Amy B. "A Checklist for Alternatives in City-County Consolidation Decisions: From Separation to Unification." *State and Local Government Review*, March 2016. Accessed May 18, 2016. http://slg.sagepub.com/content/early/2016/03/03/0160323X16634172.full.pdf+html.

29. Quinton, Sophie. "What Is a Smart City?" *Stateline*, April 26, 2016. Accessed May 18, 2016. http://www.pewtrusts.org/en/research-and-analysis/blogs/stateline/2016/04/26/what-is-a-smart-city.

30. National Association of State Budget Officers. "Summary: Fall 2015 Fiscal Survey of States." NASBO.org, December 15, 2015. Accessed May 18, 2016. http://www.nasbo.org/sites/default/files/Report%20Summary%20-%20Fall%202015%20Fiscal%20Survey.pdf.

31. Pew Charitable Trusts. "For First Time, Tax Revenue Has Recovered in Majority of States." *States' Fiscal Health*, December 10, 2015. Accessed May 18, 2016. http://www.pewtrusts.org/en/research-and-analysis/analysis/2015/12/10/for-first-time-tax-revenue-has-recovered-in-majority-of-states.

32. Farmer, Liz. "The Curious Case of Disappearing Corporate Taxes." *Governing*, January 2016. Accessed May 18, 2016. http://www.governing.com/topics/finance/gov-disappearing-corporate-taxes.html.

33. Chieppo, Charles. "State Spending and the Search for Hidden Efficiencies." *Governing*, February 2, 2016. Accessed May 18, 2016. http://www.governing.com/blogs/bfc/col-kansas-budget-crisis-search-money-saving-efficiencies.html.

34. Greenblatt, Alan. "Has School Choice Been All It Set Out to Be?" *Governing*, May 2016. Accessed May 18, 2016. http://www.governing.com/topics/education/gov-school-choice-vouchers.html.

35. Quinton, Sophie. "States to Colleges: Prove You're Worth It." *Stateline*, December 31, 2015. Accessed May 18, 2016. http://www.pewtrusts.org/en/research-and-analysis/blogs/stateline/2015/12/31/best-of-stateline-states-to-colleges-prove-youre-worth-it.

36. Kardish, Chris. "Southern Louisiana Picks a Fight with Big Oil to Save the Wetlands." *Governing*, August 25, 2015. Accessed May 18, 2016. http://www.governing.com/topics/transportation-infrastructure/gov-louisiana-wetlands-lawsuits.html.

37. Daley, John, and Jeff Cohen. "Why Colorado's Obamacare Co-op Is Falling, and Connecticut's Isn't." *Governing*/Kaiser Health News, December 1, 2015. Accessed May 18, 2016. http://www.governing.com/topics/health-human-services/tale-of-two-obamacare-co-op-insurers-one-standing-one-falling.html.